"A delightfully titillating collection of erotica written by both women and men, with something to arouse just about everyone. A wonderful resource for couples who want to increase their passion, expand their sexual horizons, and better understand the different turn-ons of men and women. It's also great fun."
—Bernie Zilbergeld, Ph.D., author of *The New Male Sexuality*

"Offers up a veritable smorgasbord of spicy fantasies."
—*Publishers Weekly*

"This collection of twenty-two short stories has been compiled as a tool for heterosexual couples to explore men's and women's perspectives on sex and to act as a catalyst for dialogue about the subject." —*Library Journal*

"A collection of fantasy fiction for couples to enhance their sexual imagination and put a spark back in a relationship."
—*Oklahoman Gazette*

LONNIE BARBACH, Ph.D., is one of the most highly regarded experts in the field of sexuality and relationships. She is the editor of two previous collections of erotica, *Pleasures* and *Erotic Interludes*, and the author of the classic works on intimacy *For Yourself* and *For Each Other* (both Signet), as well as the co-author of *Shared Intimacies*, *The Intimate Male* (Signet), and *Going the Distance* (Plume).

The Erotic Edge

EROTICA FOR COUPLES

Edited by
Lonnie Barbach, Ph.D.

A PLUME BOOK

PLUME
Published by the Penguin Group
Penguin Books USA Inc., 375 Hudson Street, New York, New York 10014, U.S.A.
Penguin Books Ltd, 27 Wrights Lane, London W8 5TZ, England
Penguin Books Australia Ltd, Ringwood, Victoria, Australia
Penguin Books Canada Ltd, 10 Alcorn Avenue, Toronto, Ontario, Canada M4V 3B2
Penguin Books (N.Z.) Ltd, 182–190 Wairau Road, Auckland 10, New Zealand

Penguin Books Ltd, Registered Offices: Harmondsworth, Middlesex, England

Published by Plume, an imprint of Dutton Signet,
a division of Penguin Books USA Inc.
Previously published in a Dutton edition.

First Plume Printing, February, 1996
10 9 8

 REGISTERED TRADEMARK—MARCA REGISTRADA

The Library of Congress has catalogued the Dutton edition as follows:

The Erotic edge : erotica for couples / edited by Lonnie Barbach.
    p.   cm.
   ISBN 0-525-93809-5 (hc.)
   ISBN 0-452-27464-8 (pbk.)
   1. Erotic stories, American.   I. Barbach, Lonnie Garfield.
  PS648.E7E68   1994
  813'.01083538—dc20
                       93–38844
                       CIP

Printed in the United States of America

To my mother, Temy Barbach, with love

ACKNOWLEDGMENTS

I would like to thank my assistant, Marilyn Anderson, for handling the enormous amount of correspondence and organizational work that accompanied creating this anthology. I could not have completed this book without her. I would also like to thank my agent, Rhoda Weyr, for her encouragement and level-headedness and my editor, Carole DeSanti, for her attentiveness to this project despite an incredibly demanding schedule.

Lucinda Mercer, Danny Slomoff, Ph.D., Deborah Shames, Scott Nelson, Ph.D., Donna Rosenthal, and David Geisinger, Ph.D., were enormously helpful in giving me second opinions on stories. Donna also helped to edit my introductory sections, and David kindly kept me warm at night and well fed during the day. I don't know what I would have done without David's support or without the joy that our daughter, Tess, brings with every moment of her being.

CONTENTS

INTRODUCTION

For the last seventeen years, the principal focus of my work has been to help women to enjoy their sexuality more fully. When I edited *Pleasures: Women Write Erotica* in 1984 and then *Erotic Interludes: Tales Told by Women* two years later, my intention was to create a body of literature that was erotic from a female point of view. Until that time, the sexually explicit material that existed had been written largely by men or aimed at a male audience. Too often, the themes were violent, objectifying, or degrading to women. Predictably, women did not find the stories appealing or arousing.

I believe that the near absence of erotica directed toward the unique needs of women made a powerful statement: if a woman is to be considered respectable, her sexuality should remain hidden; that decency and lusty sexuality are incompatible in a woman. Except for romance novels, where sexual scenes usually began as the chapter ended, explicit sexual writing from a woman's viewpoint was a rarity. I felt certain that if women could create a body of literature that was erotic from their point of view, it would eventually make a positive impact on the culture, enabling women to accept their own right to a range of sexual pleasures—rather than simply viewing their sexuality as a vehicle to provide pleasure for their partners.

My objective in compiling *The Erotic Edge: Erotica for Couples* is quite different. In this volume I wanted to create something that would appeal equally to both men and women. For example, I had discovered that while some men responded positively to the female themes contained in *Pleasures* and *Erotic Interludes*, others felt there was much ado about nothing. Their predominant complaint was that women took too long to get down to business and that when they got to the sexual scenes, they were neither graphic nor explicit enough. I felt that by integrating stories written by men with those written by women, this anthology would contain elements that would appeal to both sexes.

I wanted to provide a safe way to refresh and add variety to an ongoing sexual relationship. With a heightened awareness of the drastic consequences of divorce on health, productivity, and children, and the fear of AIDS and other sexually transmitted diseases, monogamous couples are seeking ways to work out their relationship problems as well as ways to enliven or expand their lovemaking lives in order to keep sex from becoming routine or boring.

The desire for newness or variety does not necessarily indicate the existence of a sexual problem. Many couples with otherwise satisfying intimate relationships want to broaden their sexual horizons as a way to further enhance their intimacy, much as you might add new flowers to the garden—not because you have tired of the old, but because you desire something different. I felt that an erotic anthology that men and women could enjoy separately or read aloud to each other could enhance their sexual relationships and, among other things, enlarge their erotic imaginations. In addition, the range of experiences described in the stories could enable both partners to better understand some of the differences that might exist between their sexual natures, thereby leading to greater understanding and acceptance of these differences. For example, a woman might be able to see how strongly connected a man's sexual response is to certain visual stimuli and why her dressing seductively might play an important role in his arousal process. By the same token, a man might recognize how essential the general tone of the relationship and the mental seduction are to firing desire in a female partner. By including stories written by both men and women, I hoped to make more explicit the different ways in which the two sexes approach the erotic.

I obtained the stories for this volume by writing letters of invitation to women who had contributed to my previous volumes. These invitations were passed around by word of mouth and shared at writers' groups and in writers' workshops. In addition, I posted notices at university creative writing programs and advertised in writers' magazines. I received 195 submissions, 91 by female writers and 104 by male writers, from which I selected 22 short stories. Stories came in from all over the United States and from as far away as Australia, Malaysia, and Zimbabwe.

Interestingly, the average age of both male and female authors included in this anthology is forty-two. Women ranged from twenty-eight to fifty-six, while men spanned the ages of thirty-two through fifty-eight, but the vast majority of the contributors fell between the ages of thirty-five and forty-five. Since our reproductive years extend from the twenties to mid-thirties, I find it intriguing that the best erotica is being written *after* that peak. At first I thought that this was because writing about the erotic was a way to compensate for reduced sexual activity. And while this may be one factor, I now believe that for most of us, a full appreciation of the erotic doesn't evolve until after we have had time to become seasoned. Certainly, sexuality changes over the years. Maybe it takes until our middle years before we are able to appreciate the complexities, the subtleties, the wider range of sexual expression.

This collection differs from my earlier ones in some noteworthy ways. Only one story concerning a homosexual relationship is included in this collection. Even though I explicitly stated that I was looking for themes concerning homosexuality as well as group sex or solo sex, I received an unusually low number of stories with homosexual themes (three male, eight female) when compared to submissions for my first two volumes of erotica. My guess is that because I announced that this compilation would stress the differences between erotic writing by males and females and was aimed at couples, writers may have thought they had the greatest probability of having their story accepted if they chose a heterosexual theme.

Another difference between the stories submitted for this volume and those submitted for my earlier anthologies was in the emphasis on safe sex. Submissions I received in the early 1980s for *Pleasures* or for *Erotic Interludes* rarely mentioned the use of a condom. Among submissions for this current book, however, approximately one-third of the stories that included intercourse in a nonmonogamous relationship specifically dealt with the issue of safe sex.

Finally, I found it interesting that despite the sexual revolution of twenty years ago, nearly one-third of the contributors have chosen to use pseudonyms: mostly to protect their job, their partner, or their partner's job. For example, one woman writes children's books; another's partner has a sensitive political post; one man has a job working for a telephone company in the South; and a woman from Texas would feel personally unsafe, potentially vulnerable to fanatics or psychologically unstable individuals if her name were to be associated with erotic writing. Some things change slowly.

To explore some of the differences in erotica written by male and female authors, I've divided this book into three sections. The first includes stories that, for a variety of reasons, I consider distinctively male or distinctively female. The authors' gender, in many ways, determines the nature of the material presented in both style and subject matter.

The second section deals with three of the most common themes among all the manuscripts submitted: unrequited love, anonymous sex, and sexual affairs. The first tended to be a female theme; the second a male theme; and the third, which was a favorite of both, differs considerably when written from a male or female point of view.

The third section of the book contains the stories of three couples. I call it "the perfect match," because while these couples are thoroughly unique in their sexual styles, each of them fits their mate like hand in glove. Their stories illustrate the dramatic range that can exist among successful sexual relationships.

By reading these stories before you make love, you can use them as an aphrodisiac to heighten the sexual encounter. Or you can read them to each other during lovemaking as an innovative way to spice up your sex life; or savor them alone in place of a friendly companion on a lonely night. If you do read the stories with your partner, you may want to discuss afterward your reactions to the various tales. In this way, you may learn something about each other that may enable you to be a more conscious, considerate, or pleasing lover. So happy reading and happy loving.

PART ONE

Very Male and Very Female

Having completed two previous compilations of female erotica, I was particularly interested in the ways in which the male-authored stories would differ from those submitted by women.

The first thing I discovered was that unlike stories written by women, a surprising number of those written by men contained nothing more than an opening paragraph that provided an excuse for a long sex scene: there was no literary "foreplay." The orgasm ended the story. Initially, I received so many stories of this type from men that I began to wonder if I would, indeed, be able to create an anthology of writings by both genders. As a result, I felt compelled to send out a second letter explaining my criteria more completely. The thought of having to make this point explicit in the initial invitation had never occurred to me, given my prior experience dealing with female writers, who often erred in favor of story line over sex.

Even in a fully developed story, one replete with plot and character development, there are obvious differences between the erotic writings of men and women. Typically, stories written by men concentrate on the details of the lovemaking scenes. Males tend to be concerned with explicit descriptions of the physical act of sex. Women's breasts, hips, legs, and genitals are often graphically depicted. Penetration, ejaculation, and orgasm are the main events. Fantasies are acted out; violence and aggressive sex are commonplace and four-letter words typically color the dialogue.

Whereas men focus on the physical lovemaking, women delight in everything that leads up to it. For women, the foreplay is of greatest interest, and most of it takes place in the mind: the preparation for the event, the seduction and surrender. Women's stories are often relationship-driven, with the emotional interaction at their foundation. Women focus more on what they *feel* during sex, the smells and touches, rather than what they see. Their stories are rarely violent and their language tends to be sensual rather than coarse.

However, the male authors I selected are not the traditional writers for men's sex magazines. In fact, only two of the male writers have published in men's magazines, and both of them said that the stories they submitted to me were very different from ones they would normally write for their male readership.

On the other hand, almost all of the women authors have previously published erotic writings, half of them in my earlier books. Therefore, the male authors included in this volume may actually be less accustomed to writing explicitly sexual material than the female writers. In addition, my personal bias is certain to be represented in the stories selected—in more than half of the male stories the sexuality takes place within a strong, intimate relationship. I included no stories with violent themes and few using a preponderance of four-letter words. However, the other traditional differences between male and female erotica remain evident in this collection.

The women's stories emphasize seduction, desire, and the mental foreplay that builds up to the sexual encounter. They are primarily concerned with the emotional connection between the characters. "Mirror, Mirror" by Katherine DeRosa humorously illustrates this theme as the main female character readies herself for meeting her lover. According to DeRosa, "I wanted to let the reader live through the process that goes on in a woman's mind when she is preparing for a date and looking forward to the sexual experience. She starts relating to her own body in a more sexual fashion so that the whole evening becomes a kind of foreplay for her."

Along with this interest in seduction, women show a fascination with the mystery of sex. It's not the graphic, the blatant, the obvious that arouses women, but something more subtle. To maintain some mystery, women often prefer to keep the sexuality partly concealed or to create a game of seduction that is played out in a veiled manner. "The Wager," by Anna Nymus, is an intriguing story which keeps the emotional relationship at the center, while creating a web of uncertainty that adds tension to the physical relationship. According to Nymus, "The seduction is itself a game that the two women play and the game is a kind of mystery that is left to the fantasy of the reader. The partly veiled aspect makes it more erotic, just as sex partly clothed is more erotic than being starkly naked."

According to Kim Chernin, author of "The Sacred Harlot," the mystery lies in the attraction. "To me, the essence of the erotic is the mystery of intense connection," says Chernin, "not knowing why people are attracted, but feeling that the minute they set eyes on one another, something has to happen between them." And something does happen—again and again—to Chernin's erotically charged and emotionally open protagonist.

A particular kind of romantic theme commonly found in female erotic writing, is that of the damsel in distress being rescued by the knight in shining armor. Women in this culture grow up on this fairy-tale fare, which probably accounts for the tremendous popularity of novels based on this theme. A fine example of this genre is revealed in Carroll Mavis-Raine's story, "Phantom Grey." Here, the author pairs the occult, another popular female theme, with this Cinderella form of romance, coupling elements from the Civil War era with modern-day Virginia. As Mavis-Raine describes it, "I was drawn to the way this man, who could not live out his own romantic past, was able to rescue a woman from the wounds of her own past and in so doing, heal them both."

When it comes to the sex itself, women put the emphasis on the tenderness, on the emotional or spiritual relationship as opposed to explicit physical descriptions of the lovemaking. This component is so pervasive that it is central to all but one of the female selections included in the book. For example, Carolyn Banks catches us off-guard in her surprising and tender tale, "Lucky in Love." Banks explains, "I like the idea of people with problems being intimate. I think it is the tenderness, the understanding and the caring, that is essential in a good sex life."

And, finally, it is most often the *sensuality*, as compared to a harder explicit *sexuality*, that distinguishes female erotica from that written by males. In fact, I received a number of stories by women writers that were sensual but not particularly sexual. Men, on the other hand, *always* included a specific and explicit sexual scene. "Floating World" by Wickham Boyle is an example of a story in which sensuality pervades the totality of the experience in such a way that the erotic becomes a natural aspect of every part of it. "I wanted to write about Japan," says Boyle, "because the entire countryside was very sensual, yet it's a culture where no one touches. This dichotomy heightened the eroticism for me."

Whereas only one of the stories written by a woman includes anonymous sex, four of the men's stories have no relationship base. Men are more inclined to depict the unadulterated physical pleasures of pure sex. And for men, the predominant lure of eroticism lies in the visual as opposed to the emotional.

A man's reliance on the visual to initiate the arousal process may be one of the reasons why men tend to describe their written sex scenes in such graphic detail and why, more than women, they prefer magazines devoted to photos of nude bodies. According to Clark Demorest, author of "A Matter of Attitude," "It's the sex act, plain and simple, that makes this story erotic," and Demorest describes sexual positions, actions, and organs in explicit detail.

"I think it's the passionate cries and particularly the size of the man's organ that makes my story erotic," reports B. J. Simmons, author of "Unconditional Positive Regard," a story in which the man's enormous penis inspires the turn of events.

In fact, for many men, the penis itself became a character in the drama and there was a tendency to be preoccupied with its dimensions. Men seemed to be measuring: penes were "eight and a quarter inches long," "ten inches long," in one case, "a foot long." Many stories submitted by men contained references to "well-hung" or "gigantic cocks." Women, on the other hand, were concerned with other aspects of the penis, such as the velvety smooth texture or the protruding veins; only occasionally did they make incidental references to its length or thickness.

Finally, when men write erotic stories they tend to include more sexual experimentation than women. "Unconditional Positive Regard" by B. J. Simmons is about swinging; "Waiting for Claire" by Bruce Zimmerman contains a bondage scene. Men are also far more willing to use fantasy and imagination to add variety to their stories. Among the female authors, most of the stories are largely autobiographical. Only two are not based on real-life events. However, twice that number, four of the men's stories, have no basis whatsoever in real life.

In Edward Buskirk's "Other Men," the acting out of a long-cherished sexual fantasy forms the major erotic element for the story line. "The most erotic part of the story for me is where the man has the nerve to tell his wife the sexual fantasy he's been having all these years and she reacts positively to it." In Bruce Zimmerman's story, "Waiting for Claire," the main character uses stories of his wife's erotic past to fuel his sexual fires. Zimmerman explains, "There is an aura of intrigue and mystery that develops when a woman, like the one in my story, tells her partner about the sexual adventures that happened before she met him. The fact that the man's not a part of it, and never can be, is extremely stimulating."

I have sequenced the eleven stories written by males and females, juxtaposing stories that contain similar or opposing elements. However, if you care to test your perceptive abilities, randomly pick a story. Then cover the title and author's name and see how many paragraphs it takes before you can identify the author's gender. Or play this game with your partner, reading the stories aloud to one another. I think you'll be surprised to find how easy it is to identify the sex of the author.

PHANTOM GREY

Carroll Mavis-Raine

As Lindsey exited Interstate 66, she noticed a dark blue Mazda following behind her. Her stomach muscles tightened. It looked just like Steve's car. But how could he have found her so quickly?

At the stop sign at the end of the ramp, she put on her left signal and turned toward Waterford. A sigh of relief escaped her lips as the blue car turned right and headed toward Middleburg.

It was just her imagination working overtime. Of course, it would be impossible for Steve to find her. She'd covered her tracks well.

Still, the sight of the blue Mazda brought it all back. That last day with Steve. Her twenty-sixth birthday.

She'd been in the kitchen of their home in Riverside, baking a cake for herself. No one else would do it. Certainly not Steve. He'd been so weird lately—with his sexual hang-ups and increasingly violent behavior. It was the drugs, of course. The coke was destroying him. But the last time she'd suggested he get professional help, she'd found herself on the floor with a split lip.

He'd walked into the kitchen as she was taking the cake from the oven. The scent of cherry tobacco alerted her to his presence. She straightened and saw him staring at her, his brown eyes glittering oddly. Fear clutched at her insides. She'd seen him like this before, and knew what it meant.

His grin was cruel. "What's this? Susie Homemaker?"

She turned away from him to place the cake pan on a wire rack. "It's my birthday, remember? I thought this year I'd bake myself a cake."

His face had grown blank as if he'd tired of the conversation. "Well, you can finish it later. Right now, I'm going to give you your birthday present." He began to unzip the fly of his Chinos. "Pull down your jeans and turn around."

Panic swept over her. "No, Steve! Not now, and not like that!" His face darkened at her refusal.

He took a step toward her, his hand caressing his stiff penis, now released from his clothing. "Unzip those jeans before I have to do it for you."

Lindsey's heart pounded. She knew it would go easier for her if she'd just obey him, but something inside her rebelled—finally. She took a step away from him . . . and then the phone rang.

"Don't answer it," Steve said. "Just unzip your jeans."

"It's my mother." Lindsey reached for the phone, her hand trembling. "Oh, hi, Mom! I thought it might be you. Thank you. Yes, twenty-six today." She listened while her mother told the annual story of how she'd gone into labor back in Texarkana, how she and Lindsey's father had raced along narrow country roads to get to the hospital in Hot Springs, Arkansas, arriving just minutes before Lindsey's birth.

Lindsey felt Steve's hostile gaze burning into her back. *Mama, help me . . . if you only knew what your son-in-law is about to do to me.* "Steve? He's fine. He says hello. What are we doing tonight?" She swallowed hard, trying to push away the lump in her throat. "Oh, I don't know. Nothing special, I guess. Okay. I'll tell him to take me somewhere nice." She cast a swift glance at Steve. His face was a mixture of impatience and lust. Quickly, she turned away, the photographic image of him caressing his erection imprinted on her mind. "Mom, don't go yet. How's Brenda? And the baby? Is he walking yet?"

Hands grabbed her around the waist. She gasped. "Nothing, Mom. Go on." Steve's fingers fumbled at her zipper. She tried to push him away, but his hand grabbed her chin viciously. His eyes dug into hers. A silent warning. His hands went back to her zipper.

Lindsey closed her eyes, still listening to her mother's loving voice in her ear. Steve wrenched her jeans and panties down. Violently, he whirled her around, pressing her belly against the counter.

Panic rushed over her. "Mom, I have to go! The cake is burning. Okay, thanks for calling—" His stiff penis rammed against her smooth buttocks, searching for entrance. "Mom— I really have to . . . okay, bye."

The phone fell to the counter. Her fingernails dug into the Formica as he sliced into her. She bit her lip and tasted blood. Silently, she endured his violent thrusts, but her mind was screaming. *I can't take this anymore . . . I won't take it anymore.* As her husband pumped his seed into her, her hand began to move toward the utensil drawer. He collapsed against her, breathing raggedly. Slowly, she opened the drawer and stared down at the gleaming butcherknife.

It had started to snow lightly just as Lindsey pulled into the gravel driveway and parked the car in front of the old Virginia farmhouse.

Through a mist of fatigue, Lindsey gazed up at the foyer of the old house she'd inherited. Her haven. She spoke softly to the empty room. "Aunt Lucy, you saved my life, you know. You gave me what I needed to get away from him."

It was true. This old house would be a retreat, a place where she could forget about her old life and immerse herself into her art. She'd spend the days painting . . . healing.

"Thank you, Aunt Lucy."

It was almost as if the old dusty walls were listening. She felt an incredible sense of welcome, a feeling that dear plump Aunt Lucy was standing right there, enveloping her in her apple-scented bosom. The thought of her favorite aunt reminded her of the inexplicable note the lawyer had given her. The envelope had been addressed to Lindsey in Aunt Lucy's sweeping handwriting. *"Open In The Event Of My Death."*

The note had held only two lines. "Enjoy Lee. He's kept me young for many years. Love, Aunt Lucy."

So, who was Lee? A cat or dog? And if so, where was he? No one seemed to know. One thing was for sure. He wasn't around here. The old house was as silent as a rock.

With heavy steps, Lindsey went up the stairs leading to the bedrooms. She hoped one of them, at least, would be fit to sleep in. That was what she needed most—dreamless sleep and then perhaps something to eat. That, of course, would have to wait until morning when she could get out to the nearest town for groceries.

All five bedrooms were shrouded with dust covers. She chose the one with a fireplace. It was charmingly old-fashioned with its wallpaper of lavender ribbon garnished with sprigs of the same aromatic flower. A matching cotton comforter covered the huge four-poster cherry-wood bed over a skirt of eyelet.

Lindsey felt for a switch to brighten the dusk-filled room, but nothing happened when she found it. Then, she remembered. The electricity hadn't been turned on—something else she had to do in town tomorrow. In the shadowy light, she saw a kerosene lantern on the bedside table. It was that or nothing.

After lighting the lantern with matches she found in her purse, she started a fire in the hearth. Then she stripped out of her jeans and pullover sweater and slid between the somewhat musty sheets. Only a moment after she tugged the comforter up over her shoulders, her eyelids fluttered closed.

It was a dream. What else could it be? But he was so real. He stood in the room staring at her. How she could see him she didn't know, for it was still dark. Outside, she could hear the moaning wind and the snow thudding softly against the window. Was that part of the dream, as well? She knew she should be afraid at the appearance of a strange man in her bedroom, but she wasn't. After all, he was just a dream.

The man stood at the side of her bed, tall and broad-shouldered. He had a Nordic face with high cheekbones and piercing blue eyes. Lindsey found herself mesmerized by his lips, sensuously full and kissable. Dark blond hair swept back from his face, just touching his shoulders. He appeared to be dressed in a pewter-grey uniform—one from another age.

He moved toward her and still, Lindsey felt no fear. She waited for his touch, anticipating it. When it came, she was unprepared for her body's volatile reaction. She trembled and quaked as his body slid onto hers, his hands slipping silkily under her nightgown to caress her bare flesh. They gently closed over her breasts, cupping them softly, his thumbs teasing her nipples until they stood like tiny erect soldiers. His voluptuous mouth covered hers in a deep erotic kiss that left her breathless and begging for more. But his mouth moved down to her collarbone to where the buttons of her nightgown began. Quickly, his hands left her breasts and began to unbutton her gown. As soon as her breasts were exposed, his mouth nuzzled at one nipple, then the other, sucking them gently, almost tentatively. Lindsey's fingernails dug into the sheets as the blood raced through her veins. She felt herself growing wet between her legs. *Touch me . . . oh, please touch me now.* It was almost as if he could read her thoughts.

Her thighs parted as his searching fingers slid to her hot moist center, gently manipulating her clitoris until it was stiff and throbbing.

She came quickly, gasping softly. As her heartbeat steadied, she reached for him, but at that moment, he disappeared into nothingness. And the dream was over.

When Lindsey awoke, the eerie light from the night's snowfall filled the room. Still half asleep, she stretched lazily, a soft contented sigh escaping her lips. The same dream had come to her over and over in the night, a little different each time, but always the same Nordic-looking man doing such wonderful things to her love-starved body. It was as if she could still feel his warm fingers on her bare nipples, his hot moist lips pressing against hers, his tongue searching the mysteries of her mouth. Over and over in the night, the blond stranger in her dreams had brought her to one shuddering climax after another.

Lindsey's eyes opened and vaguely, she looked around the room, not sure at first where she was. For a moment, she sensed a presence nearby, but almost immediately, it was gone. She lay still, wondering if she could summon up the strength to get out of bed. There were so many things she had to do, but she felt lethargic. Almost as if she hadn't slept at all.

Finally, she managed to swing her legs to the side of the bed and pull herself to a sitting position. When she stood and walked across the room to get dressed, she felt a deep aching inside her womb. It was a pulsating throb, unlike the painful rawness Steve's love-making always left inside her, even before his sexual appetite had changed. It was almost as if she'd really been loved last night, loved thoroughly.

"Lindsey! Where are you? We've been frantic!" Brenda's voice was shrill in her ear.

Lindsey felt a wave of guilt. She should've called home sooner, once she was safely out of the state. "It doesn't matter where I am," she said to her older sister. "I just want you to know I'm okay."

"But why did you leave like that? So suddenly—without telling anyone?"

A vision of Steve flashed through Lindsey's mind, his face a mask of animal lust. Brenda would never understand what it had been like. Not with a husband like James who worshiped her.

"I can't talk about it now. Brenda—have you heard from Steve? Is he looking for me?"

There was a long silence on the other end of the line. Finally, Brenda spoke, her voice strained. "Lindsey, tell me where you are. Jim and I will come and get you."

"No," Lindsey said quickly. "It's peaceful here. It's just what I need right now."

"You're at Aunt Lucy's house, aren't you?"

Lindsey's pulse jumped. "Don't tell Steve," she said just before breaking the connection.

She shouldn't have called. If Steve had any idea that Brenda knew where she was, he'd find a way to get it out of her.

When had things started going bad for them? Steve hadn't always been a monster. It was his slide into the world of drugs that had changed him. Unwanted memories flooded her mind during the drive back to the farmhouse, and though she tried desperately, she couldn't push them away.

For three more nights, Lindsey slept dreamlessly. But on the fifth night in the Virginia farmhouse, the dreams returned. In her dream, she was lying asleep on her stomach. She felt the man's hands sliding up her brushed cotton nightgown, lingering lovingly on her bare buttocks. Sighing, she allowed herself to move against his caress. His fingers slipped the nightgown upward, exposing her back. His breath was warm against her skin. Then she felt his lips moving along her spine, sending shivers of excitement along her nerve endings. His hands moved from her back to caress the side swells of her breasts as they pressed against the mattress.

"Please," she murmured, grinding into the mattress. Her legs parted slightly in silent invitation. "Touch me . . ."

He did. One hand slipped between her stomach and the bed, sliding down expertly to her hot center. His fingers slid into her. She pressed against them, wanting, wanting . . . and almost immediately getting release. As she pulsated against his fingers, he moved them in her wetness, tenderly, lovingly.

When her breathing slowed, she heard his voice, soft and deliciously Southern. "M'name's Lee, Ma'am, and you're just the sweetest taste of a woman I've ever had. Here, this is for you."

Her eyes flashed open. His voice was real! Heart pounding, she turned over, still feeling the wet release of her orgasm between her thighs. In the darkness, she saw a movement, a grey shadow moving away from her. She opened her mouth to scream, and then it was gone.

"Imagination," she murmured. "That's all it is."

But then she felt something soft on the bed next to her. With shaking fingers, she reached out to switch on the bedside lamp that had replaced the lantern.

And there it lay. A single red rose, fresh and perfect, its thorns removed.

Lindsey found Aunt Lucy's diary later that day. And that was how she learned about Lee.

The first entry was dated September 17, 1943. Lindsey calculated that Lucy would've been twenty-two years old. She read:

> *I can't believe it's been a year since Ted's ship was torpedoed in the Pacific. I didn't think I could go on, but somehow, I did. And I've made it through the first year. They say that's the hardest. But it's been lonely. And still, the war goes on.*

And the next night's:

> *It makes me blush to write this down, but I have to. Last
> night I had these . . . naughty dreams. I had a lover. And no, it
> wasn't Ted. This man was totally different. So sweet and tender.
> I dreamed he told me his name was Lee. Oh Lord, I'm so
> ashamed to say this, but I can hardly wait to go to bed again
> tonight. He told me he'd be back.*

Lindsey's heart began to beat faster as she read one entry after
another. *Lee came again tonight. He loved me so good. It's almost
as if he's real.* Lindsey flipped through the ink-stained pages. On
and on it went, increasingly vivid descriptions of Lee's love-making
to her aunt. Her cheeks were burning. Then, she came to the entry
that made her heart stand still.

> *Lee is real! Well, not like me. But he really comes at night.
> It isn't my imagination. His name is Capt. Leewood Jorgensen,
> an officer of the Confederate Army Calvary. I went to the town
> library and looked into the history of our house. During the
> Civil War, he and his new bride were on their way here to his
> family home when they were ambushed by renegade Union sol-
> diers. They brutally raped his bride and shot Lee, leaving him
> for dead. But he remained conscious long enough for her to die
> in his arms. It didn't say what she died of, blood loss or shock,
> maybe. Anyway, Lee managed to drag himself the rest of the
> way to this house where he died in the front parlor.*
> *Yes, died. Lee is a ghost! And he has made love to me every
> night now for two years. Sometimes, in the midst of his passion,
> he calls me Suzanne. That was his virgin wife's name. But I
> don't care. I love him, and I know he loves me. He is spending
> eternity trying to make up for the pain and suffering his bride
> went through. To give me the love she was denied.*

Lindsey drew a deep breath. Aunt Lucy was crazy. Loony.
Probably certifiable. But perhaps she wasn't the only one. Hadn't
Lindsey had similar dreams? Last night especially, when he'd spo-
ken, it had seemed so real. *Was* he real? Or was he a ghost?

She was almost afraid to go to bed that night, yet, she had to admit, the nervousness she felt in her stomach wasn't entirely unpleasant. It was a tingling anticipation, one that her conscious mind told her was absolutely ridiculous. *Nothing* was going to happen. Nothing that wasn't in her imagination anyway.

Lindsey tried to stay awake. To wait for him, to see if there *was* something to Aunt Lucy's bizarre story. But after an hour, she grew drowsy and finally, she had to give in to sleep. It was several hours later when she awoke and felt a definite presence in the room. Her heart raced. There was no sound, no movement, just a watchfulness. A scent. Yes, a heavy atmosphere of controlled sexuality. Goose bumps rose on Lindsey's skin. She was afraid, yes, but the fear was mixed with something else. Anticipation.

She sensed he'd been in the room for some time. Just watching and waiting. For what? Lindsey kept her eyes closed and tried to maintain normal breathing. Something in the room atmosphere changed. He was moving toward the bed! Her pulse leaped. Then, incredibly, he spoke in the soft Southern accent of the night before.

"Don't y'all pretend you're asleep, Lindsey. I know better."

Her hands clutched the bed sheets, but she lay still, trying to carry on her charade. An amused chuckle came from the man.

"All right, then. Have it your own way."

A sudden draft swept over her skin as the bed covers were pulled away. She stifled a gasp as his warm fingers brushed against her breasts. He was unbuttoning her nightdress! *Oh, my God! He's a ghost and I'm allowing him to undress me!* But the fact was, the fear she'd felt upon sensing his presence was quickly disappearing. Old-fashioned body heat was taking its place. She felt the cold air of the room on her bare flesh as he parted the bodice of the gown. It was quickly replaced by the warmth of his parted lips as they captured one peaked nipple. Lindsey caught her breath. His tongue leisurely traced circles on one nipple and then the other before he drew away.

"Open your eyes, Lindsey. You'll see I'm not to be feared."

"I'm not afraid," she whispered. And slowly, she opened her eyes.

A pale moonlight spilled into the room, allowing enough illumination so she could see him clearly. He was perched on the bed, just inches away from her, so close she could feel his warmth.

But he's flesh and blood, not a ghost at all! It was the same Nordic-looking man she'd seen the first night. His clear blue eyes gazed down at her. He smiled, revealing strong white teeth between his full-bodied lips. He was dressed in the grey wool coat of a Confederate officer, and strangely enough, it looked brand-new. His smile widened.

"You may touch me, Ma'am, if you want to assure yourself I'm really here. You have my word I won't disappear."

Tentatively, Lindsey reached out and touched the scratchy wool of his coat. He grabbed her hand and pressed it against his warm face.

"Can you disappear?" she asked, her voice husky.

"I surely can. Do you want me to?"

Before she could speak, his image wavered. The warm flesh under her fingers grew cool and suddenly, it was as if she were touching nothing.

"No! Don't go."

Immediately, she felt the heat of life beneath her fingertips, and once again, he was flesh and blood. "Tell me to stay, then. Say 'Lee, I want you to stay and love me like no man has ever done before.'"

Her heart gave a jolt. A heated lethargy swept through her body. A long breathy sigh came from her lips. "Oh, yes . . . stay, Lee. Stay and love me like no man has ever done before."

His mouth crushed down on hers, his tongue slipping inside easily, exploring, thrusting, then teasing and tasting. His hands kneaded her exposed breasts until they were aching and taut. Suddenly, he drew away and shrugged out of his wool jacket, dropping it casually to the floor. Beneath it, he wore a white lawn shirt. With lightning fingers, he unbuttoned it and took it off. His chest was muscular and covered with a light carpet of hair. Lindsey reached out and brushed both palms against his chest, feeling the thud of his heart beneath them. Her eyes widened in amazement.

"You're so real. How can you feel so real?"

"Because I *am* real." With a soft growl, he fell upon her again, his tongue moving down the vee of her neck to the swell of her breasts. She squirmed beneath him, trying to relieve the ache between her legs.

Lee went from one nipple to the other, in no apparent rush as one hand caressed the tip of one unoccupied breast while his tongue worked the other. Finally, his mouth slipped down the lower swell to her stomach where his tongue dipped into her navel for a leisurely taste. The fire between her legs burned hotter.

"Oh, please . . ." she murmured. "I want . . ."

"I know what you want, Ma'am," he said softly, his mouth against her lower belly. "And you'll get it. I'm a Southern gentleman, Ma'am, and we don't take kindly to being rushed. You just be patient, little lady. We have all night."

His hands were on her thighs now, stroking them lightly. He chuckled as a thumb brushed high against her inner leg and felt the wetness there. She flinched involuntarily as his touch sent an electric jolt through her.

"Right sensitive there, aren't you, sweetheart?" His fingers inched closer to her moist hot center, but not quite touching her there. She thrust her pelvis toward him and moaned. He dipped his head down to where she could feel his warm breath against her skin. "Do you want it, pretty lady? Just tell me you want it." His voice was a low rumble, vibrating against her. She knew his tongue was only inches away, and God, yes, she wanted it.

"I *want* it! Please, Lee, make me come."

She flinched again as his fingers parted the tiny hood that sheltered her nub. With the touch of his tongue, a cry escaped her lips. "Oh, *yes!*"

With his lips and tongue, he began to work his magic. At the same time, he thrust two fingers into her, moving in and out slowly and expertly, each time moving a bit closer to where his tongue was busy. Once, he came too close. Lindsey began to shudder, climaxing in warm gushing waves. His tongue slowed and finally, he drew away, his head resting against her thigh.

"Was that what you wanted, honey?" he whispered, his voice ragged.

"Oh, yeah," she murmured. "Come here."

He slid up to her, and lying on his side, took her into his arms.

They shared a deep drugging kiss. Lindsey's hands moved down
to the small of his back. Her fingers touched the waistband of his
wool trousers and slid down over his firm buttocks. Down and over
to his front. Her palm found the rock hard outline of his erection.
Very well endowed, indeed, she thought deliriously. God, she'd
never in her life felt anything like that before, oh, the talent he had
with his mouth.

Steve had never done that to her. It was dirty, he'd said. Yet
he'd always wanted her to do it to him. But soon enough, even that
wasn't enough to get him hard. She remembered the humiliation
of taking his limp penis into her mouth, trying anything to turn
him on. Once, in frustration, he'd slapped her away, snarling, "You
don't know how to do anything right, you ugly bitch."

"Don't think about him," Lee whispered into her ear. "The animal will never touch you again." He pressed her hand to his rigid
maleness straining against his trousers. "But for now, we've gotta
do something about this."

She felt for a zipper, but, of course, there was none. Only buttons. She undid them slowly, relishing the anticipation of touching
his bare skin. Three buttons undone, she realized he was wearing
no underwear. His huge shaft thrust through the opening. Her
fingers explored him as he helped to push the trousers down past
his buttocks.

"It's all yours, Ma'am. Only for you."

Lindsey got up onto her knees and brought her lips down to
him. When she began to nuzzle him, he gave a slight shudder and
pushed himself against her impatiently. She opened her mouth and
took him in, swirling her tongue around his shaft. Lee moved
slowly, tantalizingly, in and out of her mouth. Her hands worked
his cock, moving the wetness of her saliva up and down as he eased
in and out. His breathing quickened and finally, he drew out, reaching down to pull her naked body against his.

"I want to love you now," he said softly.

Gently, he pushed her down onto her stomach. With his hands,
he maneuvered her up on her knees. His rigid length brushed
against her buttocks and she gasped. Her eyes filled with tears of
disappointment. Oh, God! He was going to do it like Steve!

"Don't be afraid, love," he said. "I'm not gonna hurt you."

His fingers slid into her burning center. She rocked against them, wanting him in spite of what he was going to do to her. But when she felt him prod against her, she was bathed with relief. He wasn't like Steve, at all. Slowly, he pressed himself into her, thrusting gradually until he was in to the hilt. A wave of uncontrollable desire raced through her. She ground herself against him, clenching her hands into the sheets.

"Oh, yes!"

He began to thrust in and out slowly. With each inward thrust, she felt filled, almost to the point of explosion, and soon, it wasn't enough. "Faster," she murmured. "Please, do it to me faster."

His rhythm began to pick up. His hands slid to her breasts, pressing and squeezing. He slapped against her, hard and fast, his breath coming in gasping heaves. She moaned as the heat built up inside her, coming closer and closer with each thrust. And then, as he was pumping into her like a machine piston, she climaxed. It was even more powerful than the one he'd brought her to with his tongue. Growling, he gave one more powerful thrust and collapsed against her, shuddering.

After a moment, he rolled over on his side, bringing her with him. She nestled against his lean body, spoon-fashion. Her eyes closed. "For a ghost, you're one hell of a good lover."

His hand played leisurely with her nipple. He leaned over and kissed her right shoulder. "For a ghost? Hmmmm. I just might want to think that one over. 'Pears to me to be a backhanded compliment."

She shook her head, exhausted. "No. I didn't mean it like that . . . ," but she didn't hear his answer. She had drifted off to sleep.

When she awoke, Lee was gone. There was no evidence he'd been there at all, other than the well-loved feeling between her legs and the damp spot on the sheets. She fell asleep again and dreamed about her phantom soldier through the remaining hours of the night.

A watery sunlight filtered through the curtains the next morning, awakening her. For a few moments, she lay in bed, thinking about Lee and the magical hours spent with him the night before.

But then a new awareness crept into her mind, and she sat up, her eyes scanning the room in alarm. The entire room smelled of cherry tobacco! Her heart thudded.

Had Lee left the scent? She hadn't noticed it before. Then again, she'd been preoccupied with other things. It had to be Lee. That was the only explanation. But what a coincidence . . . that he smoked the same kind of tobacco Steve did.

Lindsey spent the day in a mental fog, her mind refusing to let go of Lee and the sensual night they'd spent together. She tried to paint, but his face was the only image she saw. Over and over, she sketched it, and was disappointed that she couldn't get it quite right.

She thought of Aunt Lucy. If Lee had done this to her every night, it was no wonder everyone thought she was spacey. But it was also no wonder the woman had been so happy. Why not? She had the most perfect of lovers, one who existed only for her pleasure. No need to worry about the anxieties of a relationship. No arguments over money, no worries over what kind of mood he was going to be in. No wondering if you'd end up slammed to the floor if you said the wrong thing.

Oh, Lee, you are the perfect man, she told herself. *And being a ghost may be the reason why you're so perfect.*

In the afternoon, she left her studio and drove into town for groceries and supplies. She moved dreamily through the aisles, wondering if it were possible for ghosts to eat. She wanted to do something for Lee to show her appreciation for the previous night.

She settled on two steaks, russet potatoes, and fixings for a salad. On the drive back to the house, she sang along with the radio, her heart light. The winter dusk was quickly approaching, and the thought made her smile with anticipation. The coming night would be magic, as would the rest of her nights, as long as Lee was around.

She brought the groceries into the kitchen and switched on the oven. "Okay, Lee, if you can hear me, I want to invite you to dinner." She looked at her wristwatch. "Say, in about an hour?" There was no response, but she really hadn't expected one. He would show up whenever he felt like it.

When the oiled potatoes were in the oven, Lindsey went into

the dining room to set the table. Where had she seen those long tapers? They'd be perfect for a romantic dinner. She stepped into the parlor to look in Aunt Lucy's china cabinet. Immediately, she was overwhelmed by the scent of cherry tobacco.

A sense of primal fear overwhelmed her. She clenched her fists and took a deep breath. It's just Lee, she told herself. Yet, her thudding heart refused to believe it.

"Lee," she spoke into the empty room. "Don't do this to me, darling. You don't know what I've been through in the last months. I'm easily frightened."

There was only silence in the room, yet Lindsey felt a change. The air suddenly reeked of evil. She felt the blood drain from her face. Her heart began to race. Fearfully, she scanned the room, knowing she could no longer deny the malevolent presence. Her eyes stopped on a black object, half-hidden in the shadows near the heavy curtains. A whip, coiled and malignant—waiting . . .

Lee's? But why . . . ?

There was a sudden movement behind her—a rush of air, an indrawn breath. Lindsey whirled around, gasping, "Lee, is that you?"

She saw no one, but her senses told her she wasn't alone in the room. Hidden eyes watched her. She tried to summon a smile.

"Please don't play games with me, Lee. I like you the way you were last night—so gentle and protective."

It came from behind her. Soft laughter with an edge of hysteria. Lindsey gasped and turned. There was nothing behind her but the long velvet curtains.

"Lee, please don't tease me like this."

But even as she spoke, she knew she could no longer fool herself. Lee wasn't her tormentor. A hand clamped down onto her shoulder. Even through her sweater, she could feel that it was ice cold. She screamed. Unseen hands wrenched her around and an icy mouth clamped down onto hers, a frigid tongue forcing its way between her clenched lips. She struggled, but the man's strength was too much for her. One icy hand pushed her sweater up above her breasts and expertly unhooked the front closure of her bra. Lindsey jerked her mouth away from her attacker's and screamed. A hand closed upon her nipple, twisting violently.

"Screaming won't do you any good, Lindsey."

Lindsey stiffened. The voice! She began to shake her head. *Oh, God—no! Not you!*

It was as if he could read her thoughts. "Oh, yes. It *is* me. And nothing can protect you this time."

Suddenly, Lindsey was free. She ran toward the door, thinking only of escape. But then, his voice came again.

"Oh, you can't leave now, baby. The fun's just beginning."

As he spoke, the parlor doors slammed shut. Half crazed with fear, Lindsey flung herself against them, twisting at the door knobs, but they refused to budge.

"Turn around, Lindsey. Look what I have for you."

Slowly, Lindsey turned. Steve stood across the room. He held the whip, one hand caressing the ivory handle as if it were a lover. He wore a sneer on his cruelly handsome face. His hard brown eyes swept over her.

"Did you really think I wouldn't find you? That your Aunt Lucy's money would protect you?" He gave a cruel laugh. "You're such a little idiot, aren't you? You can't escape from me. I'm your husband, remember? *I* take *my* wedding vows seriously. You know, until death do us part? But I'd add a little something to that. Until death do us part . . . and beyond." His eyes scanned her body and he smiled. "You're looking real sexy, Lind. I get hot just looking at you. That old problem I had is gone. I'm hard all the time now." The smile disappeared. "Undo your jeans, Lindsey. I want to put some bloody stripes on your perfect little ass before I fuck you." As he spoke, he unzipped his fly and pulled out his erect penis. With one hand, he fondled himself as he came toward her.

Lindsey flattened herself against the door. "Lee! Help me!" But she knew Lee wasn't around to help. He was far away. She didn't know how she knew it, but she did.

"Okay. So you won't cooperate. You never did, did you? You knew what I liked, but you never wanted to give it to me. You need to be taught a lesson, Lindsey. You need to learn how to satisfy your man."

He flung the whip aside and sprang at her. Lindsey slapped out at him, but one hand grabbed hers and pinned it against the door. The other grappled at her jeans. Lindsey felt the pop of the closure as it gave way. With inhuman strength, he unzipped her jeans and tugged them down along with her wispy bikini underpants. He shoved her onto her knees. "You know the position, don't you? You stay in it unless you want to feel that whip bite into your juicy flesh. You're one stupid bitch, you know that? Did you think you were going to get away with it? You wouldn't have to pay for what you did?" He grabbed her hips and with one violent shove, thrust himself into her.

She screamed. The stabbing pain shot through her core. Lindsey sobbed, praying to die, anything to stop the pain.

"Take this, you little cunt," Steve gasped with each crucifying thrust.

Locked in his animalistic grip, Lindsey could only submit, all the time wishing she were already dead. He *would* kill her this time. She knew it.

Suddenly, Steve gave a sharp intake of breath and withdrew from her. Lindsey heard a soft thud as he dropped to the floor. The tears flowed down her cheeks as she fell to the carpet, curling herself into a fetal ball. Then, miraculously, she heard Lee's voice.

"I tried, hon, but I just couldn't make it here before he hurt you." Lee stood above her, his breathing ragged, eyes filled with remorse. "But he won't ever hurt you again. I can assure you of that."

Lindsey sat up and turned her head to stare at her husband and the widening pool of blood surrounding his body. A gleaming saber pierced through his back.

She looked up at Lee. It was the first time she'd seen him in lamplight. He was tall, nearly six foot. His skin was lightly tanned and as flesh and blood as Steve had been a moment before.

But Steve hadn't been flesh and blood, had he? Lindsey began to tremble in delayed shock. "He was like you, wasn't he?"

Lee nodded and knelt down next to her. "Come here, hon."

With a soft sob, Lindsey flung herself into his reassuring arms. He pulled her onto his lap, gently pulling up her panties and jeans. Then he snuggled her close as if she were a wounded child. "I'd like to kill him again for what he did to you."

"Why . . . why did it take you so long to come?"

"It's hard to explain, Lindsey. A process we have to go through to get back to this world. So complicated I don't rightly understand it myself. But that's why it took that bastard so long to appear in the flesh. He'd tried several times before."

"You mean, you knew he was . . . coming back?"

"It was the only way we could get rid of him for good."

Lindsey snuggled against him, inhaling the masculine scent that was nothing like cherry tobacco. "I get it," she said softly. "It took a ghost to kill a ghost." She stopped as a thought occurred to her. "But how did he die—the first time?"

His arms tightened around her. He looked down at her, his eyes gentle. "You killed him six months ago. Self-defense, the courts decided. Even so, you couldn't live with what you did. You blacked it out and came here to make a new life. Only problem was, *he* was bound to catch up with you sooner or later. I just wish I'd been here to protect you when he did. I'll never forgive myself for that."

Lindsey touched his lips to stop him. "You're here now. Just stay with me."

He kissed her. As his tongue delved into her mouth, Lindsey forgot Steve, forgot dinner, forgot everything. Lee swooped her up into his arms and climbed the stairs to the bedroom.

Gently, he placed her upon the bed, his eyes gazing into hers tenderly. Slowly, his hands moved up her thighs to the waist of her jeans. Sighing softly, she lifted her hips slightly as he tugged the jeans down and tossed them to the floor. Underneath her satin panties, Lindsey felt herself growing wet—just from the look in Lee's brilliant blue eyes.

Her breathing grew uneven, her mouth parted in anticipation. Their gaze locked. Finally, Lee's fingers touched her between her legs, gently exploring her. She groaned softly, thrusting against his fingers. Slowly, maddeningly, he drew her panties down, in no great hurry. But as he turned away to drop them to the floor, Lindsey saw the thrusting outline of his erection under the wool of his trousers.

He bent down and kissed her quivering belly, his hands caressing her smooth hips. "I love you, Lindsey," he whispered. "I didn't think I'd ever feel like this again."

Lindsey moaned, parting her legs slightly. His hand slipped back to her center, delving into her wetness, opening her like a flower.

Then his tongue slid into her—flicking, nuzzling, teasing. It was almost too much. And when it *was* too much, he placed his hands under her buttocks and drew her upward, as if she were an offering to his sweet mouth. He dove his tongue deeply inside her until she thrashed in delirium, and finally, went over the edge, moaning.

Afterward, he climbed onto the bed beside her and gathered her into his arms. "I'll never hurt you," he said huskily. "I will always be a balm to your pain."

Lindsey clung to him, still gasping from her climax. He took her hand and pressed it against his rock-hard length, burning hot through the wool of his trousers. Lindsey fumbled to unbutton him. After a moment, he gently pushed her hands away and undid the buttons himself. His erection jutted out of the opening. As her hands closed around his steel-like shaft, he groaned, his eyes closing. She leaned over him, her tongue caressing his full sensuous lips. He opened to her and they kissed, tongues mingling. As her hand moved up and down his cock, he lifted his buttocks and pushed his trousers off his hips. Her eyes moved to his muscular chest. Quickly, she unbuttoned his lawn shirt and parted it. She slid both hands over his light carpet of hair, pressing her fingertips against his warm skin, relishing in the wonder of his reality. *Of the life that pulsated under that warm body.* He lay quietly under her touch, his eyes watching her.

"Come here," he whispered. And with his powerful hands, he pulled her on top of him, settling her down so her wet center pressed against his hard shaft. Lifting her slightly, he eased into her slowly. Lindsey closed her eyes, gasping at the sensations rioting through her. He pushed in to the hilt, and slowly, she began to ride him, easing up and down sensuously. It was a slow, sweet journey, the intensity of it rising steadily, leisurely. She climaxed first, slow and pulsating, hot and wet, as wave after wave of tiny shocks rippled through her. A moment later, Lee arched his back and gave one last shuddering thrust, and she felt his seed spilling into her.

Later, when they descended the stairs arm in arm and paused by the parlor door, Lindsey couldn't stop herself from looking into the room. But where Steve's skewered body had been hours before, there was now nothing but a clean carpet, a coiled whip, and a shining Civil War saber.

Mirror, Mirror

Katherine DeRosa

Miranda stood in the shower, letting the hot water pummel her neck and back. She willed the water to beat away the frustrations of her day at the office, let her mind empty as she absently watched a streak of pink form on her skin, where the steaming hot water ran down in a river between her breasts. Her eyes settled on her disposable razor lying on the edge of the tub. Tonight Jake was taking her to dinner. Would they? Probably. She reached for the razor but it slipped from her soapy hand; she jumped away from the blade as it fell. *Damn!*

She soaped up first one calf, then the other, and shaved them with long even strokes. Then she did her underarms, wincing as the razor bit the tender skin and drew blood. She washed her hair and conditioned it, then massaged the creamy conditioner into the dark triangle of her pubic hair too—what the hell, it might as well smell like herbs or apples or whatever they put in that stuff, papayas? She let the conditioner sit for three minutes; as she waited, she ran a fingertip up her wet calves, checking to make sure that the skin felt smooth.

Even after a year of dating Jake, and as much as she sometimes knew she loved him, she had never let him touch her legs unless they were freshly shaved. Maybe that was sick, but her instincts told her it was the right way to go. Jake was a good guy, smart and caring, but his attitudes were pretty basic. Anyhow, it didn't pay to let men see the real you too soon. She still preferred to make love with him by dim candlelight—and not because she had hang-ups about sex; quite the opposite. She'd learned she could really let herself go if she didn't have to worry about him seeing her wobbly thighs.

Out of the tub, toweling off, she ran her palm in circles across the steamy mirror to clear it. She liked looking at herself in the mirror right after a shower, when you couldn't see things too clearly. Reflexively she sucked in her stomach, pulled back her shoulders and thrust her breasts forward, checked out her butt from the side. Not too bad. If she worked out, which she didn't, she would have an okay body.

Jake. She dusted on the scented powder he liked, which smelled of vanilla and cinnamon—good enough to eat, he'd said. Then she cinched the towel around her damp body and plugged in the blow dryer. She hated this part; it was so boring. It took forever to dry her yard of thick, sun-bleached hair: style it, gel it, spray it, tease it into the right shape with the brush. But there was no alternative; if she didn't, she looked like hell. While she waited for her curling iron to heat up, she brushed her teeth, flossed, and used mouthwash. She curled back her lips and admired her teeth; the money for that bridgework had been worth it.

Framed by her styled hair, her bare face looked oddly flat and pale; she reached for her foundation and blush. As she labored to camouflage the same flaws she had worked over daily for the past fifteen years—lips too full, green eyes a little too narrow, an overly strong chin—she felt a flash of resentment. This was boring. Men were supposed to like women, naked women, but sometimes she wondered—did they really? If Jake loved her as she was (as he was always telling her) then why did she feel this need to make herself over? As though her natural state were somehow shameful.

It was humiliating. But she had to admit that she found these preparations titillating too—a kind of extended foreplay. With a hint of S&M. *Ouch!* Her mascara wand jabbed the corner of her eye; she wiped off the offending black smudge and started over, working more carefully. She had seen a Phil Donahue show once featuring a woman who had accidentally blinded herself with her mascara. Only in one eye, but still.

She plucked her eyebrows, biting her lip to distract herself from the momentary pain. Then she rubbed scented body lotion into her skin, from her arms all the way down to her legs, enduring the stinging as the lotion soaked into her just-shaved calves. She wanted to be completely soft and smooth. Sometimes as she made these ritual preparations of her body for sex, she fantasized that she was a virgin preparing herself for a pagan sacrifice. Kind of kinky, even masochistic if you thought about it. But sexy too.

Standing in her bedroom staring at her closet, she tried to think what Jake liked on her. She gazed longingly at her favorite black sweatshirt top, but she knew Jake thought it was too baggy. He liked it when she wore clothes that let him see her breasts. And she liked knowing he was watching. She settled on her white silk blouse; the fabric was so sheer that it revealed the precise shape of her nipples. She would wear it without a camisole, just her thin pink brassiere. But the blouse needed pressing, she saw. Irked, she stooped to plug in the iron, then set up the ironing board with a horrible screech that sent her cat flying from the room. Ironing was even duller than blow drying.

On the bottom, jeans. Again a choice: her loose, comfortable pair, or the tight jeans that made her butt look smaller but were too short in the crotch? She knew what Jake liked; she could endure a degree of discomfort to feel sexy for him. They had been having some trouble in bed lately, which was probably her fault; she ought to make more of an effort. Maybe this was the night for those lacy, pale pink panties—she didn't wear them often because the lace was so scratchy. But hopefully tonight she wouldn't have them on for long.

She poked some earrings with dangling gold balls through her ears, stepped into her highest pair of heels, and assessed the total effect in the mirror. She looked sexy, very sexy; she was a turn-on, even to herself. The knowledge gave her confidence, and she felt herself became warm and liquid in anticipation of the evening ahead. Still looking in the mirror, she pouted her lips and gave herself a come-hither look. Then she pinched her nipples lightly through the blouse, watching as they became fully erect. Jake would want to do that too.

What else? The sheets. She really ought to change them. She selected a clean set flowered with roses and struggled to get them on the heavy mattress, breaking a fingernail as she tried to force on the last fitted corner. Damn it; now she'd need some nail glue. Hurriedly she picked up her clothes from the floor and threw them in the hamper, then wiped a still-damp sweat sock over the worst of the dust on her dresser and bedside tables. She checked to make sure the essentials were on hand: candle, matches, baby lotion, condoms, diaphragm, spermicide, damp washcloth, incense, bucket of ice cubes, a tape ready to go in the boombox by the bed. The bedside clock read 7:17. An hour and a half since she'd hit the front door and headed for the shower, thirteen minutes until Jake was due. Just enough time to straighten the rest of the house, if she hurried. She lit the tall candle by the bed, then flicked off the bedroom light.

Miranda was in the kitchen, arranging cheese and crackers on a wooden tray, when she heard Jake let himself in. "Hiya!" she called. "Be out in a minute!" Hurriedly she garnished the tray with a few sprigs of parsley—they could chew on those later if the cheese gave them bad breath—and carried it in to greet Jake.

He sat on her leather couch in a white T-shirt and paint-splattered jeans, slumped in exhaustion. She noticed tiny flecks of white paint in his dark hair, which curled almost into ringlets at the back of his neck and on the shapely muscles of his bare, tanned arms. She loved the way he looked in a white T-shirt and jeans— basic, male, unvarnished. A whiff of manly sweat wafted to her across the room. "You come straight from work, babe?" she asked.

"Yeah, killer day." He pulled her down to him on the sofa, and gave her a long affectionate kiss. Miranda responded but felt distracted—she still had the cheese tray in her hands—and she couldn't help noticing the stale scent of onions on his breath. Jake took a cracker and a piece of cheese and let off the steam from his day. "We spent all fuckin' morning framing in a wall, then dildo brain realizes it's four inches too far to the left, so we spend all fuckin' afternoon tearing it down again." He cracked his knuckles, reliving the frustration. "Had to work overtime, just to get back to where we should've been at noon."

"Did you have a chance to pick up the wine?" she asked casually.

"Oh damn. I forgot. I'm sorry, babe, I'm just so beat. Why don't you see if there's a beer or two left in the fridge? If not, I'll pick some up later."

When Miranda came back in with a cold beer, Jake had unlaced his work boots and was dropping them on the floor. Thud. Thud. Miranda noticed little pieces of mud flaking off them, onto her polished hardwoods. She handed him the beer, saying, "It's the only one." Then she discreetly picked up his boots and headed out of the room again. "I'll just put these on the back porch," she called over her shoulder. On her way through the dining room, she cracked a window. She heard Jake flick on the television, flipping through the channels until he found a nature show about predators on PBS.

Miranda patted her stomach and groaned. The Italian place had been nice, but she never should have eaten that third piece of pizza. Now, snuggled on the sofa with Jake, her jeans cut painfully into her stomach and her eyes burned from the new eyeliner she had tried. Worse yet, the lace panties had crawled up between her buns and were wedged into an itchy lump. She glanced at Jake and decided he could doze off at any moment. "Time for bed, honey," she cooed. It would feel great to get out of these jeans.

In the bedroom, she punched on her Stan Getz tape, pulled off her pants and then removed Jake's, pulling from the ankle as he lifted his bottom from the bed. He lay there sleepily. "Do it to me, baby," he said with a sexy smile. "I love it when you take the lead." Miranda crawled on top of him and began kissing his ear, then his eyelids, and then slipped her mouth onto his. As their kissing became deeper; she wrapped her legs around his thighs. Then, after a minute, she pulled away.

"Do I need to brush my teeth?" she asked.

"No, babe, you're fine," Jake assured her.

She was hoping he would ask her the same question, but he didn't. Her lips hurt from rubbing up against the bristles on his chin; she wondered if he had taken a shower and shaved that morning. God, what was wrong with her? Worrying about this stuff. She should be more passionate—she tried just to focus on their lovemaking, give it her full effort. She began to lick and bite the soft skin at the top of his thighs. Simultaneously, her hand stroked and teased the erection growing inside his soft cotton underwear.

Concentrating on her technique, she thought about how they had developed a steady progression of arousal that worked well for them as a couple, and which they rarely varied. First she got him fully aroused; then he worked on her. Like the steps in a recipe; you had to do them in the right order. God, had she remembered to get the eggs for the pancakes in the morning?

"Babe, is anything wrong?" asked Jake. He reached down and lifted up her head so that he could see her face. "You don't seem like you're really into it tonight."

"No," Miranda told him. "Everything's fine." She felt guilty; she must not be concentrating.

"Sure? M'anda? Because if something's bothering you, I want to know. You can always tell me." He gave her a crooked smile and traced his finger over the outline of her nipple through her blouse, just as she had imagined.

"No, I'm fine. It's nothing really." But Miranda found herself lying back on the bed; she felt tired. "It's just . . . I don't know."

"Is there something on your mind? Or something you want me to do?" Jake asked sweetly.

Miranda tried to think—what *was* wrong? She felt herself growing embarrassed. "It's just . . . well, usually you tell me that I look pretty."

"But you *do* look pretty!" Jake said, clearly puzzled.

"But you didn't tell me."

"But you know I think you're beautiful!"

Miranda tried again. "Maybe sometimes, well, I just wish you would put more, you know, *planning* into sex." She looked at Jake but could see that he didn't understand. "I feel like you don't think ahead about having sex with me, like it means nothing to you."

She wanted to explain how long she had spent preparing for tonight, how she had selected special panties, but she stopped herself—it seemed so petty.

"So what are you saying?" Jake sounded hurt.

"Well, it's just that sometimes I feel like I do all the work."

"*You* do all the work!" Jake was incredulous. He sat up. "C'mon, Miranda, how can you say that?! *I'm* the one who does all the work. You never want to get on top. You never *initiate* anything! You just want to lie there looking sexy!"

Miranda felt confused. It was true, what he said. But was that wrong? "I thought you liked me to look sexy."

"Well, I do." Jake looked confused too.

He lay back down and they rested together quietly, listening to Getz wail soulfully on the sax and the neighbors chatting on the back steps. After a minute or two, Jake reached over and stroked Miranda's arm, then moved his hand down and ran his fingers lightly over the mound of hair under her panties, asking permission to get her excited. Miranda rolled over, away from him. She lay stiff, in stolid silence.

"I give up," said Jake. He sounded irked. He swung his legs over the edge of the bed and got up. "I don't understand you. Maybe I just don't understand women. You all look like sexpots, you act like sexpots, but when you get into bed, you don't want to *do* anything. I just don't get it. It must be me. I'm going to take a cold shower."

She lay in bed alone, listening to the sounds from the bathroom. She heard the groan of her ancient water pipes as Jake turned on the hot water—"cold shower" must have been a figure of speech. She heard him step in, heard the steady rush of water splattering against the tiles, and pictured him rubbing a bar of soap sensuously over his chest, his shoulders, his back. She sat up and looked at herself in the full-length mirror on her closet door; in the flickering candlelight, the sight of herself half undressed was exciting. She pushed pillows behind herself so that her body was angled directly toward the mirror. Then she spread her legs slightly apart, exposing the pink triangle of her panties. She watched her manicured fingers stroke herself lightly through the silky fabric.

She heard Jake turn off the water and get out. She imagined how he looked stepping out of the tub, his naked body all pink and muscled and glistening with drops of water. He would be toweling off his legs now, one foot up on the side of the tub, the cheeks of his ass spread. She glanced into the mirror again and undid the top button of her blouse. She watched herself slowly undo the line of buttons, then pull the blouse from her shoulders and let it drop onto the floor.

Now she heard him opening the medicine cabinet; he must be looking for her deodorant. Good. She stroked herself again through her panties. Next came the sound of the water running in the sink; she pictured Jake bent over the sink, the rounded cheeks of his butt fully exposed, brushing his teeth. Excited by the thought, she looked into her mirror and pulled the cups of her brassiere down until her breasts were bared, supported pertly by the underwiring. She ran her fingertips across her erect nipples, then caressed her breasts with a slow, circular motion as she waited for Jake to return.

When Jake came in, he was still toweling his hair; she noticed the way the small damp curls of dark hair all over his body sprang away from his skin as they dried. With his head in the towel, it took him a minute to notice her waiting expectantly against the pillows.

"Wow. Now?" Jake asked in amazement. "Now you want it?"

"Now. Please."

"Women!" Jake said with a grin as he admired her body, stripped to the enticing edge of nakedness. "I will never, *ever* understand!" Miranda just shot him a sultry smile. Then her gaze moved to the mirror.

Jake's eyes followed hers. For him the mirror held a freeze-frame from a soft porn film: a woman arched against the pillows, her naked breasts spilling lusciously from her bra, her legs spread seductively, her Bermuda triangle veiled in an enticing wisp of pink. Ripe and waiting. Waiting for him.

He moved onto the bed beside Miranda, letting his towel fall away and wedging his hip beside hers so that they were framed together in the mirror. "Hey. That's damn hot."

He began to caress her breasts, his touch hungrier and rougher than Miranda's own. As they watched together, she dropped her hands to the pink silk. Lifting her hips, she slipped down the panties and revealed her thick curls of pubic hair; it looked black against her pale skin in the candlelight. She caught Jake's eyes in the mirror, then spread her thighs apart against the constraining silk until her pink blossom was exposed to view.

The tension of not touching herself was excruciating. She took Jake's right hand gently in hers and guided it between her opened legs. "Now, Jake. There."

"There?" He stroked the tender skin of her inner thighs with his fingertips. "Or where?" He inched his hand higher, but not quite enough. "Maybe here?" As he teased her, he gave Miranda a deep kiss. His breath, she noticed with pleasure, tasted sweet and minty fresh, and his hair smelled faintly of papayas.

Finally his fingers found the delicious, aching, pulsing place. He stroked her delicately, using the fluttering motion he knew she liked. When her breath started to come in shallow gulps, he suddenly stopped. Miranda moaned in protest. Then she felt the warm, slick lapping of his tongue. He sucked on her rhythmically, like a nursing puppy; she came hard in a jerky, excruciating sweet-hot explosion of release.

When she could focus again, Jake was watching her with a smirk of pride. "Did I ever tell you that I get off on the way your face wrinkles up when you come?" He moved to straddle her. "And I dig that crease where your butt turns into your thigh. And the little freckles under your breasts." Locking his eyes on hers, he thrust himself inside with a sure homing instinct.

Miranda reached up and stroked his dark hair, then traced his cheek. Wrinkles? Creases and freckles? She looked into the mirror one last time. Her face was slack with abandon, her hair in disarray, her breasts flattened beneath Jake. Huh. Maybe she ought to give the natural look a try. She smiled and closed her eyes.

WAITING FOR CLAIRE

Bruce Zimmerman

Lazy peals of thunder rolled in off the Gulf, deep and hollow, rumbling from one end of the horizon to the other like loose apples in an empty barrel. The sky was black and swollen with rain, clouds shredded and frayed at the edges. I could feel the wind buffet the bedroom window. Two miles away the hard gray skyline of New Orleans braced for the approaching storm, skyscrapers reaching up into the ragged clouds like an immense cluster of steel and glass lightning rods.

"Maybe she's not coming," Gina said behind me.

"Maybe not."

"Weather like this . . ."

Gina came up and stood next to me, looking out at the city. Our indifferent tone was mannered and false. Like it didn't really matter, one way or the other. Just another Saturday in August. Claire would either come, or she wouldn't, and if she didn't there was always the movie channel on television and microwave popcorn in the cupboard. No big deal.

Nothing could have been more laughable. In point of fact, Claire's rented car swerving into our driveway on this Saturday in August was just about the *only* thing that mattered in the world. Epidemics, war and strife, the threat of nuclear holocaust—

all of it paled in importance before the anticipation of Claire's arrival. But as noon became one o'clock, and one became two, Gina and I began to wonder. Was she really going to come, or had the elaborate planning of the past five days been nothing more than dangerous talk?

I stood at the bedroom window and watched the storm gather over New Orleans. Then I looked at Gina's profile. Long, elegant nose, high cheekbones, prominent chin, straight shoulder-length salt-and-pepper hair that made her look somewhat older than her thirty-three years. She was Italian-American, with smooth olive skin, impossibly dark eyes, and bright, white teeth. It was an aristocratic face, hinting of good breeding, good schools, and enough money to have given such good fortune a big backyard to run around in. She felt me watching her and turned with a puzzled, awkward smile.

"What?" she said.

"Just watching you."

"This is kind of silly," she said, gazing back out at the skyline. "The two of us standing here at the window, staring out at the street like a couple of kids waiting for the ice-cream truck."

"Thirty-one flavors."

She smiled again, less awkwardly, and there were little flecks of mayhem in her warm brown eyes. "You *hope*."

Gina turned from the window and went back into the living room. She knelt at the coffee table and straightened out some magazines that didn't need straightening. I watched her bend to the task. She wore sandals, faded jeans, and a silky white blouse. I could see her black-lace bra through the blouse, the one that was intended to reveal more than conceal, and a strange sensation swept over me. For the first time in five days I was thinking the unthinkable. I found myself hoping that Claire *wouldn't* come. Never mind the hinted-at pleasures, the hundred erotic configurations, the unspoken promises of a page-by-page perusal of the forbidden. Gina was my wife, and I loved her. In bed she was passionate, interested, and experimental. Out of bed she was, well . . . passionate, interested, and experimental. That should be enough?

It's never smart to jump off a cliff—real *or* imagined—and Claire would be one of those leaps. No. The storm clouds would build, the roads would flood, and Claire would stay away. By tomorrow she'd be on a plane back to London. In retrospect we'd consider it a bullet dodged. An eleventh-hour reprieve from a potentially disastrous decision.

But the black bra had my attention. On a normal Saturday afternoon around the house Gina wouldn't have gone to the trouble to wear a bra. Certainly not that one. It made me wonder what else she had done differently today. A few dozen more brushstrokes through the hair, maybe. A darker shade of makeup. And it was for Claire. Claire, Claire, Claire, Claire, Claire. Despite all mature resolve, the woman's name and presence once again pushed against my shuttered thoughts like the wind against the windowpane. It was foolish to fight it.

I first learned of Claire's existence only a few days earlier, shortly after Gina and I had made love on the couch in front of the abandoned screen of a flickering television set. There'd been a discernible difference in her lovemaking. An intensity and focus several notches beyond the norm.

"Jesus!" I'd said afterward, stretched out next to her on the living room rug. "What was that about?"

Gina brushed back a strand of wet hair, uncertainty in her eyes. "What do you mean?"

"I don't know. You were . . . different tonight."

"Was I?"

I propped myself up on my elbow and stared at her, smiling a puzzled smile. "All right, let's have it. What's going on?"

Gina reached down for my hand and drew it up to her mouth and softly kissed each one of my knuckles. She wasn't smiling with me, and she waited a long time before speaking again. "There's something you don't know about me, Steve."

"I'm sure there is," I said. "And let's keep it that way. A little mystery is good for a marriage."

"No, I mean there's something *important* you don't know about. Something that happened a long time ago."

My smile faded. Stomach went a little cold. Gina was not one
for secrets, and if there was something she'd hidden from me
through eight years of marriage, it couldn't be good.

"Tell me," I said.

"I'm afraid."

"Why?"

"I'm afraid it's going to change us. Change the way you feel
about me."

"Don't be ridiculous," I said. "I love you. Nothing you could tell
me can change the way I feel about you."

"Trust me," Gina said darkly. "This might."

And so it went for several minutes, back and forth, Gina trying
to bring herself to divulge her secret, me reassuring her that our
love and trust were sufficient to handle anything. Finally, reluctantly, she gave in. Rolled over onto her back and stared up at the
ceiling and began talking.

It happened when she was nineteen years old, during the period
when she dropped out of her expensive, prissy girl's college in
Vermont and bolted off to live the bohemian life in Europe. It
caused a minor furor at the time, with family and friends pleading
with her to come to her senses. But Gina was sick of her lah-dee-
dah existence and wanted to see the world. Stroll the wild side.
Ruffle up her complacent sensibilities. All of this I knew. The dropping out of college, the fleeing to Europe, the ensuing scandal back
home. What I didn't know about was Africa.

Gina arrived in Europe in the dead of winter, so she headed
straight south, to the milder climes of Morocco. One afternoon,
shortly after she arrived in Tangier, Gina met a young British couple in a cafe. Their names were Derek and Claire. He was handsome, she was beautiful. Moneyed expatriates with a seaside home,
time on their hands, and the aura of idle decadence one would
expect under the circumstances. The three of them hit it off immediately, and Gina was invited back to their house on the Mediterranean to have dinner and smoke a little hashish. She did. One
thing led to another, and that night the three of them ended up in
bed together.

Gina paused from the telling of her story and looked over at me for a reaction. I felt relief flow through my body like warm honey.

"That's it?" I said with a reassuring laugh. "You were involved in a threesome once upon a time? My God, Gina, a lot of people—"

"It wasn't just a threesome," Gina said. She looked at me long and hard. "And it wasn't just once upon a time. I lived with Derek and Claire for over a year."

That stopped me. "A year?"

"Fifteen months."

I lay on the floor, took a deep breath, exhaled it. Assimilated the information. "So your ménage à trois lasted longer than most. It's still not the end of the world."

"You're not getting it!" Gina said. She abruptly let go of my hand and rose to a sitting position, a curious anger in her eyes. Frustration that I was so effortlessly inclined to see her youthful adventure in an understanding light. "It was more than just a ménage à trois. It was *everything*, Steve. Everything you could possibly think of."

It was hard to put an innocent spin on *that*. This time the extended silence between us had a charge of electricity. Images leapt to mind, images that fell under the heading "everything," and I immediately dispelled them.

"Why are you telling me this now?" I said at last.

"I never intended to tell you at all. Ever. I mean, Tangier was fifteen years ago. I thought it was all in the past."

"Thought?"

"I got a call today at the office." Gina looked me straight in the eyes. "It was Claire. She's in New Orleans and wants to see me."

In the following days Gina didn't actually meet with Claire face to face, but they spoke endlessly on the phone. A lot had happened in fifteen years, and there were gaps to be filled. Claire had left Derek and was now living in London, pursuing a career in the fashion industry, putting as much distance between herself and the aberrant period in Tangier as she could. But there were several crucial, unresolved things in her life that had been left dangling. Gina, apparently, was one of those "things."

I thought I handled the situation pretty well, considering. After dinner the phone would ring and it would be Claire and I would go into the living room with my book and pretend not to listen to Gina's end of the conversation. There was an intimacy in her voice when she spoke with Claire that I vaguely resented. Affection. Shared confidences. I sat on the couch, reading and rereading the same sentence in my novel, imagining the nineteen-year-old Gina making love in the African sunlight to this mysterious Claire. Seeing how it must have been. I thought of Derek. I thought of all the things "everything" encompassed.

On the third night the phone rang again and it was Claire and while she and Gina talked I tossed in the towel. Went back to the bedroom, crawled under the covers, and turned on the television. I needed talk shows. I needed game shows. I needed anything that would drown out talk of Morocco. Thirty minutes later Gina came into the room. She turned off the television and sat on the edge of the bed.

"Can we talk for a second?" she said.

"Sure."

Gina put her hand on my blanketed knee. "Claire's going back to England on Sunday. I've invited her to spend Saturday with us. Here. At the apartment. Is that okay?"

"You don't need my approval to invite people over, Gina."

"Her visit could involve you."

I took a deep breath and exhaled it. "Do you want to go to bed with Claire? Is that it? If it is, that's fine, but just say it straight out."

"I need to finish with Claire."

"I thought it was finished fifteen years ago in Tangier."

"It was ended," Gina said. "Not finished. There's a difference. That's why Claire came all the way to New Orleans to see me. But I'm involved with you now, so what involves me, involves you."

"In other words, you're proposing another threesome," I said. "Only with me in Derek's role."

"You make it sound like it's something horrible."

"So I'm right, then?"

"This isn't a quiz, Steve." Gina's tone hardened. "You don't get points for correct answers. I'm not 'proposing' anything except that Claire come over on Saturday. Period. But I'd be lying to you if I said it was only going to be tea and crumpets. If this is something you can't handle just tell me and we'll forget it. I understand. I'll call Claire right now. Pretend it never happened."

I sighed, linked my hands behind my neck and pursed my lips. "Dammit, Gina, you shouldn't have to pretend anything. I don't know how I feel about what's going on."

"You wouldn't want to take both of us to bed?"

"I don't know."

Gina put a hand underneath the covers and I felt her fingertips softly trail up the length of my leg. She caressed my balls and then made a gentle fist around the base of my erection. I was as subtle as a lead pipe. She smiled and slowly stroked my penis.

"You don't know?" Gina edged up to the front of the bed, stretching the entire length of her body over mine, and kissed me deeply. "I think you *do* know."

"Not fair."

Gina smiled, kissed me again. I felt for the edges of her T-shirt, tugged them free of her jeans, and pulled them up her rib cage, up and over her bare breasts. The flesh was warm. Gina sighed deeply. Her nipples lengthened beneath my fingers as flowering roses do in time-lapse photography.

"You'll like Claire," Gina murmured.

"Tell me about her."

Gina moved farther up my body so that her breasts brushed my neck and face, left nipple gently grazing the length of my lower lip. "She's pretty. Very, very pretty. In Tangier she had short, jet-black hair, cut with bangs, like a silent movie star. Bright red lipstick. She made me think of Zelda Fitzgerald. Deep blue eyes, and a beautiful body. A lovely body."

"Like yours?"

"No. Paler and softer. Larger breasts, but beautifully proportioned."

Gina moved her left breast slowly back and forth across my mouth and chin. Her nipple trailed the length of my lower lip, hard and full of personality. Back and forth it went across my partially opened mouth, like the loving trace of a curious fingertip, probing for secrets.

"Tell me about the first time with Derek and Claire," I said. "How did it start?"

Gina arched her back, easing her left breast more fully into my mouth. She grasped the headboard with outstretched arms and shook the salt-and-pepper hair from her eyes. "Claire started it."

"How?"

"We were sitting together on the floor in the living room, smoking hashish, and Derek left to get something from the kitchen. Claire just leaned over and kissed me. Direct. Simple. I kissed her back and she started undressing me. Before I knew what was happening we were naked, holding each other, kissing. I'd never been kissed like that before. It was wonderful. The next thing I remember was feeling Derek's hand on my shoulder. He was smiling. Claire linked her fingers in mine and led me upstairs to the bedroom."

"Then what?"

Gina slowly pushed her upper torso away from my mouth and climbed out of bed. Her arms formed an X across her chest and she pulled off the T-shirt in one motion. "Then I stretched out on their bed and waited. It was a large brass bed, with lavender sheets. A big window to the right that looked out over the Mediterranean. Derek stepped off to the side, and Claire slowly climbed in bed with me. I remember she moved up from the end of the bed on all fours, slowly, like some sleek jungle cat coming out of the forest."

Gina tossed the T-shirt aside and pulled off her shorts and panties and then pulled the covers of the bed down to the floor so that I was as exposed as she was. She climbed back in bed and straddled my chest, one knee on either side, her back to me. Then she lowered her body and I felt her hands on my hips, the nearness of her breath on my penis. Her firm, lovely ass slid slowly up my stomach, my chest, toward my face.

"Then what happened?" I said.

"Claire kissed me all the way up my leg. Every inch. So slow. So focused. I was used to overheated college boys, but Claire was wonderful. She nibbled, bit, licked, kissed. Two steps forward, one step back, and if she found a spot she liked, behind my knee or on my calf or far up on my inner thigh, she'd stop and linger."

Gina stopped talking. Her head lowered and I felt her mouth gather up my penis. She slid it deeply into her mouth, moaning slightly, and at the same time she eased her ass down onto my face. I placed a hand on each cheek and spread her apart. Ran my tongue along the soft folds of her cunt. Tasted the peppery warmth of her juices. For a minute we explored each other, then Gina took my penis out of her mouth and stroked it, hard and rhythmically, using her saliva as lubrication.

"What else happened?" I said.

"The hashish really kicked in," Gina said. "My body felt so heavy I could barely lift my arm. But that was okay. I didn't want to move. Didn't want to fight it. Claire's head was between my legs. I could see her bright, shiny hair moving this way and that."

"Where was Derek?"

"Derek . . ." Gina continued to stroke me, bending to lick my shaft, keeping me wet. "Derek was sitting on his knees, on the floor, midway up the bed, watching Claire fuck me. Just sitting there in a trance, watching, chin resting on his folded hands, inches from us. It was the way you'd sit and watch fish drift in an aquarium. Fascinated, but distant. All he did was move Claire's hair out of the way once in a while so he could see better."

"Nothing else?"

Gina turned and looked back at me. "You want me to tell you more?"

"Yes. Everything."

"Then give me your hand."

Gina reached back, found my right hand, and guided it down to my own penis.

"Now stroke yourself," she breathed. "Make yourself come while I tell you."

I did as instructed. I could hear soft moans of approval as she watched.

"After Claire made me come, I felt Derek's hand on my cheek. He was standing next to the bed, beside me. I'd almost forgotten he was there. He gently turned my face toward him. He was naked, and his cock was inches from my mouth. I parted my lips . . . it was hard and wet and I could taste Claire on him. He must have been fucking her, taking her from behind while she was between my legs, but I hadn't been aware of a thing. I was stoned. I was completely focused on what Claire was doing to me."

"Did you like sucking him?"

"I didn't suck him. He fucked me in the mouth. Braced the back of my head with his hand and kept thrusting, harder and harder. Claire rested her head on my stomach and watched. I liked it. She was so gentle. Derek was rougher. When he came I tried to swallow it all but couldn't. It was on my lips, cheek, neck . . . Claire moved up my body and carefully licked Derek's cum from my skin. When she kissed me next I could taste Derek on her tongue. I could taste me on her tongue."

While Gina talked she ground her pussy harder and harder down into my mouth, taking control of her building orgasm, using my face as she wanted. I stroked myself harder, faster, and I could feel her lips barely touching the tip of my penis.

"Come on!" she breathed. "Come on!"

I did.

Later that night I held Gina close beneath the covers and asked what else had happened on the lavender sheets in the upstairs bedroom. But she simply put two fingers to my lips and made a shush sound with her mouth.

"No more tonight," she said. "We have Saturday. No more talk until then. Let's save it."

And with that she changed into her nightgown—the unsexy flannel one—crawled back into bed, and fell instantly asleep. I rested my head against the pillow and watched my hormones light up the far end of the bedroom like the aurora borealis. Saturday. We'd save it till Saturday, when Claire's car would come swerving into our driveway . . .

As the clock struck three the skies finally opened. Rain thundered to earth with the relentless fury of a tropical waterfall. There were no more magazines to straighten, so Gina quit fiddling around at the coffee table and joined me at the window.

"Claire's not coming," Gina said flatly.

"Doesn't look that way."

"Even if it hadn't been raining, I don't think she was going to come."

"Disappointed?"

Gina nodded. "Of course I'm disappointed. What about you?"

I shrugged. "I suppose."

Gina smiled and imitated my shrug. "You 'suppose'? What about the thirty-one flavors? I've never shared you with another woman, Steve. This afternoon I was going to. The chance may not come again."

I folded my arms across my chest and looked at Gina. "Why did you put that bra on today?"

"Excuse me?"

"That bra. Why did you put it on today?"

Gina looked down at the front of her blouse. "Because it's the sexiest bra I own, and this was supposed to have been a sexy afternoon. Does it bother you?"

"Yes."

"You want me to take it off?"

"Please."

Gina assessed me for a moment or two, then slowly unbuttoned her blouse. I leaned against the window and watched her. The rain was coming down so hard I could feel it pound against my shoulder through the glass. She was deliberate, taking her time with each button. She let the blouse drop to the floor; then she reached behind her back with both hands and unclasped the bra. The thin straps slipped off her shoulders and the bra fell next to the blouse.

"Any other problems with my wardrobe?" she said.

"Your jeans."

Gina kept her eyes on me for a second. There was no coy smile, no coquettish turn to the edges of her mouth. With her eyes still locked with mine, she slipped off her sandals and pulled her jeans down to her ankles. She stepped out of them and kicked them aside.

"Panties, too."

She removed them without hesitation and stood before me completely nude. "Why don't you close the curtains," she said.

"Nobody's going to look in," I said. "Sit down on the couch."

She did, right on the edge, knees together and turned to the side, both hands palm down on the cushion.

"Lean all the way back and spread your legs."

Gina eased back into the depths of the couch, drew her knees up, and slowly spread her legs. Her breath was shallow, and her eyes were on me. "Like this?" she said.

"Wider."

She spread them wider. I walked over to where she sat, knelt on the floor between her legs, and smoothed back the freshly clipped pubic hair from her pussy. "You trimmed yourself this morning," I said.

"Yes."

"For Claire?"

She nodded. I licked the tip of my forefinger and softly trailed it between the folds of her cunt. Her thighs trembled slightly, but she kept her legs wide open and didn't make a sound.

"I liked the story you told the other night," I said. "About how it was the first time with Derek and Claire."

"I know you did."

"Why did you make me masturbate myself?"

"It was what I wanted." Gina watched me moisten my fingertip again and resume the slow, exploratory trail around her pussy. "Don't you ever ask for what you want?"

"You can close your legs."

She did, keeping her knees drawn up close to her chin, linking her hands around her bare ankles.

"Go back into the bedroom and wait for me in bed."

Gina stood and did as she was told. I rose from my kneeling position and went into the kitchen and rummaged through the junk drawers until I found the extra clothesline rope. I cut off four eighteen-inch sections and went into the bedroom. Gina had stripped the bed of its covers and she lay waiting for me on the fresh white sheets. She didn't react when she saw the rope in my hands.

"Do you want me on my back, or stomach?" she said.

"Back."

I sat on the edge of the bed near her head and she extended her right arm. I gently but firmly knotted one end of the rope around her wrist and bound the other end to the right bedpost. Then I did the same for her left hand. Then I moved down to the foot of the bed, spreading her legs wide, and bound her ankles to the lower bedpost.

"Are you comfortable?" I said.

Gina nodded. "Claire might still come."

"Don't worry about Claire." I stood and took a moment to admire Gina, spread-eagled and helpless. We'd played bondage games often before in our married life, but the binding was always more symbolic than real, the tethers loosened to give the bound partner a lot of room to maneuver. This time the rope was taut and lashed firmly to the bedposts, Gina's ability to move almost nonexistent.

"What are you going to do to me?" she said.

"You have it backward. The question is, what are *you* going to do to *me*."

I took off my clothes, folded them neatly on the bedside chair, and moved to the front of the bed. I leaned down and kissed Gina on the cheeks, nose, eyebrows, jawline, lips. When I found her mouth she wrenched her head up to prolong the kiss, to deepen it. I cupped my hand around the back of her neck and supported her. Then I left off and trailed my kisses randomly down her chin, throat, neck, collarbone. She was breathing deeply. I took her right nipple in my mouth and played with it, flicking it with my tongue, sucking it, feeling it grow firm in my mouth.

"You're tied up for a reason," I said.

Gina didn't respond. She had her head back, moving it from side to side as I fondled her breasts. The tendons in her neck were as taut as elevator cables.

"A week ago you got frustrated with me," I went on, "because I wasn't appreciating the gravity of what happened in Tangier. Remember? You said you'd done 'everything.' Remember?"

"Yes."

"A wife can't tell her husband a thing like that and expect it to just go away." I let my lips trail from her breasts down the middle of her rib cage.

"I wouldn't have told you, except for Claire," Gina said. "What do you want me to do?"

"I'm going to fuck you now, slowly, for as long as I want, however I want. And while I do you're going to talk to me. You're going to educate me about 'everything.'"

"I . . . I don't understand."

"I want to hear the wildest thing you ever did in Tangier. Whatever it is you look back on now with the most amazement."

"It turns you on, doesn't it?" Gina said. "It makes you hot. I can feel it. I felt it the other night in bed."

I moved to the head of the bed and kissed Gina softly, probingly. Ran my tongue along the edge of her teeth.

"A week ago you took the cap off my imagination," I said. "This will help to put it back on."

So Gina told me. Quickly, directly, with no lead-up. Several months after she'd moved in with Derek and Claire, some friends of theirs from England passed through. Two young guys—handsome, uncomplicated, sun-bleached surfers with nothing on their minds except finding the perfect wave and tasting whatever the world had to offer. That night the world offered up Gina. She made love to all three men at the same time, rotating them from one orifice to the next, licking their balls, trying to suck two cocks at once, losing track of who was in her mouth and who was in her ass, feeling two pairs of hands spreading her legs, feeling two sets of tongues ravenously feeding on her. They were young and full of stamina and the orgy went on for hours.

I mounted Gina and slowly slid my own cock in and out of her warm pussy as she described to me the four-way marathon, interrupting her narrative at intervals to kiss her hard on the mouth. Each kiss provoked a more private detail from Tangier; the thickness of Derek's cock, the feel of three hungry tongues on both breasts, how innocent the streams of semen looked on her breasts and stomach and thighs, like little squiggly fake worms from a child's toy box. Claire, and how she came from the bathroom to apply fragrant oil to Gina's asshole, massaging her inner thighs with it, preparing her.

Yes, Claire! Even in this kaleidoscopic blur of utter maleness, this bastion of cocks and balls and powerful hands coaxing her from one position to the next—even in this, Claire still somehow took center stage. The way she looked, sitting in the corner, nude, one lovely thigh hooked over the arm of the chair, rubbing her clit with short, tight counterclockwise circles, the other hand pinching her nipples, one, then the other, watching. Only watching. Smiling a cryptic, inclusive smile to Gina while she brought the three men to climax over and over and over again.

Gina quit talking. Her hands fought against the rope as I rocked into her, thigh to thigh, chest to chest, mouth to mouth, harder, harder, harder still, until with one final thrust I emptied into her all that was me.

When I untied her she lay exactly as she was for several minutes, eyes closed, not moving, as though the ropes still bound her. Then she opened her eyes and smiled up at me.

"That was the wildest thing I've ever heard," I said.

"Three men and a woman?"

"No," I laughed. "Squiggly fake worms from the toy box. For Christ's sake, Gina! Where in the hell did that image come from?"

Gina's smile broadened, and she moved her arms and legs for the first time. Trailed a random fingernail across her breasts.

"So that was it?" I said. "Your wildest Tangier memory?"

"Unh, unh."

"What do you mean, 'unh, unh'?"

"That was the runner-up."

I felt my laughter fade. "Then what was the winner?"

Gina brought her hand up to her mouth in a speak-no-evil gesture. "I can't tell you the winner."

"Why not?"

"You wanted the cap put back on your imagination. I think I like you better uncapped."

We were silent for a minute or two. Gina rolled onto her side and absentmindedly stroked my leg. A loud clap of thunder burst overhead and rain continued to hammer the windows.

"You asked how it started," Gina said, "but you never asked how it ended."

"How did it?"

"One morning while Derek was in town Claire came into my room and said for me to pack. She drove me to the train station and bought me a ticket and told me to leave and not come back. Just like that, after over a year together. I was stunned. Crying. Both of us were crying. Claire said she couldn't live with the guilt any longer. Said that for a young girl like me, it was too much too soon. She also said Derek couldn't be trusted. I didn't know what she meant by that, but . . . anyway, I left."

"And that was it?"

Gina nodded. "But you know, Claire said something to me that morning at the train station in Tangier that I've never forgotten. She told me the story of Scheherazade and the Thousand and One Nights. Do you remember it? How Scheherazade kept herself alive with her tales, weaving memory and experience to entrance the king?"

"I remember."

"Well, Claire said that one day my experiences in Tangier would serve the same function. Then she kissed me and walked off the train platform back to the car. I waited for her to look back, but she never did."

I left Gina on the bed, thinking of that warm, sun-bright morning in Africa fifteen years earlier, and went out to the kitchen to get some bottled water. Crossing back through the living room I chanced a glance out the window and noticed a pale yellow automobile parked in front of our driveway. Rain obscured practically all but shape and color. The engine was idling, and I could see the profile of a person sitting behind the steering wheel. A woman. She was wearing a hat, looking straight ahead, deep in thought.

I looked quickly for my pants; then in the next instant the automobile eased away from the curb and disappeared at the far end of the street.

"What is it, honey?" Gina called from the bedroom.

"Nothing," I said. "Just watching the rain."

"There'll be rain enough to watch later," she said. "Come back and join me."

Indeed. I drew the curtains on the window, turned, and went back in the direction of the bedroom.

OTHER MEN

Edward Buskirk

"I wonder if any of the other men here fantasize about their wives making love to strangers, like you do," the dark-haired woman says to the blond-haired man between bites of her chicken salad.

Brenda and James are almost indistinguishable from most of the dozen or so other couples enjoying lunch in the leafy, greenhouse-style, hotel coffee shop—thirtyish, attractive, suburban, professional-looking even in casual attire. Like the others, they are taking advantage of the Weekend Getaway special the hotel advertised all week on Lite Rock 102—two days, two nights, two hundred dollars.

The kids are at his mother's house. The neighbors are cat-sitting. They feel a little guilty about just picking up and taking off—they try to save weekends for the family—but they absolutely had to get away by themselves once in a while to keep from going crazy.

James smiles, glancing quickly around to see if anyone is listening. He leans across the table toward Brenda. "Are you still on that kick?" he says in a near-whisper. "How many times do I have to tell you that I was only kidding? You should know better than to believe anything I say when we're making love."

She fixes her eyes on him. *"Anything?"*

He rolls his eyes toward the ceiling. "You know what I mean. Things like the dumb things I pull out of thin air to say when we're right in the middle of you-know-what after a sauna and a bottle of room service champagne, and you ask me to tell you my most secret fantasy."

"You never pull things out of thin air," Brenda says. "No offense, darling, but you aren't that spontaneous. You meant every word you said. It really turns you on to think about me being with other men. I could see it in your eyes when you said it, and I can see it in them now. You're getting excited just talking about it."

He chuckles, his face reddening. "You're crazy."

She kicks off her summery flat and lifts her bare foot onto the edge of his chair, gently teasing her polished toes between his legs. "I knew it," she says with a grin.

"Have you flipped out? What if someone sees you?"

She smiles, gently curling her toes over him. "Don't look now, but someone already has. Behind you. Two men. *Young* men. They've been eyeing me ever since they came in. Maybe I should invite them over. We could tell them about your fantasy. One of them might be interested in helping you bring it to life."

"I'm sure they would," he says sarcastically, shifting in his chair as her toes move in slow circles over his thickening erection, "*if* they were really there. Now can we just forget it and talk about something else?"

"The dark-haired one's a doll," she continues, her eyes fixed over her husband's shoulder, a flirtatious smile on her lips. "The blond's not bad either, but I sleep with a blond every night. But either one will do just fine. I'll let you choose. After all, it is your fantasy. Of course, we could always take both of them up to our room with us. Would you like that? Have you ever fantasized about seeing me with two men?"

He shakes his head in exaggerated dismay, pretending to drink from his empty coffee cup.

She giggles. "How are you planning on doing it?" she asks, leaning close to him. "Are you going to sit in a chair by the bed or hide in the closet, or what? Or were you planning on joining in?"

"None of the above," he says with an embarrassed grin. He reaches down and pushes her foot away from him, fighting the urge to caress her elegant toes. "Okay, you've had your fun, honey. Now let's get out of here before they throw us out. Where's our waitress?"

She wiggles her foot back into her shoe, rising, leaning over to whisper into his ear. "I'm going to talk to those two while you wait for our check. This afternoon *is* okay to do it, isn't it?"

He grabs for her wrist but she dances away from him. Everyone is staring. He can feel it. He knows that if his face is only half as red as it feels, it must look as if he is about to go up in flames, but he doesn't turn around. He forces a little half-smile, like it is all some little game they play, and stares out the window.

Jesus, why is she doing this to him? Not that he doesn't have it coming. He should have kept his big mouth shut last night. He knew as soon as he was saying it that it was a mistake. It had been his secret fantasy for years. Why couldn't he have kept it that way?

But even so, this is not the reaction he anticipated. He expected her to be furious with him, not intrigued by the whole crazy idea. It is all she has talked about since. Of course, it is undoubtedly just a sham—her way of getting back at him for even thinking something so kinky.

He is dying to look back over his shoulder to see what she is saying to the two men—if there even are two men—but he is afraid to. She couldn't possibly go through with anything so outrageous. Sure, she loved to flirt, but it was just something she did for fun. She has always made it known in no uncertain terms that flirting was as far as she would ever go with anyone but him. She certainly wouldn't change all that overnight.

He can't stand waiting for the waitress any longer. He'll get his check from the cashier. He stands, trying to will his persistent erection away, certain that everyone will notice. He lays down a tip and turns toward the entrance, attempting to act nonchalant and amused.

The tables behind him are empty. There are no men. Brenda is perched on a stool at the counter, facing him, legs swinging like a little girl's. Her dark eyes glisten.

He breaks into a big smile. "Bitch!" he lip-synchs.

She grins, dropping to her feet and falling in beside him as he strides to the cashier. She slides her hand into his back pocket and leans close. "Are you glad that no one was really there?" she asks, teasing the wet tip of her tongue into his ear. "Or are you disappointed?"

He loops his arm around her. "Maybe a little," he says, not bothering to tell her a little of which. "How about you?"

She smiles. "Maybe a little."

"What kind of men do you fantasize about me being with?" Brenda asks. "Strangers? Famous men? Friends?"

They have gone back up to their room to change for a dip in the pool. The fantasy has delayed them between clothes off and bathing suits on. She is stretched out atop him on the bed. The drapes are partially open and the hot sun splashes over their naked bodies. James cannot remember the last time they made love in broad daylight.

"Definitely not friends," he says. He has given up trying to convince her that the other-man fantasy is a mere joke. "Friends are strictly off-limits, even in *Fantasyland*. No friends and no falling in love. The men can fall in love with you—they wouldn't be able to help it anyway—but you can't fall in love with them."

"But who are these men I can't fall in love with?" she asks, planting a lingering kiss on his nipple, slowly swirling her tongue over and around the tender button of puckered flesh before biting down ever so gently.

"No one I really know," he says, wincing as she bites down harder, playfully tugging at his nipple. "Usually it's men I hear you talking about from work—salesmen and clients and the like. Like the software rep from Boston who came to town to help you set up the new inventory control system. You spent a lot of late nights at the office with him. I had a pretty good fantasy going about you two until you told me he was gay and ruined the whole thing."

"Kevin?" She laughs, fascinated. "God, he'd die if he knew." She kisses his other nipple, leaving the crimson imprint of her lips surrounding it. "What kind of things did you think about me doing with him?"

James smiles, smoothing his hand down over her bottom, teasing his fingers in her warm crease. "You're getting off on this, aren't you?"

"I'm just curious," she says with a mischievous grin, parting her legs. "What did you fantasize about us doing? Where were we? Where were you? Tell me everything."

"I had this crazy little scenario all worked up about you two going at it right in your office, after everyone else had left," he says, stroking her plump lower lips until they are slick with her musky juices. "And by parking my car in the lot behind your building I was able to watch it all through your window."

She urges him on. "What did you fantasize about seeing? I want all the juicy details."

"Sometimes I imagined seeing you sitting on the edge of your desk, with your skirt up to your waist and your pantyhose dangling from one ankle, and Kevin between your legs with his pants around his knees. And sometimes I had this mental picture of him leaning back against your desk, with his eyes closed and his fingers in your hair, and you kneeling in front of him."

Brenda trails wet kisses down over James's chest and belly. "And just what was I doing while I was on my knees in front of Kevin?" she asks. "Was I doing this?" She kisses the spongy tip of his erection, tracing the tip of her tongue over and around his circumcision.

"Oh, yes," he says with a smile. He tangles his fingers in her dark curls, closing his eyes as she takes him into her mouth, pushing halfway to his root. "You always do that in my fantasies."

She slides slowly up and down his thick organ, licking and sucking, increasing the pressure. Just when he gasps and tenses, nearing climax, she pulls off of him, torturously scraping her wet teeth over him.

She sits up, straddling his hips, rubbing her slippery sex against him, squeezing her warm smooth thighs over him. "And while Kevin and I were making love," she says, "you were just sitting there in the car, calmly watching it all?"

He nods, grinning sheepishly.

"What are you feeling during these fantasies of yours?" she asks. "Are you jealous? Angry? Hurt?"

"They *are* just fantasies," he says. "I try not to think about those things—just about how sexy it is."

Leaning forward, she kisses him, snaking her tongue between his teeth. "Would you really like to see me doing this with someone else?" she whispers. "Or do you want it to stay a fantasy? Could you handle it if it was for real?"

His tongue touches hers. Her heavy breasts settle into his hands. He captures her hard strawberry pink nipples between his thumbs and forefingers, pinching and pulling and twisting. He feels light-headed, dizzy, dangerously close to slipping out of control—exactly like he felt the night before, when she started it all by asking him to tell her his most secret fantasy.

Just like then, he knows he should keep his mouth shut. But she is reaching for him, guiding him inside her, pushing down, squeezing her vaginal muscles over him, pulling up, pushing down, pulling up, until they are crashing over the sweet dark edge together, and his body is jerking beneath her, his hot seed spilling into her, filling her to overflowing. The words explode out of his lips. "I'd love to see you doing this with someone else," he gasps. "I could handle it. God, could I *ever* handle it!"

He dozes off. When he awakes, he is groggy. Where is he? Where is she? "Bren?" he calls.

"Right here," she says, stepping out of the bathroom, capping her lipstick. She looks stunning in her new white bathing suit. She steps into a pair of sandals and pulls one of his shirts from a hanger, throwing it over her shoulders. Dropping their room key into her oversized bag, she leans over to kiss him. "I'm on my way to the pool."

"Wait up," he says. "Give me five minutes to shower and find my trunks, and I'll go down with you."

She shakes her head, starting for the door. "Go back to sleep. I'm meeting someone."

"You're meeting someone? We don't know anyone here."

She smiles, her hand poised on the doorknob. "*Didn't* know anyone here. I went down to the lobby for a paper while you were sleeping. I didn't want to wake you, so I stayed there to work the crossword puzzle. A man sat down and we started talking. Before long we were flirting. He asked me to meet him for a drink by the pool."

James clasps his hands behind his head and stretches his legs, smiling. "Yeah right, honey," he says through a yawn. "Didn't we play this game down in the coffee shop a little while ago?"

Smiling, she blows him a kiss and is gone.

He leans back against his pillow, grinning to himself, waiting for the door to open again. A minute passes and she does not return. Five minutes. Ten. Maybe she really did go down to the pool. He'd better go down. She'll be waiting for him, a big *gotcha* smile on her face.

He gets up and pads into the bathroom. A message is scrawled on the mirror in bright red lipstick—*Be careful what you wish for, James*.

Curious, he pulls on his pants and steps to the window, lifting the drapes a few inches, peering down toward the pool. He feels a sudden rush of vertigo. His wife is sitting at an umbrella-topped table on the far side of the water, sipping an umbrella-topped drink. Across from her sits a tall tanned stranger. They lean close to each other, apparently deep in conversation. She has kicked off her sandals. Her sun-browned toes rest lightly on the man's bare feet.

Brenda glances up at the window for a split second. She smiles ever so slightly, then turns back to the stranger, leaning even closer, covering his hand with hers.

James stands watching as if in a trance. A dull ache is forming deep inside him, starting beneath his belly, spreading into his testicles and pushing up his spine. The fine hairs on his arms stand on end. A thousand emotions flash through his head—jealousy, fear, betrayal, confusion. But most of all, arousal.

He imagines Brenda kissing the man, plunging her tongue deep into his mouth, twisting it over his tongue. He pictures the man kneeling in front of her, peeling the sleek white bathing suit from her body, kissing her breasts and belly and lush brown bush, snaking his tongue up inside her. He closes his eyes and sees her beneath the man, her legs squeezing around him as she urges him deeper and deeper, wincing at his size and hardness.

James drops into a chair. His hand instinctively goes between his legs. He wonders if he is going crazy—if they are both going crazy—but he doesn't really care.

Brenda steps out of her wet swimsuit and tosses it into the bathroom. It lands on the tile floor with a loud *plop*.

James lies on the bed, watching her, an Elmore Leonard novel placed strategically upside down and open on his stomach, as if he had been reading. The ache still permeates his body, but so does the excitement. They smile at each other, but it is different now. It is more than just a silly game.

Fluffing her damp pubic curls, Brenda climbs onto the bed with him, straddling his thighs. She leans forward and kisses him. Her damp hair falls across his forehead. Her swollen nipples brush against his chest.

"He wants me to meet him in the lounge for drinks later tonight," she says, nibbling on her husband's lower lip. "And dancing and whatever."

"Do you want to do whatever with him?" he asks, sliding his hands down over her back, pulling her close.

"Only if you want me to."

"That doesn't answer my question."

"You could sit at the bar and pretend you don't know me, and watch me flirt with him," she says. "And his room is right across the pool from ours. When we go there—*if* we go there—I can ask him to leave the drapes open and the lights on, and you can watch it all from here. Just like in your fantasy."

The ache intensifies. So does the arousal. They reach for his zipper at the same time.

"Who is this guy?" James asks. He leans in the bathroom doorway, watching her apply her makeup. Her lipsticked message to him is still scrawled on the mirror. "What is he?"

"He's a lawyer," she says. "He's in town on business. He planned on flying home yesterday, but his last meeting was postponed until Monday, so he had to spend the weekend."

"Is he married?"

Her eyes meet his in the mirror. "I didn't ask. Does it matter?"

"Does he know you're married?"

"Yes," she says. "He thinks I'm here visiting relatives and you're back home in Wisconsin or Michigan. I can't remember which I told him, so I hope he doesn't ask again." She smiles. "Don't worry, I didn't tell him about your fantasy. I didn't want to scare him away."

She shrugs out of her robe and examines herself in the mirror. "Do I sag too much to go without a bra?" she asks.

"You're perfect," he says. "But you never go braless."

She squeezes past him. "That was the old me," she says, brushing her lips across his. "The old me never slept with strange men, either."

She pulls black panties from her suitcase, contemplates them for a moment and tosses them aside, stepping naked to the closet. She takes the little red cocktail dress she had packed to wear for him from its hanger and pulls it over bare skin. She wiggles her toes into his favorite red pumps, grabs her bag and reaches for the doorknob.

"I can't believe that you're really going through with this," he blurts out. "You're terrific. I love you."

"Just don't forget the *I love you* part," she says with a smile, kissing him and slipping out the door.

He doesn't know which he wants most—to go after her and hug her and ask her to stay, or to let her go. He doesn't know which she wants most either.

James dresses in the dark, pacing their room, staring out across the pool toward the window she pointed out to him. All he sees is darkness.

When he gets downstairs, the lounge is crowded and noisy, and it is all he can do to find a place to squeeze in at the bar. A band is playing seventies oldies across the room. The dance floor is packed. He doesn't see them anywhere. Could they already be up in his room, together in the darkness? Something about that thought—about the intimacy of darkness—makes him woozy.

Then he sees a flash of red in front of the band, between the other dancers. He sees her dark and lustrous hair, her sparkling eyes, her unbound breasts and smooth bare legs. He sees the man from the pool, all capped teeth and salon-tanned skin and leering eyes.

The band slows the tempo, shifting into a familiar old ballad. As the two of them turn to walk off the floor, hand-in-hand, she spots him. Their eyes meet. She fights back a grin. She moves in front of the man, stretching up to kiss him. She slides into his arms, maneuvering him back onto the dance floor. All the while, her eyes never leave her husband.

"I see you've spotted the lady in red," the bartender says with a grin, sliding a scotch and water across the bar to James. "Something else, ain't she? Five bucks says she doesn't have a stitch on under that flimsy little dress."

James tries to ignore the bartender, his eyes fixed on the dance floor. The man from the pool pulls Brenda close, pressing against her, lewdly hinting at what is to come. His hands slide down over the small of her back, onto the gentle swell of her bottom. He leans closer to her, whispering into her ear, his hands moving lower and lower. She smiles, her cheeks reddening. They might as well be making love, their movements are so as one.

James feels a slow heat creeping up the back of his neck. The dull ache from earlier in the afternoon has returned to the pit of his stomach, only ten times more intense now.

The bartender chuckles. "And another five says that wedding ring of hers didn't come from her dance partner. I'll bet she doesn't dance like that with her husband."

The words echo through a mounting roar in James's ears. He wants to scream at the bartender to shut up so he can hear himself think. What he is thinking is that maybe this isn't such a great idea, after all. As badly as he wants to let the fantasy play out, it isn't going like he imagined it would. Maybe it's the wrong man. Or the wrong time.

It excites him to watch his wife and the tall stranger perform their ritual mating dance, but it is not the kind of excitement he anticipated. It is the chest-clutching, nausea-inducing excitement of impending disaster—like watching a traffic accident happen right in front of you, knowing that you are doomed to be a part of it, too.

"Yeah, hubby's probably back home feeding the kids," the voice comes from behind the bar, "thinking his sweet little wife is curled up in bed with HBO and his photo."

James spins around. "Doesn't anyone ever tell you to mind your own damned business?" he snaps, surprising himself as much as he does the dumbstruck bartender. He angrily slides his scotch and water back across the bar, watching it fly off the other side and crash onto the floor.

Without even thinking about it—if he thinks about it he will never do it—he fights his way through the crowd toward his wife, muttering, "Excuse me. Pardon me. Sorry." He hates scenes and he knows he is about to create one, but he pushes on, stepping onto the dance floor, elbowing his way through the swaying couples, ignoring their dirty looks.

Brenda watches him over the man's shoulder, breaking into a delighted smile.

James taps the man on the shoulder. "Can I cut in?"

The man ignores him. Brenda bites her lower lip, laughter bubbling just beneath the surface.

"*Excuse* me, pal. I'm cutting in."

The man twists his head to look at him, eyes flashing. But as he says, "Take a hike, bub," he loosens his grip on Brenda. She slides effortlessly into her husband's arms.

The man stands there red-faced and open-mouthed as they glide away from him. He finally shuffles off, humiliated, eyes on the floor, seeming to shrink a little with each step he takes.

People are staring at them, whispering. James's face burns with embarrassment but he cannot stop grinning. Brenda kisses him, teasing her tongue between his lips. "Take me out of here," she says. "*Now.*"

He reaches for the light switch but she stops him. She steps to the window in the darkness, pointing across the pool toward the man's room. The lights are out, but the drapes are open. They can see his silhouette and the glow of a cigarette behind the glass.

As she stands at the window, he flicks on a lamp, then steps behind her, kissing her neck, sliding her dress over her shoulders. She turns to face him, giving a shrug. The dress settles in a crimson puddle around her feet. She leans back against the cold glass, pulling him to her.

He kisses her lips, her chin, her neck, moving slowly down over her breasts, lingering over each excited nipple. She gasps when he drops to his knees in front of her, his lips touching her dark bush. She grabs his shoulders to keep from collapsing as, drunk with her musky aroma, he moves lower and lower, lapping up her salty-sweet juices. But just as he pushes his tongue between her slick lower lips, she suddenly starts laughing.

He looks up at her, his face wet with her excitement. "What's so damned funny?"

"I was just wondering if he's enjoying the show as much as you thought you would have."

He grins. "Somehow I doubt it." He sees the man across the pool angrily closing his drapes.

She leads him to the bed, tearing at his shirt, loosening his belt. He falls between her legs, kissing her, pressing his hard organ against her.

"Did you ever have any intention of really letting me do it?" she asks, taking him into her hand, guiding him inside her.

He pushes to his root in her, marveling at the way she seems to ripple over him. "Did you ever have any intention of really doing it?"

She smiles mysteriously, wrapping her legs around him, holding him deep inside her as her hips move in ever-quickening circles beneath him. "I'm not telling you until you tell me."

"Well, I'm not telling you until you tell me." He is laughing. She is laughing. He doesn't know which feels better—the love-making or the laughter.

They pick up the two kids—the boy who looks like her and the girl who looks like him—at his mother's house the next morning. The children run to them, leaping into their arms.

His mother beams. "Do you two have any idea how perfect you are together?" she gushes. "Everyone says so."

"Well, almost everyone," Brenda whispers to James as they walk out to the car.

* * *

That night, after the kids have been kissed good night for the last time, they climb into bed, she in her baggy T-shirt, he in his baggy boxers. He turns to her and says, "You never told me *your* most secret fantasy."

She smiles at him over her reading glasses. "Didn't you know? I lived my fantasy this weekend."

"You and another man?"

"No, stupid," she says, planting a wet kiss on his forehead. "Being rescued from another man."

She goes back to work on her crossword puzzle. He goes back to his Elmore Leonard novel. A few seconds later, he peeks at her out of the corner of his eye, still wondering what she would have done if he had let her go with the man.

She smiles, her eyes and pencil never leaving the page. "You'll never know," she says.

THE WAGER

Anna Nymus

A stranger in a roomful of strangers. What makes this one special? I nudge Odette. We are standing near the jukebox in a corner of the bar. "You see that guy next to the wall?" She looks over. "Him?" she says dismissively. Probably doesn't see what I see. Pale, angular face, well-cut dark hair falling over his forehead. Not drinking much, looks down into his beer as if, for all he cares, he were alone in this place. The gesture he makes, lifting his head to flick the hair back out of his eyes. It is because of this I know I can take him.

Odette glances back at me. She knows what I'm up to.

"Listen," I say. "This guy's a Scorpio."

"Scorpio, is he?"

I nudge her again. "I'm telling you. He's a Scorpio. Aren't you going to ask me how I know?"

"You met him at astrology class," she drawls, with that indolent sarcasm for which she is famous.

"Never set eyes on him before in my life."

"I get it. He's a Scorpio because . . . of the way he drinks beer?"

I put her hand against my cheek. Her hand is ice because I'm burning. "If there's one of them, just one, in a whole room full of strangers, I know."

She lights a cigarette, tips back her head to let the smoke out, very slowly, through her nostrils. "Yeah," she says, "so he's a Scorpio." She unzips her jacket, takes out the onyx charm I gave her in place of a wedding ring, tosses it in the air. Now she's got that smile I've been expecting. I have to win it back, to win her all over again, to keep love going.

He's sitting in the corner, leaning on his elbow. Saturday night, the place is crowded. Hair oil, perfume, loud music, bitter smoke and he sits there staring at a glass of beer. I have to squeeze past the man standing next to him. I push in sideways, rest my elbow against the bar. So now I'm here, I'm looking down at him.

In a few minutes he's aware of me. He'll look up, won't be interested, not much, in what he sees. Dark circles around dark eyes. Nevertheless I'll take him.

He reaches out for the pack of cigarettes on the bar. I reach faster. I shake the pack, hold one out to him. He frowns up at me, doesn't smile, holds my eyes for a few seconds, shrugs, takes a cigarette. We repeat the same little game with his lighter. Again he gives in. Moving closer now I light his cigarette. I wonder what he makes of me, smiling down at him the way a conqueror, sure of conquest, smiles.

"Seen you here before?" he says. Good sign, his having to speak first. Me, I keep silent. I move closer, getting my thigh up close against his thigh. He clears his throat, shifts about on the bar stool.

I say nothing, more tension. My thigh hard against his hard thigh. His fingers play with the lighter. My fingers move over his hand, taking it from him. This time, when he looks up at me, he doesn't look away.

"I told my lover you were a Scorpio," I say and fall silent again.

He has light eyes, a rim of darkness around the pupil. He's younger than I thought, more vulnerable. He passes his tongue across his lips. Looking up at me, looking away, his eyes drawn back to mine, he says, "How'd you know that?"

"Can't you guess?"

By now he's wondering if he should get up fast, leave his cigarettes, get the hell out of here. He glances at the man next to me. Male proximity. It won't do him any good. The place is too crowded. If he takes off, he's going to look like a man in flight. He flicks his ash with the edge of his thumb, puts his cigarette between his lips, straightens his shoulders.

I take a drink from his glass without saying a word, so now he laughs, in spite of himself. A good laugh, boyish, yielding. There's a fine line of sweat on his upper lip. He's watching me as if I were a snake charmer.

Maybe I am.

Imperceptibly, he leans toward me, closing the tension, locking it between us.

I will put my left hand on his shoulder. It takes a special courage to do this. That's what Odette admires. When I reach out to touch him there will be no turning back.

I have placed myself fully between him and the man next to me. I glance down at his lap. There's that distance, impossible between strangers, between the place I'm touching now and where I'm going. I give him time to figure it out, to refuse me. My hand grows heavy on his shoulder. I take the cigarette from his lips, set it burning into the glass ashtray. I keep looking at him. A few years ago, on a good night, when I was new to it, this was enough, sometimes. My hand moves to his waist, comes to rest on the leather belt, takes hold of the thick buckle, plays with it lightly.

We are so damned close to one another, my breast pushed hard against his shoulder, my knee moving to push his knee against the bar, I can't tell for sure who is breathing. I guess that's my breath in the dark hair that curls over his ears.

My hand moves slowly, willing him to stop me if he still can, over the rough cloth pants, his body hammering against my palm. I stroke along his bulge, around it, pretending this isn't serious. It's up to him. My touch is delicate, he can ignore it if he wants to. Fingertips and nails, I stroke, I size him up, I trace his shape. Then I cusp him with my whole hand as though ready to take him. But I don't. He draws his breath in with anticipation. I hover, cusp him. Demand that he give himself over to me. I know what will happen. I send Odette a glance saying, You're gonna lose that bet, honey, right now. He's getting there. He'll let me know he's mine.

He can't wait to let me know. He is sweating. He pushes against me desperate to feel my enclosure, to bulge even larger, to grow out of himself, out of his mind, to be gripped.

I'm not moving, my hand is absolutely not moving in his lap. He's the one who has to move so there can be no doubt which of us wants this encounter between strangers, which of us asks for it. I keep my eyes on Odette while he lifts himself on his bar stool to press himself again, then again into my hand.

"*Plaisir d'amour, ne dure qu'un moment . . .*" Odette, sending me a message from the jukebox. We are rocking here in a dark corner of the bar, his sex filling my hand. I have unzipped him. I curl my fingers around him, stroking. "Don't come, make it last, don't come," I whisper into his ear, knowing Odette has started counting.

He's trying to keep his breath steady, face calm, shoulders still, hands gripping the bar. He's biting his lip hard. I keep stroking. Across the room the song has started up again. Odette, promising what comes later.

Before he comes, his eyes glazed with the effort to pretend nothing is happening, I glance over at Odette. She is sipping her drink as she leans against the jukebox, watching.

I hold up the onyx charm, flipping it between my fingers. That's when his body starts to shake. He jerks back from me once, his boot sliding against my calf, his left hand grabbing at the ashtray.

On a scale from one to ten, I would say that was an eight plus orgasm. I'd like to hang around to see him recover. But Odette wouldn't like it if I lingered.

THE SACRED HARLOT

Kim Chernin

I knew there was a reason to keep an eye on her. I felt it from the moment she arrived at Esalen with her husband. We had been expecting him since morning. "Don't worry," I assured the group, "famous men always come late."

Slightly balding, he was wiping his forehead with a crumpled handkerchief as he stepped out of the rented car. He wore a white shirt, sleeves rolled up to the elbows and striped, faded pants in need of pressing. When we went over to greet him, he smiled grudgingly, thrust out his barrel chest, drew up his sagging trousers with his elbows. Magnetism and something decidedly slovenly in this man. I introduced myself as the organizer of our conference, accepted his handshake, then ignored him. His wife had just stepped out of the car.

We had heard about her too, had been expecting her. We were an international clique, inbred, inclined to gossip. She hung back while the others welcomed her husband. I, who stayed behind while the group of them walked away, was free to give my full attention to her. Born in Naples, raised in New York by her father's aunt, she was arriving, we had heard, in California for the first time. I said hello to her in Italian, nothing else seemed possible. Younger than I had expected, a good thirty years younger than her husband, she looked as if she might have stepped off a canvas by di Giorgio. America had not touched her. She spoke Italian with hesitation, in a low, soft voice that gave the impression she would have spoken any language reluctantly. Small, very delicate, a dense forest of dark hair falling over her shoulders, it was the long, slender fingers, enormous eyes with their expression of dreamy disengagement that were her language. And then, walking along beside me over the gravel path toward the redwood house we had converted to a meeting room, she took my arm with the easy, confiding gesture of a small child who has just decided to trust a woman, a stranger. "Please call me Francesca," she said, and smiled up at me with an expression of wistful relief that made me conscious just how stressful the arrival must have been for her.

I felt an unexpected irritation with our famous guest, who had certainly brought his child bride with him in order to show off with her, but was already neglecting her. She was carrying a small overnight bag of embroidered cloth, was dressed in a simple white shift trimmed at the neck and wrists with lace. Childlike, painfully laconic, I could sense in her a latent power to charm that promised someday to hold its own against her husband's more extroverted (could one say, institutional?) charisma.

She was worth keeping an eye on, although of course I did not yet know what she had brought with her to our northern coast. It was dusk when we sat down for dinner, the kerosene lamps lighted on the lawns, fog rising up from the ocean and drifting over the edge of our grounds like a hesitant hand. It was late autumn, too cold with the coming of night to take the meal outside. Francesca was disappointed. She had been looking forward to a picnic on the edge of the cliff, to the famous view, the wild ocean that sometimes, she had heard, would send its foam up over our lawns and the sulfur tubs at the northern edge of our land. She spent most of the meal with her hand resting lightly on her husband's knee, staring out at the illuminated swimming pool, neglecting her dinner until her husband whispered to her. She looked up at him, then at me, with an apologetic smile, began to pick at her enchiladas dutifully, indifferently.

The conversation, during dinner, should have interested me. We had assembled at our conference the most prominent renegade

Gestalt therapists in the world, most of them newcomers to our rough California coast. Among us, schools and schisms and party lines had already developed, so that our gatherings were certain to be filled with heated disputation and erudite locking of horns, none of which this evening made any impression on me.

Our little Francesca sipped occasionally at her carrot juice. She ate most of the desert (an apple pie with whole wheat crust, and of course no sugar). During tea, she leaned on her elbow to let her eyes wander about the room, with an expression that seemed to suggest she'd spent her life in places that had taught her to see.

We had gathered in the beamed conference room, with its stone fireplace, Indian rugs, brightly colored weavings, to participate in a workshop with Dr. Roazen, a European analyst who had early broken with Freud, moved to California and established his own dramatic school of Gestalt therapy. We were an incongruous sight, some of us too well dressed with new arrival, in suits and button-down shirts, our shoes off, ties loosened, jackets folded across the backs of chairs, others in shorts and sandals, sitting on the floor, as one or another went forward to report a dream, a memory, a waking fantasy, which Dr. Roazen would instruct us to enact, making use of pillows, sometimes chairs, to represent parents, spouses, long-dead siblings.

Francesca sat close to me, her arms held tightly around her waist. She looked, if anything, even younger than when she arrived. I had the impression she had not met Dr. Roazen before, although he was her husband's mentor. She seemed awed, maybe fascinated, perhaps a bit put off by the old man, with his unkempt beard, shoulder-length hair, terry cloth jumpsuit. But soon I noticed that whenever a participant laughed or raged, beating at a pillow, tearing a sheet of newspaper between his teeth, although she sat perfectly still, her head lowered, looking at everything it seemed through her veil of hair, Francesca was weeping or raging with them. She did not volunteer; she did not reach out as we did to congratulate or comfort those returning from their self-exposure. She did not raise her hand to ask a question. She said nothing, scarcely moved, and yet I was aware that more, then more attention was being drawn toward her.

Her husband puffed his chest perceptibly, took her hand,

brought it to his chest in tribute, I supposed, to this impression he had evidently known she would make. His turn would come to-morrow; for tonight he was a participant along with the rest of us, nodding his head in a knowing, considered way as the great man strutted his stuff.

At first, it was the women who glanced at her, sensing the power of her emotion. Then, one of the men who had been working with Dr. Roazen sat down in front of her, on the floor. Soon, I noticed, everyone who volunteered to go forward glanced at her before they stood up. If she had seemed lovely before, her beauty was now visibly ripening, taking on a rapt quality that reminded me of Vanni's Saint Catherine in the San Domenico in Sienna. The old man himself, sensitive as always to the undercurrents in the room, had long since picked her out. Now, he made a quick, wel-coming gesture, calling her forward to work with him. She shrank back against her husband, who shook his head at his mentor with a bemused smile.

Dr. Roazen shrugged, pulled at his beard, looked around at us. We sat with suspended breath as though aware that Francesca too was holding her breath. She seemed to have drawn herself in, to have shrunk to the size of a small girl. Her dread cast a hesitation, a sudden doubt over the assembly as the great man scanned the audience, his small, close-set eyes pouncing, rejecting, circling. Those of us who lived at Esalen knew his work. We knew he would not take no for an answer, would not bow to any resistance. I had the impression Francesca knew perhaps too much about this ex-ercise of power, that her knowledge drew the old man toward her, steadily now with his shuffling step, until he veered sharply to her left to put his hand on the shoulder of a young man, Raoul, the younger son of one of our members, who looked in that moment particularly hesitant and confused.

I saw Francesca grab her husband's arm, her knuckles white. Her husband looked down at her, the corners of his mouth pinched with reassurance. He gave the impression of a man long-suffering from his wife's tendency to react strongly where other people saw only reason to be calm.

I hardly knew Raoul. I had heard rumors that he was in some kind of trouble, suspended from his football team, perhaps because of drugs. I asked Francesca, in a whisper, "What is it, do you know this boy?"

She shook her head vehemently. Then, she turned again to pluck at her husband's arm. "Stop him," I heard her say. "You must stop Dr. Roazen. Don't you see what will happen?"

Apparently he did not.

Looking back, I can't say anything very dramatic happened during the quarter of an hour Raoul struggled to work with Dr. Roazen, trying to "get in touch with his feelings." At the time, I was far more interested in Francesca's response than in the young man's failure. He made efforts to follow the Doktor's instructions, closed his eyes, crouched down, couldn't come up with much, stood up again, shrugged his shoulders and looked, I must admit, very embarrassed.

Francesca kept urging her husband to interfere, to call the whole thing off. Her husband put his arm around her, placating, indifferent. He did not seem to notice that the old man, his mentor, was by now performing for his wife. Or perhaps he noticed and took pride? Certainly, he seemed to be enjoying the spectacle, the frail old man lording it over the athlete who could not come up with a single emotion, not one, not even impatience, no matter how hard he was pushed. I suppose it might even be said that Dr. Roazen was deliberately humiliating him.

Of course, the boy was making the old man look less of a master than he had seemed previously, with his unfailing ability to cut through surfaces, break through denial, reach the emotional core. The old man had once bragged he could unlock a human being the way Billy the Kid could open a safe. This time, he explained to us, not very convincingly I thought, that he could not abandon the boy without first having helped him.

At these words Francesca rose up protesting to her feet but was quickly drawn back by her husband. He whispered to her, frowning severely. Her agitation visibly subsided, she clasped her hands in her lap, shook her head sadly, regained possession of herself.

Certainly, the boy looked crestfallen and unhappy; he made a few halfhearted attempts to reach his "animal rage," crawl on all fours, growl, rear up on his hind legs, but he was out of his element.

If Dr. Roazen was performing for Francesca, the old man had taken on more than he bargained for. I felt this instinctively.

The boy returned to his seat, the evening progressed, the old man regained his mastery, but Francesca never looked at him again. She had leaned back in her chair, was gazing at the athlete, trying I thought to send him some brief word, a gesture of sympathy. He sat bent over his knees, stoic, humbled, a warrior defeated by a power he will never be able to grasp. If he was aware of Francesca, he gave no sign.

And so it went for another hour or more. People wept, raged, embraced the old wizard, sat down with radiant faces. Only Raoul, the athlete, had failed. The muscle in his right arm throbbed perceptibly but he never lifted his head as the success of other participants added, drop by drop I imagined, to his shame. Finally, the evening was brought to a close when Francesca's husband went forward, clapped his arm around the old man's shoulders, applauded the show of mastery, led Dr. Roazen off, giving the impression the great man might otherwise have gone on performing until morning.

Most people went off to bed, to the cottages or tents set up back in the woods or close to the edge of the cliff above the ocean. A few of us remained behind in the smaller room to dance. I stayed to keep an eye on Francesca. Her husband looked back into the room, walked over to her quickly, gathered her up in a bear hug. But she, who had been standing by herself near the window, shrugged him away. He bent over her again, talking to her in what I took to be a consoling fashion. She shook her head. He insisted. She looked up at him with that reproachful child's expression, then petulantly turned her back on him.

I imagined he was eager to get some rest, knowing what lay ahead of him the next day. Dr. Roazen would not be an easy act to follow. I certainly didn't envy any man who considered himself his disciple, and anyway, he and Francesca had been en route from Texas since early morning.

Her husband seemed eager to avoid a scene. Who wouldn't be? We were all by then in a collective state of sensitivity, excitement, stress. Sensing this, I suppose, one of our older members went up to introduce the famous disciple to his wife. They were quickly joined by another man who, I had noticed at our last meeting, had an irritating way of holding his chin pressed against his chest whenever he talked. The doors were open onto the lawn. The group of them strolled outside, leaving Francesca to herself.

The young man, Raoul, had left the room before the dancing began. He did not speak to Francesca, nor she to him, I am certain of that. Not one glance was exchanged between them. Perhaps she was watching him from the window, but I doubt it. She impressed me now as someone lost in herself, drifting. She was startled and disturbed when Dr. Roazen approached her, touched her lightly on the shoulder and then, with a low bow, lifted her hand to his lips.

I don't know what passed between them but I can imagine. Dr. Roazen had his reputation. I did, however, notice that her husband peeped into the room, saw his mentor bent over her hand, frowned and then smiled much too broadly when the Doktor caught sight of him. Francesca, whose cheeks were very pale, stared at her husband without a smile, refusing to join him when he pointed at the overnight case he was carrying. He went off alone to bed.

At that moment I was called from the room. It was late. There were only a few people left standing about on the lawn near the pool to say good night to one another. I wasn't in the room when Francesca started dancing. Perhaps if I had been, I might have tried to stop her? On the other hand, what business was it of mine!

She was, I admit, a remarkable sight. I imagined she had danced like this by herself for years, late at night when the old aunt had thought she was sleeping. I am not sure she was aware that anyone was still in the room with her. Her face lifted in rapture, eyes closed, she slowly undulated her body in an innocent sensuality that reminded me of a Balinese temple dancer, or perhaps a vestal virgin naked by moonlight in rites no man was ever permitted to behold. The look in the old man's eyes, as he watched her, seemed to me a desecration.

I've already said it was late by then. Others, I knew, had gone down to the sulfur baths where I had promised to join them. Suffice it to say, I stayed as long as I could, and therefore I witnessed the moment the old man came up to her, shuffling in front of her in a hideously awkward dance that seemed after a time to draw her out of her rapture. I heard him say to her, with a slight catch to his voice, "And you my dear, are femme fatale?"

She had been standing on one foot, the other tucked behind her ankle, one hand on her hip, the other wrapped around her waist. But now, in a single instant, before my eyes, he had ripped off her girlishness as if it had been a merely ornate shawl. Her face had taken on an expression of deep sexual knowledge, hauteur, disdain for the desire she had called up in her spectator. With a single cut, with those words Dr. Roazen had penetrated her, laying her open to a depth she had perhaps never before touched in herself.

I cannot tell whether she was captured by his recognition or by her power over him. I watched her walk from the room with the old man. He had a house of his own there, set back slightly in the woods, its upper story commanding a wide view of the ocean. They walked down the gravel path with its kerosene lanterns, his arm tucked through hers in a possessive embrace, well satisfied with the evening's trophy. I did not see her again until she came down to the baths, perhaps an hour or two later.

It was a full moon. The fog had cleared while we had been in the baths near the edge of the cliff. The old stone tubs lined up along the wall, fed from the sulfur source in the mountains through black pipes, were lit with a pale light that gave back to the kerosene lamps their flickering evasion. Francesca came down the stairs toward us with her shoulders back, small breasts, arms easy, then the quick, sudden curve of the full buttocks as she turned to hang her towel from a hook. I was in the larger tub with several others. She seemed indifferent. Raoul, the young football player, was alone in one of the small tubs, his massive shoulders visible above the water with its sulfur fumes.

She stepped down into the tub and moved toward him through the water with a gravity that brought to mind something long-forgotten, as if we were called to witness the most forbidden of ritual acts. And then, with the rest of us looking on, she pressed herself against him without a word, put her arms around his neck, very slowly leant her head against his shoulder.

The boy had his back to us. Her face we could see in the moonlight, eyes open, lips parted. She whispered to him, lifting her head to press her neck against his lips, the dark hair spread out behind her, combing the water as he rocked her. She had, I was sure, come to him directly from the old man, from his bed, from the thick rug in front of the fire where I myself had once been honored by his attentions, from those knowing hands that made good the failure of other potencies; she had come as if certain the boy would be waiting, as if it had been silently known between them, as if we too had known and were there to witness it. The boy had wrapped his arms around her and was slowly walking with her toward the edge of the tub. He held her against him tenderly I thought, her legs curled around his waist as he climbed up out of the tub to carry her the few steps to the stone bench.

Bending forward, very deliberately, he laid her down beneath him on the rough stone. He looked like a faun I thought, not human, as he hovered over her, breathless, his limbs hewn, his member erect, potent as ancient stone. His nymph spread beneath him, arms curled back in the glistening web of hair, and she, too, suspended. Then she arched her back, breasts rising, head thrown back, mouth opening, craving rain, her entire body already receiving, the faun's face torn open in possession.

Many times I told myself to turn my head, to close my eyes, to leave the place, to take the others with me. None of us moved. We stood there, waist deep in the steaming bath, as they rocked each other, his curved back, the strained power of his neck, the muscular buttocks so beautiful I felt at moments an impulse to shout with admiration, even with encouragement, as his fans must have done when he made some spectacular move on the playfield. Supporting himself with his hands, he rose above her, arched above her, as though he were worshipping a vestal he desecrated and possessed.

It might have been the way her hands trembled when she stroked him, I had the impression no one had ever made love to her before; or the way she cried to him, as if she could not wait to discover what she had not yet known, hands clasped on his back, drawing him down to her as he withheld himself, resisted.

Did he imagine the old man had followed her down to the bath, was standing at the door to the dressing room, watching? Was he showing off, showing himself to us, trying to prove his prowess, his mastery? What was he waiting for, his body beginning to shake violently now as she twisted beneath him, coaxing, calling, enticing, cajoling?

I thought the night had lasted some ten thousand years by the time he threw himself over her and then immediately withdrew from her, slipped down onto his knees beside the bench, spread her thighs, buried his face in her lap. Pushing herself upward, her whole body stiffened, her back arched, her hands clutching as she cried out in Italian, "Yes this time yes my love my prince I possess thee."

I buried my face in my hands. Was it transgression or some forlorn sublimity torn back from an unthinkable age? When I looked up she was kneeling on the bench in front of him. He cradled her head in his hands, moving her toward him with a strangely forsaken precision, then in the last moment holding her back to gaze down into her face as she struggled to free herself, to reach him. The moonlight, indifferent to the rest of us, poured over them, as if they were the only thing on earth worth noticing. Immobilized, beyond us, the boy shuddering, her mouth closing on him, he arched himself back, reaching up suddenly with one hand to cover his eyes.

There was a roaring so vast I thought I could hear water moving beneath the earth. And then, the boy had visibly dragged himself away. Lifting her in his arms, he seemed to wake to our presence, glanced over at us and smiled with a fine sullen triumph as he began to carry her, curled up against his chest.

It was I who reached out for her. I reached out for her and he placed her in my arms. She came to me as willingly as she had gone to him, wrapping her arms around my neck, smiling blissfully as she cradled herself against me.

I did not think about her husband asleep or at work in his lonely cottage, perhaps waiting anxiously for her. I did not think about the old man, who might have followed her, unseen, on whom she had just enacted the revenge I myself, years before, must have longed to bring down on him the following morning when he had thrown me back among the others, too small a fish for his keeping. Part water nymph, part child, in that moment perhaps the sacred harlot who worships by giving herself to strangers, this woman curled up in my arms was sweeter than any revenge I might have imagined as the boy's hands closed on me while still I held her, the others part too of this strange rite, during which I dipped my head to her breast, barely daring to graze her with my lips, awed by the quick falling away of the forbidden, its irrelevance in the face of greater mysteries. Of course, it may have been I who lifted her but I thought it was she who bent back in my arms so that my mouth was filled with her.

We passed her between us, floating her through the steam, a spread white lily. Her eyes closed, she let herself be moved, stroked, kissed, consumed, with a smile of unearthly innocence, while the boy stood behind me, pressed so close against me he might have felt my desire bleed for him through my veins.

Her laughter came later, when it came to the boy carrying me to the bench. Was I too taken with the wish to let the boy triumph over the old master who had humiliated him as he had once humiliated me? Why else did I reach for him as she had, as if he were mine to inscribe with resurrection? Francesca stood beside the boy. She stood over us, arms lifted, laughing. Was it in mockery, in surrender, in victory? From desire's assertion of its archaic rights? Obedient to the complex revenge in which she had involved us, caught up in the transgression that had flung itself so unexpectedly at the feet of the sacred, he lay over me, never taking his eyes from her as she smiled down at us from her immaculate height.

Then once, with the cry of a soul lost, redeemed now momentarily as it seemed forever, the moist, stabbing heat of him finding me as never before, he spoke her name.

Francesca, a name I myself have had reason to repeat, not often perhaps in the many years since then when nothing like her has descended on us in our remote community at the cliff's edge.

By the following morning she had left, followed somewhat later by her husband, who after all did not hold his workshop that day. Raoul, who had driven Francesca to the bus in Monterey, kept close to me all morning, bound by an eccentric chivalry I suppose.

Forgetting cannot be willed, I had known that already.

I could tell the old man had put two and two together, either because he had been told or because he had seen us. I could tell from the way he stared me down at breakfast, from the way too, just after lunch, he drew back suddenly behind a bush to study the boy's solitary, naked body in the swimming pool. I watched the old man, our sage of the mountain, shuffle past Raoul on the way to the next discussion group, pretending not to see him.

Of course, I returned to my office routines when our visitors had departed, but the community was never again the same, not for me, the story's guardian. Therefore it was inevitable I suppose that one night I caught sight of her in the baths, an unknown young woman turning to hang her towel, the brief, meaningless gravity of a girl moving through water. I saw him too, in an arched muscular back, in the sudden, unthinking gesture of a man putting his hands over his eyes.

Others, suggestible on an overcast night, have seen them as well. The boy cradling her head, pulling her to him, her head and hair flung back on the stone bench, the boy on his knees. And so the baths have held them, moonlit, transgressive. Or they may have been caught by the tutelary spirits of the place. Perhaps, I have liked to think, an admonishment to the old man who never again came down to the baths, where indeed he must have followed her that night. Something about meddling with the shuttered alleys of the soul, their essential silence.

A Matter of Attitude

Clark Demorest

We were supposed to have been closed, but the two hardbodies were still naked.

I figured that watching might help my mood, so there I was, squatting down in the dark with the plumbing, one eye pressed to the hole behind the cracked Pepto-Bismol-pink tile, while soapy water washed over their ripe breasts, nipples crinkled from the stiff spray that was now peppering an insolent red on the tops of their insolent, little butts. As usual my leg cramped. But as usual, I ignored it and watched the fingers of white suds flow over their button-shallow navels and down their flat, brown bellies, the foam collecting in their neatly trimmed, furry patches. Little, white froth-penises dangled between the smooth tan of their thighs while they laughed and talked, before dropping, weightless, into the milky water that swirled about their precious, pink-enameled toes.

One was a blond, the other wanted to be.

Bitches.

I stood and rubbed out my cramp, then dug around in my jock to rearrange things a little and told myself, again, that it wasn't because I hadn't scored in over a year that I watched the hardbodies in their shower. No, really. See, I figured that once you knew what they looked like naked, it was easier to swallow their line of shit.

My sneaks scruffed on the gritty concrete floor as I sidestepped crablike out of the damp, narrow pipe chase and out into the hall; it was late, and I wanted to go home. Somehow I had gotten grease on my new shirt. Damn hardbodies.

Thought maybe I could hustle the little darlings up, so I cracked one of the double-doors marked LADIES' LOCKER, sucking out a puff of warm steam, heady with a sweet-and-sour collage of girl smells: powders, socks, sprays, underwear, soaps, lotions, perfumes, periods, and sweat. I hollered into the cloud:

"Hurry up, please. We're closed."

"Like, keep your tool cool, dude," came the answer.

"Yeah, fur sure," came another.

Fur sure, my ass.

The door oozed quietly closed by itself while I headed for my office—at least that's what it said on the sign: OFFICE. Wasn't really mine, but at least in there I could wait sitting down and enjoy my pissy mood in comfort. Most of the clients cleared the spa before nine; damn hardbodies took their own sweet time.

They say that how much shit you gotta eat depends on how bad you need the job. That's profound, you know? I landed the assistant manager's spot here at Body D Light Spa after being laid off and finding that my ex had thoughtfully cleaned out the excess cash from our bank account and run off with a chiropractor from Phoenix. Well, I figure by now, I must have munched a turd a mile long for the privilege of picking up towels, adjusting exercise machines, unjamming the drink box, picking up trash in the parking lot, and posting client ledgers.

The owners of the chain probably hired me because I had a little college ten years or so ago and could keep books some—God, I'm starting to think in decades. I also cleaned the whirlpool some, the sauna some, and the showers some, and plunged the commodes a lot when the hardbodies flushed their maxies.

The yellowed card with "Bob Williamson" scribbled in blue marker had fallen from my locker door again and was now upside down on the floor next to the cement blocks and five-pound weight

that held up a corner of the wobbly excuse for a desk I shared
with Houston, the manager. Houston.

Hello, my name is Houston and I'll be your aerobics instructor
this morning.

Shit.

Hello, my name is Bob and I'll be picking your pubic hair from
the whirlpool filter this evening.

Damn hardbodies drooled all over his steroid ass, but wouldn't
give me the time of day. Not that I wasn't in reasonable shape—
I watched my weight and even jogged some, but I couldn't spend
all my time strutting around in a tank top, scratching my nuts, and
impressing myself pumping iron. But I didn't mind. Not really.
Besides, all the women weren't like that—chubbette housewives
and the lonely plain Janes. Of course the hardbodies, being equal
opportunity cunts, dumped on them as well. And Houston only
gave them the help they paid for when he had to, so most of them
had stopped coming.

Yeah, Houston. I figure what really griped my butt was having
to work for a troglodyte whose cognitive brain functions were split
between his balls and his brow ridges. But someone had to do the
grunt work, and like I said, I needed the job.

I picked up the card and a junk food wrapper from under the
desk. Taped the card back in place with some tape I found in the
center drawer under one of Houston's socks. Put the wrapper in
the trash. Needed to make extra nice for a while. The new regional
manager, a C. J. Baxter, was supposed to start regular monthly
visits, probably in the morning. I already had the lobby, the common area, and the Men's standing tall, and soon as those two bim-
bos with the bra-size IQs left, I could do the Ladies' and go home.

Finally, I heard the front door crunch open. Hardbody voices
shouted in unison, "So long Mister Spa Dude," the long U careen-
ing down the hall as the door scraped itself shut.

I locked up and attacked the Ladies'—took me over an hour.
Even stacked the laundry bags in the corner for the morning's
pickup. Hit the shower afterward; spray felt good on the back of
my neck. I was tired from the inside out and still had the mood—
men are messy, but women, damn . . . Like the lipstick on the
mirror: FOR A GOOD TIME GO JERK YOURSELF, DUDE.

Shit, get a life.

I figured women probably got off just knowing I had to clean up after them—especially those arrogant, ex-cheerleader types who let their 'tards ride up into their ass, then shine their twenty-two-year-old buns around just so they can give you the What-are-you-lookin'-at-Asshole? look while they slowly run their thumbs down their butts, pulling the spandex from their cracks.

But that's all right, I had the last laugh. Like I said, I've seen them all naked. Seen their razor-nicked bikini lines and their little red butt-pimples and heard them pop farts when they thought they were alone. There's even one who gets herself off by letting the water spray just right on her pussy.

I was face-first in that same hard spray, lost in the rush of the water, letting it blast away at the night's frustration, when a woman's voice came from behind and startled the bejesus out of me.

"And who are you?" Her tone was more to announce her presence than to find out who I was.

I turned around, grabbing my washcloth to cover myself the best I could. It wasn't easy—between the stinging shower and the thinking about the naked hardbodies, I was almost a hardbody myself.

"How in the hell did you—?" My tongue sputtered like a wet fuse and went out.

Tall and regal, reigning barefoot in the splash and steam, stood an alabaster goddess robed in a skimpy spa-towel. It was tied, sort of, under her arm, but majestic, Olympian breasts pushed the edges apart, revealing a seamless, pearl-smooth curve of waist, hip, and thigh. The dressing room light behind her seemed to explode in the sparkling mist, crowning the waves of red-gold hair that spilled about her face and fondled her naked, white shoulders. This was no dippy little hardbody. No sir. This was Woman.

"Master key," she answered, silently adding "silly boy" with her eyes before continuing. "You must be Mr. Williamson."

I managed a nod. "A-And you are—?" I asked, knowing damn well who it had to be. Still, when she told me I about shit.

"C. J. Baxter." She cut a glance at my bulging washcloth.

Now what? What's protocol for meeting your new boss while

you're naked in the ladies' shower and fighting a boner? Shake hands? Or maybe just let your dork stand and salute.

"C. J.?" I asked, being cool.

"Candice Jocelin."

"Candy? Or do you prefer Candice?" I pressed, being cooler.

"I prefer Ms. Baxter." So much for cool and so much for the bulge in my washcloth.

She brushed past me to a vacant nozzle, peeling off her towel, and like an empress donning her vestments, she wrapped it about her head, folding her hair inside, and stepped into the spray.

"Do you usually bathe in the ladies' side, Mr. Williamson?" she asked. I only half heard her words; they sort of whooshed over me, mixing with the hiss of the water. I tried to think of some studly answer, but I just stood there—my mind, mush—reverently gawking at her proud, nearly Rubenesque backside. God. I was in the presence of *gluteus magnificence.*

I finally mustered an intelligent "Huh?"

She turned.

My jaw fell, slack.

Ruddy pink nipples, drawn tight into eager, sanguine thimbles, were boring straight at me, pushed by melon-round breasts that were high and firm and confident—breasts that most men would die for. Breasts most women would kill for.

That did it! My fallen soldier sprang to his post and anxiously peeped up at me from behind his terry parapet.

"I said, 'Do you usually bathe on the ladies' side, Mr. Williamson?'" Her eyes were appraising me through my shrinking washcloth. Part of me wanted to throw the damn thing away and just stand there like a wet hatrack, but most of me still hoped to convince the new boss that I wasn't some kind of pervert. And up to then I hadn't done too well.

"The doors were locked, Ms. Baxter, and I was cleaning up in here anyway. I didn't think it mattered." I was trying to sound so professional.

Yeah, right. Naked, erect, and professional.

"No, I don't suppose it does," she said, returning to her spray. And taking a bar of courtesy soap from the wall tray, she massaged it slowly between her hands, the suds pouring down her arms and off her elbows.

So far, so good, I figured, as she lathered her breasts. But now what? No way could I move on her—no matter how hard the blood pounded behind my trusty washcloth. Like I said, I needed this job. But still, what's next? Quietly leave? Ask her to pass the soap and finish my shower like nothing happened? Offer to wash her back? Ask her to wash mine? Or maybe just stand there behind her and jack off like a gibbering idiot.

The Gibbering-Idiot option was ahead in the polls when it hit me—what the hell did I think I was doing? She was just like the rest of the stuck-up bitches: she was only playing with me. Only wanted to see how big a dipshit I could really be.

Throwing down the washrag, I spun my ass around and marched my hard-on and me the hell out of there. We grabbed a towel. I was sanding away at my wet hide when Ms. Baxter called out to me from across the locker room.

"Are you leaving, Mr. Williamson?"

She had unwrapped her towel/turban and was standing next to the pile of laundry, blotting her luscious body. Again, I responded with scintillating repartee.

"Huh?"

"I asked you if you were leaving, Mr. Williamson." She sounded just like Miss Terkle, school librarian, but she sure as hell didn't look like her. Common sense was screaming at me to just grab my pants and go—this job was history. But you've got to understand, generations of pagan fertility cults have made blood sacrifice to far less than what was standing there in the locker room, dewy-naked and shaking out her hair. Then the unbelievable happened.

I think I whimpered when she sat down on the laundry pile and held out her hand to me. Mechanically and with stupid all over my face, I stumbled over to her, gave her my hand, and let myself be pulled down next to her. And I just sat there, helpless on the shifting bags, trying to think of something clever to say to this naked goddess, while the scent of her hair pumped through my veins, swelling my reawakened soldier.

Suddenly, she lay back and pulled me to her breast. Damn! I

looked up at her. I couldn't figure what my new boss—ex-boss—
was up to. I just couldn't believe— Like I said, my mind was mush.
Anyway, she sort of smiled and gently pushed my face back to her
breast, guiding its rose tip to my lips.

Well, I figured I didn't need another invitation, so I straightened up and began to crawl on top of her. And made a grab for
her crotch. Wrong! Bad move. I was rewarded with a hard, stinging slap on the rump. Ms. Baxter raised her hand, threatening
another, and held her breast to me. I took the hint.

I also took the nipple.

Now, I know this is going to sound like something that weird
little doctors with goatees and bent pipes write about in slick, pompous journals and get obscene amounts of government grant
money to study. But it wasn't like that at all. No. See, sometimes
a man just needs— Shit. Look, after the last coupla years— Well
dammit, it's one of those things that you can't explain; either you
understand it or you don't. But believe me, Ms. Baxter understood.

The locker room, Houston, the hardbodies and their maxi-
pads—everything melted away, my universe becoming warm and
white, smelling all safe and clean and female. She kissed my forehead and cooed to me and gently rubbed the tingling slap spot on
my butt while I nuzzled and suckled away months of anger and
frustration.

Minutes or hours later—maybe weeks later, I really didn't
know—we were lying together, my cheek nestled on her soft,
warm tummy. I was contemplating the canyon of her bottomless
navel when she shifted us around, me ending up between her
thighs, her legs resting over my shoulders. She spoke to me from
beyond the nipple-tipped horizon of her mounded breasts.

"There is something I wish you to do, Mr. Williamson."

Now, if I had taken time to think, I might have resented what
happened next: technically, I suppose, you could call it sexual harassment. But trust me, I wasn't feeling very technical, much less
harassed. You see, I was now face to face with—no, actually I was
more nose to—

O Sweet Jesus, there it was.

Looming up at me was a Mount Everest mons, rounded and
full, and crowned with straight gossamer fluff, so fine that it flut-

tered from my breath as I brushed my cheek over it. And no sir, she wasn't pretending to be a redhead.

Anyway, she specified exactly where I was to touch, how, and with what. How I was to part her pudgy cleft and drag my tongue across her most private spot. It was incredible, my new boss—by then I figured I still had a job—was ordering me to pleasure her, detailing every . . . well, detail. And as I complied, I felt privileged. See, she was sharing with me—*me*—very personal and secret needs.

I swear I never knew half as much about my ex. And thinking back, it wouldn't have been worth the effort: after the honeymoon, she had stopped pretending. Sex with her quickly degenerated into using her cold cunt as a masturbation aid, then into nothing. It just wasn't worth the effort, you know? (Her chiropractor friend has probably found that out by now, poor bastard.) Nope, Ms. Baxter was firm, but she never once bitched or whined about what I might be doing wrong. She encouraged and coached, and being the willing employee, I learned. Boy, did I learn.

I was soon on my own, working only with unspoken commands: a twitch, a sharp intake of breath, fingernails cutting into my shoulders. I slowly searched out each crease, savoring every secret fold, kissing and nibbling and licking at her glistening, female pinkness. I captured her magic kernel between my lips and was probing it with my tongue, when suddenly, violently, her hips arched high, bucking us above our laundry-bag cushions. I held on, and from deep inside her came a cross between a startled scream and a desperate groan that crashed and echoed about the concrete and steel of the locker room.

Now flailing her head from side to side, Ms. Baxter grabbed my hair and forced my face, hard, into her crotch, holding me fast between her thighs and frantically raking her heels across my back. I shoved deep, and ruthlessly pushed her to the top, then sadistically held her back, tonguing her and toying with her, letting her teeter at the edge. I pushed her hard, again and again, and she screamed and grunted and cried and clawed at my hair. Then suddenly, it was over, and she lay still, mewing softly, her breasts heaving.

Out of breath myself, I rolled onto the concrete floor and lay spread-eagled on my back, listening to myself throb; so much blood was diverting to erectile tissue, it's a wonder I didn't pass out. Anyway, I just lay there with my eyes closed, awed. I had never heard a woman make that kind of sound before, much less been the cause of it.

A moment longer of mutual heavy breathing, and I felt her kneel between my legs. I opened my eyes; her chest was an irregular splash of strawberry, glowing hot and vivid against the cream-white of her breasts. Her face radiant, she brushed back her hair: the scarlet had continued up her neck, even to her ears.

Women can fake the orgasm, but never the blush, and she had wanted me to see.

God, I was proud.

I was wallowing in macho when she reached down and gently squeezed my poor, twitching soldier. That did it. I hadn't pre-lubed since high school, and I tried to control it, but in spite of my best efforts, a large, clear drop erupted from my little sentry and ran down his helmet to her fingers. Then with a wicked, almost evil, laugh, she pulled my erection painfully forward and let go. It slapped back against my belly with a loud, wet flop.

She jumped up and spun away, but I was quicker. Scrambling to my knees, I locked my arms around her waist, and with my face pressed between her sacral dimples, I wrestled her down.

I was hornier than when Sally Ann Middlebrooks showed her titties on a dare behind the bleachers during ninth-grade gym class. Shit, I was beyond horny. I was on fire when I forced her to her hands and knees; every bone, muscle, every square inch of skin screamed for release as I pushed her head down and forced my knees between hers from behind, my manhood standing tall, wedging upright in the soft valley of her proud, female behind.

Ms. Baxter grunted and fought, and for a moment I thought maybe I was getting too rough and was about to let her go when suddenly the tip of my sword slipped down between her legs and pressed against the damp opening of her scabbard. I froze. She froze. Then with a high-pitched, almost pitiful little cry, she dropped her head—her hair heaping on the floor—and swayed her back like a cat in heat, rolling up her luscious bottom at me in a posture both supplicant and demanding.

For a moment I didn't move; I just knelt there behind her, pressing against her opening, wet, yet yielding to my pressure only ever so slightly, expanding over my warrior's head with agonizing slowness as I ran my fingernails around her bottom and up the small of her back, chasing the goose bumps that raced to her neck while she rolled her head, inhaling and exhaling through her teeth with a throaty, feral rasp.

I held my breath and caressed her shoulders, her back, her hips and her thighs. I was leaking again, and it was all I could do to keep from impaling her with a single thrust, but I forced myself to wait and savor the moment. Savor her desire. I took shallow panting breaths as she slowly dilated, each millimeter of entry sending new and different waves of pleasure-pain screaming from my genitals, across my hips and down my thighs. Then all at once I was deep within her, curved and stone hard. Filling her. She, stretching and yielding, yet firmly encasing me in her wet heat. Snug and tight against my entire length. And again I paused: her sharp, female scent was reaching up, caressing me with long piquant fingers. I inhaled her sex and again the world faded away: I was dizzy-headed, consumed by her hunger.

Suddenly she constricted herself around me, rhythmically gripping and squeezing my erection. So help me God, I never knew women could actually do that, at least not that hard. Then she looked back at me through her hair, and her eyes locked into mine—eyes that were pleading, yet giving, eyes bright with lust, pure and unashamed. I dug my fingers into her hips and she pushed back against me, flattening her cool buttocks against my thighs—her hunger, her demand, as unmistakable as mine.

And that night on the floor of the Ladies' Locker at the Body D Light Spa, we mated.

I was Cro-Magnon, ancient and primeval, bellowing in the storm atop the mountain as lightning burned my thighs, and thunder, rumbling low from my loins, summoned forth the hot torrential release that gushed and streamed from me into my Woman, my slave, my lady, my whore and goddess, who raged with me, our voices rejoicing in our union while she hungrily consumed my spasms, invoking the next, and the next. And the next.

And the next.

And the next.

When it was over, we lay cuddled like puppies on the floor in a panting, twisted pile, intoxicated by the afterglow. And we were wet: backs and bellies shone from our sweat, thighs from our sex. I tested the red of her renewed passion rash with my cheek; it felt hot to the touch. And she giggled when I explored her navel, teasing my little finger into its deep, oval crevasse, extracting the drop of perspiration pooled at the bottom. I looked up into her sleepy eyes and sucked the drop from my fingertip; it was salty and tasted of her. And I swear she was actually purring when I kissed away the hot dew shining beneath her breasts, while she fondled my tired 'nads, gently testing the thickness of my scrotum with her fingers. I kidded her about the scrapes on our knees—the cement floor had really done a number on us—and told her that next time we'd have to use the laundry bags.

Suddenly, she rolled away from me and stood. She was sobered by more than just the chill of the concrete. She hurried into the shower. I followed, lost. What had I done?

We washed in silence and erased the evidence of our copulation, the steam of the hot shower cleansing our lust from the air. I spoke once to offer shampoo, she declined.

I turned off the water and brought dry towels.

They were small; I gave her mine and went for more.

She complimented me on the condition of the spa and the accounts while we peed, naked, in adjacent stalls.

I thanked her.

She dressed and left.

I stared at the closed door for a long moment.

Put our towels in the hamper, moved the mop around a little, filled the tampon machine, dressed, carried the trash to the dumpster, and left.

I don't use the hole anymore.

The sign on my office door says MANAGER, and Body D Light has the highest efficiency rating and the fewest client complaints of any spa in the region. Last quarter, Ms. Baxter recommended me for the corporate profit-sharing program.

I know it sounds weird that it's still "Ms. Baxter" and "Mr.

Williamson," or that I still work for her after . . . after that night.
It took me a little while to figure it, but believe it or not, our
relationship had been strictly professional from the start. Listen,
you think she just accidentally walked in on me that night, not
knowing I was there or who I was? No sir, Ms. Baxter doesn't do
things by accident: she had done her homework on Body D Light
long before she drove up. Believe me, those tight-assed, Ivy league
business schools could learn a lot about management theory from
our Ms. Baxter.

Anyway, she's taught me a lot about the business and people
and a lot about myself, too. Like she says, it's your attitude that
counts. You've got to care about folks before they'll give a damn
about you. Like when I spend extra time with the chubbettes and
the lonelies, help them with the machines and just talk a little—
encourage them, you know? You gotta mean it or it won't work,
but the right word, a smile, maybe a fanny pat, and they'll glow
all afternoon. Feels kinda nice, you know? Besides, they tell their
friends—good for business. And I've dated a couple, too. Listen,
some of them are really shaping up.

And get this. Some of the hardbodies even made moves on me.
No, really. They're not so bad. See, I figure they know they're not
going to keep the tight bods forever—biological clocks ticking and
all that. Anyway, I just don't get all bent anymore when they pretend not to be flashing their tails on purpose, or when they make
like they really don't know how much their titties show through
their sweaty T-shirts. Once I figured out where they were coming
from and understood their needs, we got along just fine.

Even hired a couple of hardbodies, part-time, to help out. Boy,
you ought to hear the hell raised when someone trashes the locker
rooms now.

Yep, like Ms. Baxter says, it's all in the attitude.

UNCONDITIONAL POSITIVE REGARD

B. J. Simmons

Between sips of wine and tokes of pot, Luke and Hannah slowly and voluptuously brought each other to a fever pitch as they watched an adult video. Several thin shafts of late sun squeezed past the window blinds, slicing through wisps of pungent smoke, threatening to expose their erotic activity. The television splashed bright colors across the floor, its throbbing music in synch with the meaty thrusts of a pair of muscular men into two magic-tongued women.

Unable to wait any longer, Hannah eagerly scrambled up and sprawled jackknifed across the arm of the sofa, presenting her up-thrust bottom to Luke in all its naked splendor.

Luke positioned himself behind his wife, planting his feet firmly on the blue carpet, his trim, nude body tensed into a partial crouch. Cool, conditioned air swirled about his pendant genitals. His whole skin felt like one big supersensitive glans, every capillary blood-charged by the pot. The drug slowed time, isolated nerve endings, allowed him to relish each touch with extended ecstasy. Totally focused, he was intensely committed to giving and receiving maximum pleasure. He lavished drawn-out caresses over Hannah's lush, pliable buttocks, poetic in their stretched tautness, created explicitly for this purpose.

Luke gently rubbed the top edge of his hand back and forth in the wet heat between her distended nether lips. She whimpered, hunching, pressing down on his hand. He pulled her buttocks wide apart. Saliva gathered in the corners of his mouth as he gazed lustfully at the clenched brown spot peeping up from its rich nest of silken black hair. Mewing and sighing, Hannah squirmed in delight when he gently sank his thumb up to its first knuckle into the tight opening.

Just below, lovingly prepared by his tongue, the glistering pink petals of her cunt flared open. Its taste clung to his lips, her compelling musk strong in his nose. While easing his thumb in and out, Luke slowly worked his achingly engorged penis into her heated, lubricious sheath. She pushed up and back to meet his thrusts, undulating frantically, trying to stuff both orifices as full as possible.

In control, prolonging the incredible pleasure, he held her down, gradually pressing deeper, the wide head parting, slowly and snugly sinking in. "Oh!" she yelped, thrashing her head. Muscles rippled in the clean, smooth curve of her back. "Deep . . . so deep!" Her orgasmic cries galvanized Luke, stiffened him even more. He began to stroke in and out slowly, in and out, changing angles, up, down, side to side. The salacious sight of her cunt lips sliding along his shaft, a gripping ring demanding his flesh, was almost too sexy. She thrust back eagerly to meet his every stroke.

They soon lost themselves in the compulsive, rapturous spell of the ancient rhythm.

Hannah's asshole suddenly began clasping and unclasping his intruding thumb. He shivered at the thrilling, ultra-intimate sensation. She was there. Her hot, slick vagina clutched and unclutched, fluttering spasmodically along the length of his jacking cock. Luke's nostrils quivered, his neck and chest swelled, a shocking numbness started at the top of his spine and flashed down his hunching body.

Gasping in ecstasy, he ejaculated forcefully, squirting far back into Hannah's greedy flesh. Each repeated, paralyzing spasm seemed to echo in his head.

Her joyous, lusty cries rang out. "Oh, Luke! My god! Oh my god!"

Panting and replete, they remained locked until the acute sensitivity of his glans subsided enough for him to withdraw. He gave her backside a final, lingering caress, reluctant to leave it. But he padded quickly to the bathroom and washed his hands, bringing back a damp towel.

After helping the cramped and trembling Hannah stand, Luke lit cigarettes while she used the towel. Then, limp and relaxed, they sat on the sofa. She leaned against his chest while they smoked. The television flickered blankly.

Hannah's face was happy and slightly puffy, short black hair tousled, dark eyes moist. She touched his cheek. "That was remarkable," she said in her low, precise voice. "I love you." He didn't answer right away. She insisted. "Do you love me?"

The question—its timing, the plea in it—suddenly irritated Luke. Not her usual style. It wasn't something to be asked for, like a goddamned hobo asking for a quarter. He pulled her head against his shoulder to avoid those eyes waiting for the automatic answer to a question he himself would never ask.

Murmuring into her soft neck, he said, "Sure, you know I do."

Luke went to the television and ejected the tape from the player. Still buzzing, dry-mouthed, he rubbed his feet on the carpet while studying the couples depicted on the label. He glanced across at Hannah. She sat on folded legs, one arm along the top of the sofa. Her narrow shoulders seemed too small to support the heavy, dark-tipped breasts.

Behind a covering grin, Luke asked, "Have you ever thought of swinging?"

Her quiet, watchful eyes widened and a touch of pink brushed her cheeks. He'd never mentioned this, though he'd thought about it. Breasts swaying, Hannah reached for another cigarette. Poise quickly regained, she looked serenely up at him, reflecting.

"No, Luke," she said lightly, smiling. "You're more than enough for me." A pause. Then, with a hint of challenge, she asked, "Am I not enough for you?"

"You know that has nothing to do with it." He'd have to be more subtle, she wasn't easily led. Waving a hand, he smiled and said, "No big deal. Just crossed my mind, that's all. Forget it."

He slipped the tape into its cover and inserted it into the book-

case that lined the wall. Then he walked over and picked up the
towel. Holding it away from his body, Luke glanced at his petite
wife of six months.

"Guess I'd better get my things together." He had to be in
Atlanta early the next morning. Dried sperm tugged at the inside
of his thigh as he strode toward the shower.

Driving home to Jacksonville after his third day on the road,
Luke checked into a south Georgia motel. Strolling through the
sultry summer twilight toward the restaurant, he stopped a moment beside the brightly lit pool. A laughing young mother struggled to boost her chubby child onto a bobbing, plastic green
alligator. Big white teeth sawed the gator's watermelon red mouth
and fat blue tears rolled from its long-lashed eyes.

Luke smiled at their happy efforts. Wearing sport coat and
slacks, he was a tall, fit man of thirty-five, tanned from hours of
reading beside motel pools. He had neatly trimmed brown hair and
steady gray eyes. Though his face seemed open and friendly, an
indefinable detachment hinted that he was a man who spent much
time alone.

He bought an *Atlanta Constitution* from a vending machine
and went into the restaurant. The gnawed fingernails of the sullen
blond waitress who took his order made him think of Hannah's
small, delicate hands. Sighing, Luke stretched his aching back and
glanced about the large, sparsely occupied room. After ten years
of traveling, selling electronic equipment for an Atlanta-based firm,
motels bored him. Two waitresses stood idly by the kitchen
counter, smoking and watching a group of elderly couples seated
in a corner. The cashier, a thin boy with a shadowy mustache,
watched the waitresses. The tables nearest Luke were empty.
Canned music competed with clinking sounds from the kitchen.

His steak arrived and, as was his habit, Luke was soon en-
grossed in the paper, reading as he ate, unaware of his surroundings. Several articles expressed amazement at Carter's nomination
for president. As he sipped a final cup of coffee, scanning the back
business pages, a strange, nagging feeling made him look up.

A pair of shocking green eyes stared directly at him from the
next table. They glowed in a deeply tanned face, which was framed

by a mass of coiffed copper hair. Spray of freckles across a proud nose. The collar of her lime blouse opened over the lapels of an expensive white linen suit.

About his age, the woman radiated health. Crimson nails flashed as she gaily tilted her glass at him. Their color matched her smiling, wine-wetted lips. Suddenly jerked back into the world, Luke managed a weak smile of his own and lifted his cup in puzzled greeting. She brazenly challenged him with her mature, confident beauty. There was no mistaking the invitation in that look.

Luke glanced down at the paper, out the window, back at the paper, back at the woman. She obviously enjoyed his reaction. After a few moments under her scrutiny, he had to move. Fighting back the impulse to approach her, Luke finally grabbed the check and stood, smiling ruefully at the living dream. He walked self-consciously to the register, silently bemoaning his married state.

Pausing outside the entrance, he lit a cigarette to calm down. After a few moments, clicking heels approached from behind, bringing a provocative breath of exotic perfume. Luke turned around. Mocking eyes like melting emeralds.

She stood very close, breasts thrusting, her nearness and aroma powerfully seductive. Smiling, she asked, "What's a good-looking guy like you doing dining alone?"

Luke stared entranced at the soft lips as they moved, imagined being engulfed by them. "I could ask you the same thing," he managed to answer.

Looking deep into his eyes, she grasped his forearm with a strong brown hand. Her other hand held a flat briefcase. "I have an unopened bottle of good bourbon in my room. How about a nightcap?"

After an indecisive pause, he held up his hand and wiggled a gold-banded finger. "You don't know how sorry I am, but I can't."

"A minor legality. Since when did that stop anyone?"

Good question. Her friendly hand moved to his bicep. He hesitated, pinned like a struggling butterfly under her gaze. "Can't . . . sorry . . . I want to, but I can't."

She frowned slightly. "Well, if you change your mind, I'm in the room directly above yours."

She swung about, copper hair glinting, and strode away, swing-

ing the case, long legs scissoring, tight rear flexing under the clinging skirt. Pride in his restraint faded with the retreating scent.

He gave the redhead time to get to her room, then went to his
own. Disgustedly throwing off his clothes, he flopped nude onto the
bed. Half-hard, he fondled himself as he used the phone.

"I'll see your smiling face tomorrow," he told Hannah when she
answered.

"Great. I'm sure ready for my traveling man."

"You can't know how ready he is for you."

"Have a good trip?"

"Good enough. Helped our bank account. Say . . . there's something . . ." He hesitated. Should he?

She laughed. "What is it?"

"Well . . . what if . . . I can't seem to get the idea of swinging
out of my mind."

"Oh, Luke! Are you serious?"

"Damned right I'm serious. Why can't we try . . . if it's no fun,
if we don't like it, what have we lost?"

An awkward silence. Then, "Luke, you know I'd do anything
for you. But let's not talk about it now. I miss you."

"Okay, sorry. I miss you, too, and I'll see you tomorrow. Sleep
tight."

"I will. Don't forget my play tomorrow." Her voice softened. "I
love you Luke, and please drive carefully."

"Same here. See you tomorrow. Bye."

He hung up the phone and fell back on the bed. He was fully
hard now. A toilet flushed overhead. She was moving around up
there.

A woolly red muff nestled between long, tanned legs.

"Fuck!" he muttered viciously at the ceiling. Then he turned
out the light.

As Luke arrived home the next afternoon, Hannah's Toyota
parked in the drive reminded him that her play opened that night
and she'd ridden to the theater with a friend. She was a licensed
psychologist and worked as a family counselor for the state of Flor-
ida. A second interest, however, was drama, and she was active in
community theater. He ate lunch and did several hours of paper-

work. Making sure he had a fresh suit in the car, he then drove to
his health club.

After so many hours alone, the club seemed unusually crowded
to Luke. Straining bodies huffed and pulled at gleaming chrome
equipment, everything multiplied by the mirrored walls. He added
to the huffing, diligently following his routine, working out the car
kinks.

He soon found himself doing more looking than lifting. Scantily
clad young women cavorted all about, threatening to burst out of
packed costumes. So much firm and luscious flesh exposed, sweating and grunting, gyrating and contorting, squatting and bending,
curly edges of pubic hair escaping, plump nipples jutting, clefts and
cracks opening and closing. He wasn't tempted this strongly when
he was single.

Wasn't thirty-five too young for a midlife crisis? Hannah wasn't
athletic, but she was all woman. He'd known many women, had
nothing to prove, was happily married. Still, it was sobering to
realize that he'd never again touch bodies like these. By god, he
had to talk Hannah into swinging. What was wrong with wanting
the excitement of variety, new thrills, new reactions? To hear unfamiliar moans of joy as he buried himself in the freshness of a
young stranger?

A distant thunderstorm rumbled as Luke walked through the
hot, still air to the theater. An usher gave him a pass and he
threaded through the large, well-dressed crowd to his seat. The
playbill indicated Hannah's character was a feisty old lady in the
comedy. She didn't appear until near the end of the first act, and
he waited expectantly, nervously hoping she'd do well.

Then Hannah skipped onstage—he needn't have worried. Luke
hardly recognized her. Voice, gestures, the way she held herself—
she *was* a funny old lady!

And what a performance! His serious and shy wife had this
sophisticated audience in stitches. Chills of pride washed over him
when he stood with the others and applauded vigorously as her
part concluded the first act.

Backstage afterward, he pushed past enthusiastic admirers to
hug and kiss Hannah, pleased to see her so alive and happy, bask-

ing in the praise of her fans. Her made-up face and eyes glowed, framed by hair that had been sprayed gray. Then they went to someone's home for a celebratory oyster roast. There was much animated talk and laughter, champagne flowed. The play had been a ringing success.

On the return home, thunder and lightning moved toward them as Luke drove the company Pontiac across one of the city's several bridges. Hannah snuggled close when they met the rain. He turned off the radio and put on the wipers. The wet tires snicked over metal section dividers. Intermittent lightning lit the choppy St. Johns River flowing far below them. Between flashes, it was a wide black ribbon bordered by colored lights.

Exiting the bridge, traffic piled up as usual for the despised tollbooth. Stop and go, stop and go. The driver just ahead flicked an empty hand at the toll basket and sped on through the red light. Luke, however, stopped, dutifully tossed a quarter into the basket, then waited for the light to change before driving on.

Hannah snickered. "Good Citizen Luke. You're a trustworthy soul, aren't you?"

"Lucky for you . . . a traveling man is often tempted." A nearby thunderclap startled her. "Some weather!" he exclaimed.

"Yes . . . wuthering weather."

"E. Brontë . . . too many ghosts in that book."

"A love story by a woman who never knew love . . . I like her poetry."

"Tell me some."

Hannah thought a moment, then quoted, trained voice distinct above the drumming rain: " 'Riches I hold in light esteem / And love I laugh to scorn / And lust of fame was but a dream / That vanished with the morn.' "

He thrilled to the ringing, mellifluous words, so much more powerful than the printed page. They left the storm behind, driving down a broad avenue lined by wet, glistening trees. "Thanks. I'm glad you know that. Sad, though."

"She lived a sad, short life . . . death all around her. But she had spunk . . . listen: 'Let us part, the time is over / When I thought and felt like thee / I will be an ocean rover / I will sail a desert sea.' "

"Sounds like she wanted to break loose." He touched her face with his free hand, smelling champagne and the unfamiliar makeup. "Which reminds me . . . doesn't the idea appeal to you at all? Two men at once, another woman . . . watching each other do it with a stranger. Does it offend you?"

She lifted her head from his shoulder and sat up. He sensed her staring at his face as he drove. After a long silence, she said, "You're not going to forget it, are you, Luke? No, it's not a great moral dilemma . . . just people having sex." She hesitated. "I like watching our videos. Maybe I'd like to see you inside another woman. After all, Freud said that biology drives us, civilization's just a veneer . . ."

"So?"

"There are other theories of personality. Rogers said we seek those experiences that satisfy and avoid those that don't."

"My point is that you can't know what's satisfying or not until you try it. You were so alive and happy tonight and I'd like to see it more often. Open, saturated with life, boiling over with raw sex. Lawrence wrote that a man and a woman together make an angel."

Laughing, she put her head back on his shoulder and caressed his thigh. "Does several doing it at once make a host of angels?"

"One way to find out."

"Well," Hannah continued, "Carl Rogers says we all need unconditional positive regard. Swinging does sound exciting. But your positive regard for me may fade when you see another man fucking me."

Her warm breast pressed against his side. "No way. It's my idea . . . I want to see it. Our special adventure. We just quit if we don't like it."

He pulled into their driveway under gnarled oaks draped with Spanish moss. Hannah said, "I've missed you, Good Citizen Luke," and kissed him passionately. Then she opened her door. "Carl Rogers also said that a fully functioning person is open to experience."

Luke laughed as he went around the car to join her. "That guy was a wise man." They started arm in arm to the house and she groped for his crotch. "Hey, lady, if just talking about it does that, what will the real thing do?"

After they had made love, Luke lay back in the king-size bed, sated and exhausted, snug at last between crisp home sheets.

Hannah cuddled against him. She murmured sleepily into his throat, "I know a teacher . . . Rick . . . in Gainesville. He swings . . . I'll call him if you like."

Luke patted her belly and smiled in the darkness. He had actually talked her into it!

Barefooted, in jeans and T-shirt, Luke paced before the window, now and then peering between the drapes. He had to leave early tomorrow and hoped their visitors wouldn't be late this Sunday evening. With the help of Hannah's friend, they'd arranged by phone for a married couple to initiate them into swinging.

Hannah fixed snacks on the coffee table. She didn't show it, but Luke knew she was nervous. Also barefooted, blue shorts and a white blouse showed off her tan. Her short-cut black hair gleamed. He'd persuaded her to forgo underwear, and pert brown nipples peeked through the blouse. What would these people be like? Would Hannah join in or hold back? She must be ready—he sure was. They hadn't fucked for three days now, just touching and teasing, stoking their fires for this encounter. As she bent over, Luke lusted to run his hand between her legs, to feel that soft, thick bush simmering behind the thin cloth of her shorts.

Everything was ready. He'd helped Hannah dust the colorful books lining their large bookcase. Freshly cut flowers scented the cool air. He'd even polished the carved Don Quixote figurines adorning the seldom-used fireplace. Gray ceramic lamps at either end of the blue sofa cast a soft glow upon white-draped windows and framed art prints. Chopin's intricate trills tinkled softly from the stereo.

Hannah was teasing Luke about the two showers he'd taken when their guests finally arrived. Betty had elaborately styled blond hair. Medium height, mid-thirties, several years older than her husband. Luke quickly noted that her full figure filled out a yellow blouse and short brown skirt very nicely. Taller and heavier than Luke, James was dark and had curly black hair. Luke and Hannah showed the others about the house. Talking, becoming acquainted, everyone exceedingly polite, the real purpose of this get-together was carefully avoided.

Betty's sharp blue eyes darted about, taking in every detail, especially Hannah. She spoke in a slow, pronounced drawl. "Your names are straight out of the Bible . . . are y'all religious or something?"

Luke and Hannah exchanged amused glances. "No," he said, as he led them back to the living room sofa, "it just happened that way." He and Hannah sat across from them, separated from their visitors by the goodie-laden coffee table.

"Hey," James said in his deep bass voice, "check out all the books." Luke noticed that his smoldering brown eyes brazenly examined Hannah as she left her chair to pour wine. He was craggily handsome and virile-looking. Thick hair curled at the collar of his short-sleeved shirt and on his strong arms. He wore too much expensive cologne.

Hannah seldom looked directly at James. Was she attracted or repelled? He's sure rugged-looking, Luke thought, not exactly Hannah's type. Ambiguous emotions briefly cooled Luke's enthusiasm as he noted James's hot gaze undress Hannah's delectable body. But prurient visions quickly overcame his doubts. What the hell, they weren't here to discuss literature.

"Nice legs," James said to Hannah as she sat and elegantly took up her wineglass. Ignoring Luke and Betty, he asked her, "So, you two are new at swinging?" His tone implied that he certainly was not. Hannah looked at Luke for an answer.

Luke hesitated, aware of his inexperience compared to this seasoned pair. "Yes . . . we decided to try it." He took his stash from the bookcase, but James waved it away and gave them each a machine-rolled joint.

"Oh, we love it!" Betty said. Luke guessed that her husband loved it more than she did. She smiled at Hannah. "We travel all over to parties . . . you'd be surprised at how many couples swing." She took a puff. "I own a furniture store. Since James came, business has boomed, especially from the lady customers. Before we started swinging, I was jealous . . . now I join right in." She waved her glass at Hannah. "Ever have two men inside you at the same time?"

Hannah blushed. "No, I can't say as I have."

"Well, I don't mean James was one of them . . . that would be impossible. Oh, honey, just you wait! They never forget James . . . always calling us for a party. You're in for the ride of your life!"

James glanced at Luke, gauging his host's reaction. He squared his big shoulders and grinned, teeth startlingly white in his dark face. "Don't scare this little thing, honey. You just take care of Luke."

While Luke pondered this exchange, Betty took a large conch shell from the end table. James began asking Hannah about her work. Betty watched them a moment, then put the conch to her ear and listened eagerly. The shiny pink convolutions of the shell always reminded Luke of a vagina. Her eyes widened. "These things are so neat . . . the ocean and all!"

Luke smiled at her and took another toke of the strong reefer, feeling sexier with each puff. "You don't hear the ocean. That's blood pulsing in your inner ear."

"Is that right?" The skirt rode up her pale thighs as she leaned to put the conch back. She wore no panties. Grinning lewdly at Luke's rapidly expanding crotch, she began slowly opening and closing her legs. Luke couldn't think of anything to say, just stared and swelled.

With a final check on the talking James and Hannah, Betty came over to Luke, taking off her blouse. She straddled his leg and kissed him, tongue probing. Luke pushed up her skirt and clasped her naked ass, so excitingly unfamiliar. Her heat burned through his jeans as she rubbed herself vigorously against his leg.

Lifting a freckled breast to his face, she stuck the nipple into his mouth. As Luke sucked, feeling it grow and stiffen, he glimpsed Hannah wistfully looking their way. He dimly heard James say, "Why not come over here, honey?"

Luke helped Betty jerk off his jeans and shorts. His penis flopped into her waiting hand. He gasped when her warm, wet mouth engulfed it. She gently manipulated his scrotum while her tongue lapped exquisitely at the underside of his glans, alternately sucking it against her hard palate. Luke closed his eyes and threw his head back, thrilling to her expertise. He dimly heard James exclaim, "Man, what a set of boobs!"

Luke was soon grunting along with Betty's lascivious smacking
sounds. Was that the back of her throat? Despite the pot, he was
already getting close. His cock surged as she suddenly fingered his
anus. He had to squeeze the chair arms to hold back. "Wait! I'm
gonna . . ."

Her warm mouth suddenly released him into the cool air. She
stood up, touching herself. "Not yet, honey. My turn."

Luke lifted his head, dazed by lust and pot and wine. Then he
remembered Hannah.

She was on her back, naked, one leg high along the top of the
sofa, one foot on the floor. Except for shoes, James was still
dressed. Hannah's hands twisted in his hair as his head moved
between her widely spread legs. He clutched a breast in each hand.
Hannah's head arched back, tendons standing out in the slender
neck, her face flushed a bright red.

Betty pulled Luke up and called, "Come on James, time to
party!" As she tugged him along, Luke glanced back. James effortlessly lifted Hannah into his arms and followed.

Luke turned on the light and pulled off his shirt while Betty
dropped her skirt and flopped onto the broad bed, holding out her
arms. But Luke paused to watch the other two. After James sat
Hannah on the other side of the bed, he stood before her, avidly
fondling her breasts.

Concerned, Luke asked Hannah, "Are you okay?" It occurred
to him that they didn't use pet names such as "baby" and "honey."
Black hair mussed, lips smeared and swollen, eyes bleary, she was
obviously high and aroused. She looked nervous, but Luke saw that
she was determined to take on James.

Hannah gave her husband a weak smile while James massaged
her voluptuous breasts, squeezing each nipple, tugging and twirling, clenching his teeth. Hannah sighed. James gritted out, "Un-
buckle my belt, baby."

The three gazed expectantly at the incredible bulge shifting in
James's trousers. Luke held his breath as Hannah unbuckled the
belt, unzipped the fly, and, with difficulty, pulled down the pants
and shorts.

Hannah's mouth fell open with a gasp.

Betty giggled. "Never seen anything like that, have you, honey?"

Luke stared, astounded. He'd seen overdeveloped men on video, but this was real and up close, quiveringly alive, unreasonably huge.

Hannah looked dumbfounded. Timorously, she cupped the pendulous nutbag. It drooped over the sides of her wrist. The trembling, delicate fingers of her other hand fluttered along the veiny, swollen monster. It swelled even longer and thicker, rising fully erect and vibrant, stiff and massive in her small hand. Hannah licked her lips nervously, eyes wide and fascinated. She slipped the foreskin back and forth, covering and uncovering the great, fleshy knob, shiny and dimpled like an apple. Luke could even smell the vital, tangy maleness of it, sharper than the women's rich aroma.

"Suck it," James said. Hannah released his sac and the weighty testicles sagged. She grasped the shaft with both hands and struggled to work her mouth around it.

She pulled back, licking her lips, staring in wonder at the magnificent dick jutting from her hands. "I can't . . . it won't . . ."

James peeled off his shirt, baring a ridged chest, hair narrowing to run in a thin line down his flat belly. He laughed and said, "That's okay, doll. Just lick it a little."

Enraptured, a wanton expression on her face, Hannah gazed spellbound at the rock-hard cock. Afraid and admiring at the same time, she fondled its thick girth as though it were a jeweled, dangerous dagger. Luke sighed in recognition as she palmed one dangling nut, gently squeezing it while she continued working the foreskin back and forth.

Then she obediently leaned forward and began rolling her tongue over and under and around the sculpted, flaredback glans.

James grunted. "Ah, yes. Lick it baby, lick it. It likes you. That's it."

Luke stared, mesmerized. Suddenly, Betty pulled him between her spread knees and said, "Come to mama, Lukie."

Suppressing his concern for Hannah, Luke slid into Betty easily on the first try. She squirmed, locked her mouth onto his, wrapping her legs about his waist, pumping.

After a few moments, the bed shifted as James added his bulk. Luke's erection dwindled. He pulled out to check on his wife, but Betty pushed his head down between her legs.

Luke spread Betty's legs wider apart, hungrily inspecting the inviting pussy. Burying his face in her eager wetness, he reveled in the smell and taste, craving it, and began pleasuring her with his tongue. Yet his concentration kept slipping, drawn to the other bodies so near. Especially to the sounds . . .

"Oh no!" Hannah cried. "Easy . . . go easy, please."

"Don't worry, honey," James reassured. "I won't hurt you . . . um . . . relax, let me do the work."

The bed rocked.

"Uh! . . . my god! . . . please go slow . . . oh! . . . let me adjust . . . uh! . . . yeah . . ."

"Ah yes . . . no hurry . . . yes . . . tight hot pussy!"

Betty whimpered and squirmed. "Eat me baby, eat me!"

Hannah's voice rose higher. "Uh! . . . god! . . . it's . . . oh, god, it's incredible!"

James coaxed. "Better . . . um! . . . oh, baby, that's better . . . it's liking it now . . . easy."

Luke hurried—he had to see. He drew Betty's clit into his mouth, nipping gently, softly sucking. She squealed and began bucking rapidly against his teeth. Warm secretions filled his mouth, wet his face. He swallowed. Her body suddenly tensed and quivered, out of control, legs clamping tighter about his ears. She yelled, then abruptly relaxed. "Oh, honey . . ." Luke wiped his face on the sheet and eagerly lifted his head to look.

James's muscular back writhed, extended arms straining to hold his weight off Hannah while forcing her legs wide apart. The view was shockingly erotic. He's a master at this, Luke thought. James's buttocks rippled, pressing carefully in and out. Right before Luke's eyes, the mighty shaft was impaled halfway into Hannah's furry nest.

Hannah stared upward, unseeing, face flushed and contorted. Her body hunched in short, quick jerks. The anxious tone of her voice gradually changed to one of intense pleasure. "Fuck me! . . . oh, fuck me! . . . uh! . . . oh, yes, oh, yes! . . . uh! . . . uh! . . . I can't stand it . . . what a . . . good god!"

The musky odor of sex mingled with James's cologne.

Luke lustfully watched James work on Hannah, squeezing it slowly in, ignoring her elated thrusts. James bulled, delving deeper inch by salacious inch. After each partial withdrawal, more of the invading dick shone with Hannah's lubricant. A lot of it was still dry.

An irresistible impulse came over Luke.

Betty laughed. "Go ahead, honey. Touch it, he won't mind."

Luke ran his finger up and down James's damp, hairy crack, lingered on the crinkled anus, feeling the powerful buttocks clenching in effort. Loosely encircling the hot column with his other hand, he let it slip slickly between his fingers, feeling it going in and out of Hannah's body. Odd, thrilling sensation. Prickly pubic hair, living human junction, jostling egg-balls in wrinkled pouch. He fingered James's warm hole, pressing in lightly to assist each forward thrust.

"Uh . . . uh! . . . it's so . . . yes," moaned Hannah. "Like that. Fuck me, James! . . . god, that's good!"

Betty moved up and held Hannah's thrashing head so she could kiss her. She fondled Hannah's breasts, tenderly pinching the stiff nipples. She brushed damp tendrils of hair off Hannah's forehead while Hannah stared fixedly up at the implacable James.

Betty's pale, heart-shaped bottom, resting on callused heels, caught Luke's attention. He lovingly caressed the satiny buttocks. What a work of art is a woman's ass. She lifted to allow his hand to slip under and finger her steamy slit while he thumbed the neat, pink asshole. She squirmed in delight. He was as hard as he'd ever been.

Betty pulled her head out past James's arm. Turning and squatting lewdly before Luke, she spread her labia wide apart. Grinning lecherously at him, she slipped two fingers into her pussy and worked them in and out. Then she rubbed the slickened fingers over Hannah's lips and nostrils. Hannah opened her mouth and greedily sucked them. "Oh, James," Betty cried, "she's a hot one. Give it to her!"

Luke lay on his side, his face a foot from the intense coupling. Betty moved down to see, fondling Luke as she hungrily watched her husband drive Luke's wife out of her mind. Luke took Hannah's hand, letting her know he was there. She squeezed back in time with James's thrusts.

Hannah's bottom was lifted high, straining anus protruding from its black-thatched cleft.

Achingly aroused, high and lusting, Luke avidly watched.

James suddenly shoved it all the way home.

Hannah's head jerked up off the pillow, eyes springing wide open. She yelled at the top of her voice. "Oh my god!"

James grabbed her buttocks, pulling her snugly against him. Hannah thrashed her head, gasping rapturously, completely skewered now, impossibly full, utterly ravished by sensations she'd never known. "Oh goddamn! That's too . . . uh! . . . yes!" Oaken arms bulging, James suddenly held himself still and rigid, plugged tightly into the rhapsodic Hannah, rocking slightly from side to side. "Do it! Fuck me!" she cried.

At last, James withdrew an amazing length of gleaming flesh and began long searching strokes, in and out, unhurried, masterful, generating utmost bliss. At the end of each deepest penetration, he gave a little twist as his bag settled down over Hannah's crack.

Betty's hand worked Luke's cock. "My, my, Lukie. This little pulser sure woke up!"

Muscles rippling, James grunted. "Um! . . . that's it . . . take it, baby, take it! . . . ah, yes!"

Betty's supple mouth clamped over Luke's erection.

Hannah's feet drummed spasmodically against James's back. Her bottom bounced compulsively upward, impaling herself repeatedly on the stiff dick, smacking into James, taking it all, thrilling to it. "Uh! . . . uh! . . . so . . . don't stop . . . god don't stop! . . . fill my cunt!"

Luke ejaculated tremendously, feeling as though his spine was jerked out with it.

James suddenly tensed, shuddering. "Oh shit! . . . now . . . now! . . . um! . . . um! . . . um!"

Hannah yelled fiercely, crushing Luke's hand. "Give it! . . . give it! . . . oh god, I'm coming . . . oh god, I'm coming!"

Rubbing his stubbled whiskers, Luke peered wearily through smarting eyes into the cone of light splitting the darkness. Moonlight silvered the broad fields floating past on either side of the speeding car. It was half past two in the morning. He tried to find a different station on the radio, couldn't, dialed it back to hillbilly, and cursed as it twanged out that drinking beer would cure a broken heart.

Another hour to go. Where the hell was Hannah?

She hadn't answered the phone for three nights now. Her office told Luke that she'd taken a week off. So unlike Hannah. Where could she be?

She'd been sound asleep when he left early Monday. A well-earned sleep, he thought. She had to be sore. Jesus, that guy had a hammer on him! Must use a vacuum pump or something . . . guy oughta be in porn movies.

Had Luke's insistence on swinging made her mad? No, she had definitely gotten into it . . . never seen her so wild. He got hard just thinking about it. And after that weird couple left, Hannah didn't act ashamed or angry . . . just snuggled up as usual and went to sleep.

It had been damned sexy, no doubt about it. Was it sordid? Not really . . . as Hannah said, just people having sex, no big deal. Why does it bother you then, Luke old boy? Lukie?

Enough of that swinging crap. Not sorry we tried it, but we don't need that. What if things had gotten out of hand? I'd never have been able to handle that big bastard. I'll pay more attention to her. He visualized Hannah wearing a white dress in a majestic pecan grove, quiet and pensive; her animated eyes as they discussed books; moon-cast palm shadows laced across her nude body on a midnight beach.

Where can she be?

At last, he pulled into the driveway and got out, leaning on the car to do a few deep knee bends. It didn't seem like home, all quiet and lonely. Ghostly streamers of Spanish moss swaying in the dim light from the porch. The faint bark of a distant dog.

Luke unlocked the door, feeling like a burglar, and entered, clicking on lights. He immediately saw the note, blue paper held down by the conch shell, and rushed to pick it up, anxiously scanning the familiar, elegant script.

"Dear Luke, I know you won't understand, but I've gone to

Miami with James and Betty. They have a lot of friends down there. I need some time to think about us. Take care and don't be sad. I'll be in touch."

Waves of numbness crawled over his skin. He crumpled the note in his fist and blindly groped for the sofa arm with his other hand before realizing that it still held the shell.

Surprised, he lifted the shell almost to eye level and stared at its pink, convoluted interior. The silence of the empty house echoed loudly in his mind.

Luke's hand trembled as he gingerly set the conch back on the table.

LUCKY IN LOVE

Carolyn Banks

Marianne stooped in order to see herself in the side mirror of the Buick at the curb. With one chapped hand, she rearranged the fringe of curls on her forehead. Oh, she wished she'd been able to shampoo. Right after a shampoo, her hair always seemed to have a life and lift and gleam of its own. But anyway, it was too late now, she was thirteen minutes away from meeting Roy if the clock at Chauncey's on the corner was accurate.

Roy. Her heart hammered just thinking about him.

Last night, alone in her bed, it was more than her heart. It was all of her body as well, all of her body yearning to press against his. She'd held the pillow flat up against herself, pretending.

She had worked it all out in her head, the way they'd start. The way he'd hold her, the way she'd take in the smell of him, her nose uplifted and brushing at the edges of his collar. Then her lips, partly open, just about to touch the thick, ruddy skin of his neck.

Oh, she'd known from the moment she first saw him that he wasn't like the rest. He hadn't eyed her hungrily or spoken to her coarsely. He hadn't *assumed*. Instead he'd smiled at her almost shyly and he'd asked her name.

"Marianne," she'd said, and she'd stuttered a bit, prolonging the M sound in a way that made her blush.

But he hadn't seemed to notice that. What he'd done was repeat her name, "Marianne," as if savoring it. He had a bit of an accent, a brogue perhaps, and that lent a sort of softening to his masculinity. "My name's Roy," he told her, his thick hand reaching for her birdlike one and giving it a squeeze.

And damned if she hadn't done exactly the same as he. She'd repeated "Roy" as if it were a prayer.

It might have been a prayer, she thought now as she awaited him under the big Chauncey's clock.

Today would be special, he'd promised. Lord knew what special might mean to a man like Roy, a man who'd been all over the country, indeed, all over the world. Oh, he'd regaled her with stories of this place and that, places she'd only seen in magazines and in the movies. "It's only natural that a man my age would have been around some," he'd said when she'd oohed and aahed at the tales he told. He was sixty-five.

But where had she, just ten years his junior, ever been? Nowhere. Only here, in Beaumont. Only here, in this one town.

"You look sad, Marianne," he'd said while she was thinking this. "Perhaps I can brighten things for you a bit."

And then he'd cupped her face in those rough hands of his and he'd looked deep into her eyes and he'd said, "You deserve a day especially fine, Marianne, and I'll see to it that you get it."

Oh, she thought now, even if he never showed up, even if he'd never so much as planned to show up, she was grateful to have felt the deep-down stirrings she'd thought long dead.

Last night, imagining what today might bring, she'd been full of those stirrings, and she'd yielded to them. In the darkness, she'd thought of him as she rubbed at herself with the fingers of her hand, rubbed at herself pretending that his voice was in her ear and his breath was on her face. She'd tossed and pressed against the bedclothes as her hand moved and carried her along with it. Just as she went over the edge, she'd almost whispered his name aloud instead of in her heart. Ah, but "Roy," her heart sang now as then, "Roy."

She glanced into Chauncey's big glass window and for a moment thought she was hallucinating, dreaming him, for there he

"I suppose I haven't told you I'm a rich man," he said. The sunlight flashed along bright strips of chrome.

"Oh, I guessed it," she teased. "But I don't see the chauffeur."

"He'll be along. I wanted to be alone with you."

"Oh," she said, trying hard to sound as if she were accustomed to such things. "I see."

He pulled the rear door open and she bent to enter the car. In that brief moment when her buttocks bloomed out behind her, she thought of Roy's penis again, hoping to feel it pressing against her from behind.

But then her concentration was broken. "Oh, Roy!" she breathed.

"I told you it would be special."

There were real leather seats and even a little fold-down table. On this he'd arranged a few things: a battered paperback volume of Victorian poetry; a white kerchief; a single chocolate candy nestled in a pleated paper wrapper.

"I'd have brought more sweets, but it seems all women are dieting," he said.

"Oh, I am for sure," she told him. She was reed thin, always had been.

He took the chocolate from its wrapper and held it up beneath her nose. "How does it smell?" he asked.

"Rich," she said. "And delicious."

"Have a bite then," he said, lowering the candy so that it abutted her lips.

Marianne opened her mouth and took the end of the chocolate in it. She closed her eyes and savored its flavor as it melted in the warmth of her inner mouth.

"Go on," he said, "have it all."

She obeyed him, pulling the entire piece into her mouth. She chewed at the candy's center. It was cool and tasted of mint. "Mmmm," she said, opening her eyes and smiling.

"Allow me," he said, poking a finger into the kerchief and using the tip to wipe at the corners of Marianne's mouth. Done, he put the kerchief and the candy wrapper into his pocket. He raised the book of poems. "Shall I read something to you?" he asked.

She closed her hand over his. "In time," she said. And then she leaned into the limousine's soft seat. "I've never in my life been in a car like this," she confessed.

"I hoped you hadn't," he said. He took the book and folded the table back upon it. And then, at last, he sat close beside her and laid a hand upon her knee.

Without thinking Marianne opened her legs a bit wider, and yes, yes, his hand moved upward just as she had hoped. "Oh, Roy," she kept saying, sucking in long draws of breath each time she said his name.

He laughed delightedly, but took his hand away. She caught hold of it then and hoped the look in her eyes would urge him to keep on.

"We have the whole day ahead of us," he told her, reaching into a little cabinet near the floor and taking out two tiny glasses and a small amber bottle. "Brandy," he said.

She shook her head at the thought of brandy before noon. "None for me," she said, thinking of how her head would swirl if she were to drink.

He drank though, and she watched his throat again, and then he placed his arm around her shoulder and leaned back contentedly. She laid her head on his chest and breathed in the thick brown scent of liquor on his breath. Without letting go of her, he eased forward and with a single hand replaced the cap on the bottle.

She snuggled against him gratefully. She felt his lips and then his chin moving against her hair. She took his free hand and laid it where it had been on her leg and then she brazenly raised her skirt.

"Marianne," he said, his voice deep and appreciative.

She let her own hand fall over his penis and yes, it was long and hard and she'd been dead right about the underwear.

"It's been so long," he said, as if an apology.

"Yes," she said, "for me, too."

And then he turned toward her, pressing her backward against the leather seat, his weight coming down upon her just as she'd hoped.

Oh, it was wonderful, even the fumbling with his zipper and the yanking at the elastic legbands of her underpants. He used his fingers first, and she could hear the sound of her wetness sucking at his fingers as he played with her. She squirmed with delight, sometimes closing her legs tight upon his hand and in other moments opening as wide as she was able. And all the while, his eyes were upon her, as if her pleasure were all he'd ever hoped to see.

Then she had him lean back and she, in turn, held his penis and ran her palm up and down the shaft and round and round the flowerlike tip of it.

"Close your eyes," she said, and he did, but only for a moment. "It's you I want to see," he said.

It was wonderful, all of it, the probing and the touching and the smell of leather and brandy.

"What's your pleasure?" he whispered, as if her pleasure hadn't yet begun.

She couldn't speak, but instead tried to guide his penis toward the place where his hand had been. And meanwhile, his lips were everywhere, at her cheek, her nose, her eyelids.

"Wait," he said, and he pulled away and reached both hands under the bunched-up fabric of her skirt. "Let's take these down properly." She had to laugh at the thought of the way she'd been trying to jam his penis up through the leg of her underwear that way. He caught hold of the waistband of her panties and she leaned back, locked her hands behind her head, a princess being waited on.

He inched her panties down, and she saw where his eyes had fixed, saw the wonder in them as her dark-haired bush appeared. "Ah," he said, taking the panties over her feet and only then, at the last, yanking off her shoes.

He knelt on the floor of the car, spread her legs and covered as much of her as he could with his mouth. What she felt at first was gratitude and then it mingled with the sweet sensation of his tongue against her pinkest, most tender flesh. The thought alone made her moan. "Aaah," Marianne heard herself say, and then "Aaah," and "Aaah," again. And when she came he kept his mouth there to receive the rush of fluid she'd released. Her arms shook and she dropped them to her sides and tried to sink her fingernails into the leather as if that would stop them from shaking. And then her hands were up and she was pushing his head away as if she could not bear even the smallest second more of pleasure. "It's too, it's too . . ." her arm braced, her hand holding his head away.

But in another instant she had changed her mind. She was pulling his head deep into her, she was straining at his mouth with her hips and her thighs and, yes, yes, with her soul.

And afterward he'd looked up at her, the smell of her on his lips and he'd teased, "Was it special enough for you, Marianne? Was it indeed?"

In time he'd pulled her skirt back down to cover her thighs and he'd handed her the panties saying, "You'd better put these on yourself, eh?" and, while she was wriggling into them, he'd zipped his penis back inside his pants.

She felt that she'd cheated him, and weary as she was, she wanted him to come too. She'd do anything he liked, really, and she told him so. Anything.

And he'd poured another glass of the brandy and this time sipped at it. "It's been years for me, Marianne," he said, by way of explanation. "It's given me pleasure just to have satisfied you."

"It's the drinking," she chanced.

"It might well be." He looked at the glass.

"I want to try," she said, taking it away and wolfing down the contents herself.

"It could take all day."

"All day in a limousine with a fine man like yourself. Sounds awful. Sounds like bloody hell." She reached for him and right away she felt his penis swell. "This is going to be easy," she told him.

"It isn't getting it up that's the problem. It's keeping it up."

"Oh, keeping it up," she said, changing places with him, his turn now to sink his bulk into those deep leather cushions, hers to kneel on the plushly carpeted limousine floor.

At first she only rested her palms upon his thighs and dropped her face down between his legs. She moved her face from side to side, feeling the tickle of his pubic hair. Then she slid her hands around to his buttocks and pulled him toward her as she opened her mouth to receive him.

He was big inside her mouth and grew bigger, bigger still, and she kept her mouth there, pulling toward and away and toward

and away. Time ceased as she gave herself to the rhythm. He sat
stock-still—as if it were a dream and any movement might bring
wakening. Even the muscles along the tops of his thighs seemed
made of stone beneath the palms of Marianne's hands. Still, she
knew from the deep and guttural sounds that he made that she
was giving him the same sweet pleasure he had given her.

His penis grew harder and the tip engorged so that, if she'd
been capable of thought just then, she might have wondered if the
intensity of it caused him pain. But his hands answered any of her
fears in that regard. His hands, indeed, spoke of the deepest pleasure. His fingers were like the brush of a feather, the wings of a
bird, even when his orgasm shook through him. His ejaculate
spilled into Marianne's welcoming mouth and she swallowed it,
then buried her head in the dampness between his legs.

"We're lucky people, both of us," he told her, stroking her face,
then urging her upward so that he could kiss her face. "Lucky
indeed," he said, his lips soft against her own.

"Lucky in love," she said, emboldened.

" 'Love that endures for a breath,' " he said. And then, when
he saw the way she was looking at him, he had her sit beside him
and he took out the volume of poetry. "That was Swinburne," he
told her, finding the page and indicating the line. "I'm a man of
education, you see." He searched her eyes, squeezed her hand.
" 'Ah, the singing, ah, the delight, the passion!' That is Swinburne
too. Or is this, my Marianne, too much like school?"

"I loved school," she suddenly remembered, though, after Vin-
cent, she'd never gone back. She shut her eyes and let Roy tell her
his own story, tell her when the sure, forward movement of his
own life had stopped.

Later she looked for the sun. It was just above the roof of
another car, a Desoto, she thought, an aisle away. "We'll miss dinner," she nudged him.

"You're right," he said. "We'd best be getting back."

He got out first and held the door for her. She ran her fingers
over the leather seats. Then she slid toward him and out.

He patted the sleek white surface of the door with the flat of
his hand when he closed it while she moved around toward the

back. She grasped one of the big white fins. "I love these," she said. "This must have been quite a car in its day." She stood back, taking in the whole of it.

He came and stood beside her. Together they appraised the limousine: its upraised hood, the yawning space where its engine had once been. The front, where the driver must have sat, had been stripped down to the metal frame. Even the steering wheel was gone, a rusted shaft remaining.

"Still," she said, gesturing at the skeletal remains of the ordinary cars that surrounded it, "this car is very special."

He pulled her toward him, his eyes bearing down on hers. "More special than I'd dared to hope," he said.

And arm in arm, stepping carefully, Marianne and Roy made their way out of the junkyard and back through the streets to the Salvation Army shelter where they spent their nights: he in the basement with the men and she with the women on the second floor.

FLOATING WORLD

Wickham Boyle

A tall, blond American woman in Japan is what they assured me
I'd be. My brown boy's bob had been heavily peroxided as a signal
that I was beginning an adventure outside the work of daily pa-
pers, classes, and Ivy League correctness. I had a fellowship and
was on leave for a summer. My sole charge was to fill my eyes,
mind and soul with the pace and scent of Japan.

I wanted to see the neon of Tokyo, the ancient Kabuki, the
cherry blossoms in Kyoto, the indigenous island Inu people, the
resonance of Hiroshima, and the pace and beat of life on the other
side of the world. A world I imagined was at once so blatant and
subtle—modern and antediluvian—so much so that the populace
snapped back and forth like viewers at a tennis match—now ro-
bots, now geishas.

I had read also of the Japanese floating world. It is a world of
the senses and pleasure. Many Western fantasies are built on the
Japanese attention to this ephemeral land. In my imaginings I pictured this pleasure kingdom existing somewhere between waking
and dreaming. Even as I researched architecture and culture, the
floating world always inserted a presence. It has existed for
centuries.

In Samurai times, lavish attention was paid to women who

would be available to service warlords. Today, the sex shops, massage mansions and services for men are everywhere. One of the amazing contradictions in Japanese society is that although marriages are often arranged, preordained couples escape from their parents' homes by visiting Love Hotels that ubiquitously dot the landscape. In Tokyo, the Love Hotels can resemble the American White House or Disney World or prehistoric caves. They have colonial servants, cave women or vibrating beds, condoms in different colors, sizes and styles. Everyone knows why you go to a Love Hotel. There is no pretense needed. It is a sector in Japanese society where women need not laugh coyly behind their hands or defer to men. A man or woman may suggest a rendezvous at a Love Hotel. Because they are everywhere, if the mood strikes between Tokyo and Nagoya, please exit to the nearest pleasure dome.

My first morning in Tokyo and I insinuated myself into a rigid queue and readied myself for my first rush-hour onslaught Japanese-style. The train smoothed into the station, a silent cylinder on rubber wheels. A conductor with white gloves pushed the more recalcitrant passengers into the fray. No one spoke, no one complained, but they all stared at me. At nearly six feet with my spiky blond helmet, I was more than a head above them. I was a white giant in a land of uniformed workers. Many of the men were crushed right at breast level (and the grandeur of my mammaries even outranks my height). They gawked and pressed closer. Despite censorship rules forbidding the showing of pubic hair, men clutched comics in which males and females hacked at each other's members with violent precision. On other pages right under my nose, I saw lovely smooth drawn cocks dripping with semen. I watched the passengers' eyes rove from page to page until I felt a hand on my thigh.

I couldn't move. I could barely maneuver a glance to ascertain the possessor of the gentle touch. The train rolled and rocked, stop to stop, as the hand followed a steady course. I felt excited and repelled and immobile. My blood began to tingle and against both my will and my judgment I let my thoughts and juices go to my moistening center. Pleasantly lost to a somnambulant ardor, I fantasized about the arm connected to the hand and saw a muscled shoulder connect neatly into a crisp, hairless chest. As my fantasy moved to engulf the landscape of the body, the wiggle and thrust of my own pleasure bubbled up to my nipples and began to ready itself in a sweet taste in my mouth. Suddenly, the train stopped. The hand moved and walked off with its body to begin a working day.

Exhausted from five hours of sightseeing, Japanese-style, complete with bento box lunch, I navigated my way through the station to the green line train. I had carefully copied my station stop onto a morsel of paper secreted in my bra; I could lose my purse and still find my way home. The Japanese characters for my stop were a ladder, an upside-down house, some running water, and a mouth. It was the running water that attracted my attention. I remembered reading that the Japanese see Westerners as stone, but regard the Asian countenance as water. When I observed myself crossing a crowded room, pushing with a solid stone gait, I vowed to become water for a summer. I began by infusing a physical flow into my movement; no sudden jerks or abrupt changes in direction. I would point myself there and float. A solid Western stick on a vast Eastern river. The voyage was on.

I mastered the Metro. I toured the temples and the museums, and ate acres of noodles while sitting on cushions, but Tokyo exhausted me. I was alone, and wedged into a tiny coffinlike hotel where even my quiet actions of masturbation seemed exaggerated. There was no one with whom I could share my discoveries and the crushed quality of life pressed in on even my new water self.

I planned my escape to Kyoto, the first capital of Japan. My escape hatch was the bullet train *Shinkansen,* two hundred twenty miles an hour and no bumps. It zoomed past museum landscapes and watercolor mountains. The ridges rose up abruptly and their proximity made the gradations of gray, green and blue seem tender and palpable. The leafy, verdant tea plants appeared everywhere in tiny gardens tended by men and women with towel-wrapped heads. These tea guardians bent lovingly over the mounded humped tea bushes as the train ripped past and the mountains created another painting. The mist outside my window lifted and parted as scene after scene took shape.

My loneliness turned to desire. Other than my inaugural touch on the subway, I had not been held, hugged or even had my hand shaken in ten days. Japan: the land of the bow and the proper face.

At the Kyoto station, I found tourist information—in English. I expressed my excitement and emptiness. "Kyoto," the agent said, "is a gentle, full city. You will want for nothing here. The food, the palaces, the blossoms along the river all invite you." She directed me to a beautiful traditional Japanese hotel called a ryokan, with shoji screens and sweet-smelling tatami mats on the floors. My bed was a futon, a cotton baton mattress piled with clouds of white quilts. After settling in, the proprietor showed me the bathhouse. A small building in a mini garden. The walls and floor were cedar slats and herbs grew in the cracks of the stones. Crushed smells wafted up each time our wooden sandals bumped tender shoot to stone.

Through the hotel manager I made a late appointment for a massage at the bathhouse. Then I rode my borrowed bike along the graciously paved and terraced river. Golden carp jumped, boys fished, and girls chased each other. The boys flung their lines and the girls flew alongside with pointed black braids echoing the angles of the fishing lines. I was returned to serenity and ready to float.

Kyoto had been spared from the bombing that tore Tokyo apart and necessitated its complete modernistic rebuilding. Instead, old, wooden buildings graced the narrow back streets of Kyoto. Paper lanterns hung outside minuscule shops whose windows were wonders of design. The shops sold glass vessels filled with small orange, green, and brown crackers; boxes wrapped in silk and filled with candies shaped like fish, watermelon or lotus blossoms. Samurai kites and folded stacks of writing paper adorned graceful bamboo shelves.

I pedalled through Kyoto until I came to the tiny restaurant recommended by my ryokan. The entrance was marked with a black-and-red flag. Dinner was simple and sublime. I knelt on pillows around a table. Silent women passed tidbits of white, spicy, sweet and slippery food. On the walk home, I followed the turns of the river, which were lit by paper lanterns glowing pink. I stopped at one of Kyoto's oldest teahouses, just a slight detour before my massage. The walls were open to the air and small char-

coal fires burned in flat portable stoves. I left my shoes at the
doorway and folded my legs beneath the table. The green tea was
served with wrapped, roasted rice candy on sticks. A sweet sticky
treat with a charcoal taste, it was the Japanese version of marsh-
mallow, which had evolved to a subtle, gloriously served delicacy.
I loved the assault on my senses. I tasted, smelled and felt so much
more in Japan, perhaps because I had no words to describe my
sensations. I jumped into the pool of floating Japanese culture; all
lay suspended.

The winding path back was strewn with delicate white blossoms. Petals chased my cheeks and scented the route. I looked up
and there in the window was a geisha serving a table of business-
men. These were not the drones of Tokyo, "salarimen" hiding from
their wives in *Pachinko* palaces, playing penny-ante pinball. These
were the smooth of Kyoto. The handsome, monied, muscled men
of power enjoying an ancient tradition of seduction on a crystal
night. Her black lacquered hair and slash of red mouth punctuated
the powdered face which was painted to amuse the men. She was
pouring liquid carefully into tiny cups. I watched the geisha bow,
then walked on to my bath, my massage, my attentions.

At the ryokan I was given a blue cotton robe printed with sym-
bols and crisp from washing. Every transaction was conducted in
silence and a gesture conveyed instruction and obeisance. I took
the robe to my room. I deposited my Western clothes with no great
ceremony except to note the scale and lack of grandeur. Naked, I
felt regal and ready for the bath and ministrations of the masseur.

I padded, wood sandals on stone, across to the bathhouse. I
hung the robe on the round peg and stretched down to open the
wooden cover concealing the roasting bath. The steam rose. Not
yet. The bath is for cleansing the spirit, cleaning the body comes
first. I folded my lanky limbs onto a tiny stool. Wood, cool and flat,
it snuggled up over my vagina and held my round butt, my melon-
ous American ass that through years of weight lifting and dance
had become a ball of inviting sinew coated in a light down. My
body undulated muscle. I noticed it more acutely after entering
Japanese bathhouses where a profusion of soft women's bodies dot-
ted tiled floors as they squatted decorously on cedar stools. Now
I was alone for the first time in a bath in Japan. The steam, the

scrubbing, the endless touching of brush and cloth and slippery soap began to work wonders on my loins. I rubbed myself, relaxed and began to flow. What goddess would drip from between my legs tonight, I mused.

So deep in thought was I that I failed to hear the clicking of stones or catch the scent of herbs as the masseur made his way to the door. A silent whoosh of cool air announced his arrival. I flinched and reached for my robe to cover myself, to protect the private space I had constructed in the secluded hotel bath. As I looked aghast over my shoulder, my eyes met a serene moon descended from heaven, a wide planet of a face with almond cuts for eyes. The light pouring forth from these deep eyes was brilliant, as if a candle lit his beautiful skull from within. "I am Taka," he said. His delivery told me that he spoke no more English. This was his phrase. It was perfect. He was perfect.

He was young with long black hair pulled back tightly in a priestlike ponytail. His small hands and dainty feet emitted an incredible strength, ready to pound and pounce on my waiting corpus. His skin glistened and a smile parted full lips and soothed me, so I dropped my robe, enamored of his sweet Oriental way.

Wordlessly, he took the brush from my hands, our first touch. My large flat palms outstretched to his tight small fist. The exchange was charged, but Taka went directly to his task. He held me round my shoulders and his kimono fell to the floor, leaving him in tight bike shorts and a marble torso. His forearms and shoulders seemed to be a condensed version of the American ideal. His bunchy small torso was a distilled creation that I had never seen and never fantasized. Every muscle showed and was covered carefully in smooth tawny skin. Like all of Japan, the silent, diminutive rippling Taka was a shock and a mystery.

Stunned and pliant, I sat on the tiny stool. His hands worked around my body, my arms were bent back, my shoulders rubbed, his hard hands under my large soft breasts. He circled them, he moved like a breeze working the brush, the loofah, the cloths, his hands. I closed my eyes as a sense of sweet confusion rolled over me. When the brush faded into the tingle of skin, I shuddered. Taka kept an unwavering connection to me. No sign, no motion, no flinch deterred him. There was a map seething from my downy flesh and he was reading it. At each new turn, he tore at the map and burned it from my skin. No one would pass this way again. No explorer would follow Taka's path.

He moved down my legs, kneading, rubbing, and reaching upward to the source of the map and the moisture that lay there. A quick return to my electrified cunt just to touch base before he ran down each leg to my ankle bone. He squeezed the small of my heel and bit furiously into the arch of each foot. Then he bent back my toes and moved his head leisurely down my inner thighs.

I thought perhaps I was hallucinating. I was afraid to blink, to stir, to breathe deeply. My respiration came from the top of my breasts and escaped in bitty baby breaths that kept me from reality. In a swoon, Taka's arms were lifting me from the cedar stool and leading me, lowering me into the tub whose steam had been filling my lungs. The water was scalding. I saw my skin prickle and go from porcelain to rose. My entire body stood at attention and waited weightlessly. Taka slid in next to me and insinuated his body under mine like a slippery water beast. I put my head on his chest, my arms round his back, touching the point of his black tail hair.

He continued to work his hands across my shoulders, up to my cheeks and under my furrowed brows. Wiggling, speedy, deep fingers and strong legs wrapped around me. His rocklike heel just resting on my black mound. His aim was true to my center. His heel settled powerfully, but then dug deeper and finally floated to the surface. My body followed his arc. I didn't want to be separated from his touch. I adhered to him, a perfect dancing partner; I followed. I questioned this descent into the floating world as little as I did the chanting at Kabuki or the silent hidden laughs of the women walking down the side streets. This was my journey.

Taka began to move in earnest now, his hands working under my ass to separate every fold of skin hidden in my vagina. Skin supple, water jiggling into the folds and his fingers tapping on every tiny mound and complicated convolution, he was inside me pounding at the water from deep within my mound. One hand pulling up on my nipples as they rose from the bath. He pulled them to twin Mount Fujis, sacred points in a gray misty world ready to be worshipped. His heel was at the base of my anus pushing me into his hand. I was trapped in a body tied in tiny knots, a sailor's folly, and then I felt the change. His hands, the water, the steam, the scent of fresh green rose and slowly I felt the knots loosen. I was coming slowly from my center. Taka rolled and rubbed the folds like a tiny magician with an array of scarf tricks. And the silky scarves released the knots everywhere in my body. Emotions flowed and a wave, a release, passed from my clenched teeth. Taka's hands sprang off me and he pressed his body deep into the tub causing me to pop to the surface like a cork shot from a bottle. Flashing brain, clutching cunt and scent of cedar and herbs so confounded my senses that I lolled and gasped for breath.

Taka rose and extended an outstretched hand. I stepped out of the bath and he folded the robe around me and led me to my room. I floated on the clouds of futons, an incredulous visitor to the floating world. I lay between dream and reality until the exhaustion of foreign words, touches, smells, and pace ate away at my waking state and I was free to wander in the floating world of my dream life.

I slept in deep dreams of colors and smells. As the morning sounds woke me, I stretched my mind to find images and personages to attach to my sensations. In my mental struggle, I walked back and forth from my room to the bath feeling my body reverberate from the touch of the previous night. Real or imagined. I questioned myself and regaled my psyche with details of Taka's touch. The residual tingle in my loins left me no doubt. I relaxed in bed as the sun shone through paper walls and a swish of feet brought in my tea tray. I will always be an incredulous visitor.

PART TWO

Common Themes

In this section, I have chosen to explore three of the four most common themes contained in the erotic stories I received. They revolve around an affair, the unrequited love story, and the one-night stand.

A fourth popular theme, rape and forced sex, is notably absent from this collection. Of the stories submitted by men, almost twenty percent dealt with these issues. The protagonists of these stories, usually male authority figures—judges, policemen and teachers—use the power of their positions to get women to submit sexually. Only one woman wrote a story based on coercive sex. I included none of these stories because I believe that without the consent of both parties, the sexual experience is really about coercion or violence, neither of which is compatible with eros.

A fulfilling sexual encounter, however, can be erotic to both parties and still have negative consequences. This often happens with a sexual affair. Sex with someone other than the main character's spouse or partner was an extremely popular theme among both male and female writers. An affair contains all the elements that make a story inherently erotic—it is new, forbidden, intriguing, and dangerous. The essence of the relationship is often sexually based. However, males and females tend to deal with affairs quite differently, and the two stories I've included illustrate some of these differences.

For women, an affair is not simple. It is more than a sexual liaison. The emotional relationship is as important as the sexual one, and concerns about consequences are addressed from the beginning. Suzanne Miller's story, "Taos Spring," is an excellent example of how a female author examines a woman's marriage, her feelings about herself, and her approach to life before she enters into an affair. "I'm writing about how sexuality can become central to power struggles in long-term relationships and how a woman's understanding of her own sexuality can affect all other areas of her sense of self," says Miller. "In this story, the female character's sense of self has eroded because of her husband's need to control her. When she encounters a stranger who admires her both intellectually and physically, she awakens to her desirability and begins to question the nature of her marriage."

For men, however, an affair is typically an affair. Men are more able to isolate the sexual and emotional aspects of a relationship and create an encounter that is based entirely on sex. If male writers are concerned about the emotional repercussions of an affair, these concerns often don't surface until afterward, as illustrated in Shimon-Craig Van Collie's story, "Preliminaries." In addition, the sexual connection is a rather immediate one. Instead of the theme of "will they or won't they" so typical of women writers, men look for assured gratification. "What is erotic for me," says Van Collie, "is when you feel attracted to a woman and you get instantaneous feedback; you don't have to say anything. When the woman in my story rubs her toe on the man's leg under the table, he knows that the connection is there equally for the both of them and all possibilities are opened."

The unrequited love story was another prevalent theme, but one appealing primarily to women. These stories are distinctly different from simple romantic tales where everyone lives happily ever after. Sweet tales with happy endings were submitted equally by male and female writers. But women seem to be the ones captured by the tragic ending—the loss of a major love, a story where the man of their dreams turned his attentions elsewhere. Even one story submitted by a man that didn't end up happily, had the woman as his main character, and, as usual, she is the one abandoned.

It is as common for women to write unrequited love stories as it is for men to write rape and forced sex themes. Men are the transgressors, women the transgressed.

Now I have to admit that I don't like the findings of this informal survey. It confirms a rather distasteful bias I see in the American culture, where, in the sexual realm, both sexes tend to portray women as the victims, the masochists in the emotional and sexual arena, the ones who get emotionally or physically hurt by love.

I wonder, though, if there is not another, yet equally valid interpretation for these findings. It may not be that women are drawn to emotional injury, but rather that they deal with the loss of love differently. Men are wounded by love as frequently as women, but men tend to deny or suppress their feelings. Women express them. And with the expression often comes a form of healing. Both Hope Katz, author of "Glorious Reunion," and Dina Vered, author of "The Accident," felt that composing their stories was a healing experience. According to Katz, "Writing the story allows me to touch him, to keep him in my mind, and that acts like a salve." Vered said, "I trusted this man. He saved my life. Yet the story has remained a big mystery for me. Writing about it helped to put it to rest."

Erik Jendresen, one of the very few male authors of an unrequited love story, also felt that writing his story had a healing component. According to Jendresen, "The writing of 'Nighthawks: From a Painting by Edward Hopper' was disturbing because, like the lover in the story, I was forced to relive the experience while writing it, but it was ultimately liberating because by confronting it, rather than denying it, I was able to make the memory more comfortable."

So while the theme and even the autobiographical nature of Jendresen's story make it less traditionally male, the specific lovemaking has a visual quality common to stories written by men. And the approach to the story is quite male in that the relationship evolves through the sexual content as opposed to the typical female author's technique of building the relationship slowly before any explicit sexuality is broached.

Another aspect of the unrequited love story that may account for its draw is the intensity generated by the impossible situation. We are captured by the incomplete experience, the unfinished gestalt, the unreached potential. According to Jendresen, "The characters live on their memories, or they live on the possibilities for the future, even though such prospects are virtually hopeless. This creates incredible erotic tension." For Hope Katz, the erotic power of the relationship is a direct outgrowth of the inability to attain her love. "It's the wanting and longing for something that's just out of your grasp that makes this experience so erotic for me," reports Katz. And, in truth, many women and men are hooked on the impossible relationship, moving from one intense but unhappy love affair to another.

Now, for the one-night stand, a predominantly male theme. Since men are better able to fashion the erotic out of the excitement of the lovemaking while women look more toward the development of the relationship, it is understandable that men should prefer the casual or unencumbered sexual liaison as the theme for an erotic story. In this respect, Rob Scott's story, "Espresso and . . .," is typically male. In Scott's story, the sexuality and eroticism are built on total anonymity. "What is erotic to me," states Scott, "is the chance encounter, situations that are unusual or out of the mainstream." And he develops this entirely unexpected moment—tinged by aspects of the forbidden—into an original and enticing vignette.

Marsha Powers' story, "11:30 P.M.—Saturday Night," however, is unusual for a female writer. The sex is extensive, explicit, and graphic. The main female character is sexually engaged purely for the pleasure of the experience, no strings attached. In fact, Powers says, "The eroticism for me is the discovery by the female character that she could take a man to bed for the pure experience of the sex without feeling shocked or embarrassed by it," a statement that reveals how uncharacteristic for a woman the author considers this action to be.

Interestingly, Powers is also the only female contributor who regularly publishes stories in men's magazines. Her extensive experience writing in a style that will appeal to men may be what makes her story so different from those of women who write erotica for other venues.

As you and your partner read through these stories, you and your partner may want to compare your reactions to these various themes. Which do you find the most exciting? Why? You may also want to use this opportunity to share some of your own fantasies and see if they tend to fall along typically male or female lines.

TAOS SPRING

Suzanne Miller

Happiness didn't enter wholly into it. She was safe. Her life with Larry, whom she had always wanted to call Lawrence, was what she imagined marriage to be, safe and secure. When she was awarded the artist-in-residence, which would require an entire month away from Larry and their home, it didn't occur to her to demur. Larry always supported her in her independence and her work. He would come out to the desert at the end of her residence and they would take a few days together. She would call him each night before sleep. Her calls were all he required to feel secure in her absence, no matter how mightily he was affected with loneliness.

The week before her departure she had a dream. She was resting at the edge of the woods. There was a large tree at her feet and brush at her back. She was in a light sleep when she heard a rustling sound behind her. Three deer had pushed their noses through the shrubs. She felt heavy with no will to move, though she thought they might step on her. It was a dream within a dream. Another rustling sound came from the tree at her feet. She looked down, and there, having come from around the base of the trunk, was a man: dark curly hair, tanned skin and a look which combined knowledge with intensity. He did not speak, but just

145

stared at her. He moved to her side and she saw that he was half-man, half-animal. He motioned to her with his head that she should mount him. She rose without hesitation and climbed upon his back, holding him fast around the neck as he galloped off into the forest. The ride was heated and she sensed that his phallus was filling with his pounding blood. As it rubbed insistently against his belly, she felt his desire to mate with her. Even dreaming, she wondered how they could merge. He was of mythic proportions. They came to a circular clearing in the forest and she dismounted. They mated in a fierce collision which the dream could not articulate. She awoke drenched with sweat and shaking with the hard contracting release of her orgasm.

Larry lay next to her, undisturbed. She wanted to touch him, to bring her dream desire into their own union, but she couldn't. Their erotic life had diminished slowly over time. It was Larry's choice, not hers. When he was pursuing her, their lovemaking was a daily ritual. She never felt deeply satisfied with their sexual relationship, but believed that it would improve with time. She did not anticipate its fading into the background of their shared life, as if it were part of a romantic phase, only a memory. She lay there feeling disappointment and overcome by the desire to go back to the dream, to the centaur, to the forest.

They showered together the morning of her departure. She had become used to this economic ritual of waters devoid of intimate contact, inured to the efficient strokes of their shared Norwegian brush, brisk and therapeutic. As they toweled off, Larry, in an unexpected manner, asked her not to go. She was shocked. It was too late—her bags were packed, the ticket paid for, and she was determined to go. If he had only asked her earlier, when she had hoped that her impending absence would stir him into renewing his claim on her. At the last moment he sounded more like a forlorn boy separating from his mother than a man who desired his wife and resented the world's claim on her.

The long treacherous road along the Rio Grande was an exhilarating drive, a favorite of hers. The small cabin granted her for the month was adequate, though rustic. She set up her typewriter, pens, dictionary, paper, the accoutrements of her craft. Nomadic in her nature, she had also brought with her the softness of her favorite down comforter, some favorite bath oils, brushes, lovely soft throws. She set up candles here and there. When she was finished she had transformed the old adobe into a place of serenity and beauty. She set the piñon wood fire in the corner adobe fireplace. Larry always complained when they traveled that she carried too much, but he always enjoyed the beautiful worlds she could create with a few pillows, colorful blankets and soft lights. As she stood and surveyed the loveliness that surrounded her, she felt she stood for the moment in the best of all possible worlds: Larry, safe and patient at home, the privacy of her own cabin, and an entire month to work without external demands.

She began to work and the writing went well. It was spring, and birds were nesting in the trees, which gave life to the compound surrounding the artists' cabins. She would take her morning tea outdoors, sitting on an old uncomfortable chair, letting the clear air of the high desert fill her body and the first heat of the day's sun strike her skin to life. She wondered who the other artists were, what they were creating. Some she knew were painters, others composers. Most of the reclusive inhabitants were writers. They were all to meet within a week—the Foundation hosted a small cocktail party which she would probably avoid. She inevitably felt self-conscious at those gatherings. They were there at the Foundation's expense to work, to be in solitude, and to respect the privacy of one another. She had her ritual evening margarita at the colorful Taos Inn and her nightly calls to Larry, which she made from pay phones, as there were no telephones at the compound.

Larry was upset to learn that he could only reach her through a third party—the Foundation office. She enjoyed the fact that the absence of a direct line would upset him. Her enjoyment was not born of a desire to cause Larry discomfort, but more to inspire longing in him, which their constancy had seemed to erase. As always, Larry maintained a calm demeanor; only a slight protest suggested his irritation. He sent her cards daily, filled with sentiment and loving thoughts. She was writing a story about a passionate obsession and was acutely aware of the total lack of passion in his missives. She shrugged her feelings off as ungrateful. After all, Larry was devoted to her. The sting of dissatisfaction would just have to be borne. She did not want to do anything to upset the smooth surface of their lives.

She was writing in her journal one afternoon, sitting in the garden behind her cabin. The heat was especially penetrating. She wore her old battered straw hat to shield her eyes as she read through her dreams and daily meandering thoughts. She felt sleepy and lethargic. Suddenly there was a rustling to her right and a shadow cast across her, obliterating the outlines of her writing. She turned swiftly, hand to her hat as if the suddenness of her motion might knock it off. She looked up. The sun was too bright, and she could not make out clearly the face of the dark man standing so quietly at her side.

He apologized for interrupting her and introduced himself as Lawrence, explaining that he was staying at the cabin behind hers. He ran every morning by her front door and couldn't help hearing the clamoring of her typewriter keys. He was, he said, impressed by her discipline. She was nervous and unsettled by this rent in the cocoon of her privacy. He sat on the ground at her feet. He was extremely tall, broad of back and had a strong deep voice. She thought how different he was from Larry, who was slight, almost adolescent in his body. She knew that this Lawrence had had the body of a man early on. He was careful to say that he did not want to disturb her work, but was anxious to know what she was working on and to talk with her about writing. He was so serious and compelling she invited him to join her later, after her afternoon's labors, for coffee. He accepted immediately and left her to her silence. She watched him return to his cabin, and heard, soon after, the sound of pounding typewriter keys. She left her journal and returned to her own story.

Their meetings after that first one in the garden blended into a kind of timeless pleasure. They lost themselves thoroughly in conversation. He understood everything about her writing. His work, he said, was completely different. She liked that, that they were so different. Her thoughts and feelings about him were weaving in and out of her hours without resistance. She couldn't wait to read her newest passages to him. He was much younger than she was. Yet, when they were together, the years between them vanished. Larry, who was closer to her in age, seemed younger than Lawrence by lifetimes. The fact that they shared the same name was disconcerting. She was glad that Lawrence used his full name.

One night, after they had talked through twilight, she invited him to dine with her. They walked though the small town together, talking ceaselessly. This was the first time they had been together outside of her cabin. She felt uncomfortable. Since her marriage she had not spent intimate time with anyone but Larry. Larry had women friends outside of their marriage, which had never bothered her. He, however, had courted her male friends, subtly disallowing her to have intimate friendships with them.

That night, as always, Lawrence focused on her completely. When she was with him she experienced how the world could fall away when two people truly meet with heart and mind. Their love of the written word was their bond, the tireless wordplay of artists, the vanguard of their minds shooting out against existential realities, a balm against the unendurable.

During dinner she began to feel an awakening of desire, and this awareness made her uncomfortable. She told Lawrence that she was beginning to feel disturbed by him. She imagined, because of his youth, he might be flattered by her attentions. This was not his reaction. At her opening, he rushed forth with feelings he had been holding back, fearing he would frighten her. He thought she was utterly lovely, desirable. She could barely take it all in. She sat in a mild state of disbelief. She hadn't considered that a woman in her early forties might be found desirable by a man in his late twenties. Larry's seeming indifference to her sexuality had proclaimed her midlife transition and the diminution of her beauty. She had accepted this without question. She had foolishly fallen into a trap of profound manipulation. Larry had controlled her by slowly undermining her belief in her desirability.

Lawrence was beside himself. He followed her out of the restaurant, undaunted by her protestations. She tried to convince him that she had not meant to create an untenable situation between them. She simply wanted to let him know how attractive he was. She realized, too late, that these things were never simple. He told her that her husband should never have let her go for so long a time; he begged that he be allowed to hold her hand—*to hold her hand.* She simply could not believe that he was pleading to hold her hand. Her defenses forced her to shove her hands into the pockets of her coat. She would not let him hold her hand. His ardor was like an insistent heat. Finding herself walking down the wooden sidewalks of this ancient desert town hand in hand with him would draw her into a circumstance which was frightening to consider. She already felt out of control. She was so narcissistically wedded to her life and its seamlessness, she hadn't anticipated his reaction. If she were to touch him, she felt her very life would be threatened. What would happen to Larry, her home, their bond, however flawed it appeared. She had never considered an affair. Her nature was strong and passionate, not given to surface liaisons and the inevitable deceits of covert living.

Her caution made Lawrence relentless in his pursuit of her. He knew her words were the opening he feared would never come; she was so contained and focused on her work, language, fiction. He often wondered if she used her intellect as a defense against passion. Her marriage represented safety for her—this was anathema to the woman he felt she was. He knew what they could share together as lovers and as artists. He imagined there were rivers in her that no one had ever discovered, lands that no man had explored. He felt the fire of her and he wanted her badly. She suspected nothing of his knowledge and he was glad of it—for he did not want her to pull away from him.

She looked younger than her years. She told him she was an obsessive swimmer. Each day she would walk to the old town's recreation center and swim in a heated pool. When he had watched her enter her garden those first mornings, he knew he wanted her. She was so graceful. She was older than he was, but how much older was a mystery. He didn't consider it important. He knew with his dark hair and beard he appeared ageless. He had lived through the aches of creating, the torments of artistic angst, and he had tasted the bitterness of the poverty of his bohemian lifestyle. He had recently been turned down by the university where he had hoped to do his doctoral work. With nothing in his past to hold him, he was prepared to follow her home west and derail her lifeless marriage. He was unconventional, and had lived fully enough to find the courage to pursue what he wanted; the traditions of a sick culture and its prejudices meant nothing to him.

Everything he possessed was in his old battered car. Her other Larry was an attorney. He hated attorneys and agreed with Shakespeare that they should be eradicated. This particular one he would get rid of himself. Her indifferent husband might send sentimental notes, but would never seek her out and down through to the marrow of her bones and the wisdom of her blood. There was no part of her he would not touch, that he would not taste. But he would be patient, he would begin with her hand and travel the lands of her body past the boundaries of flesh into the very matrix of her soul. Yes, he was young, he knew he was young, but he was also as ancient as the mountains of the desert, as wild as the roaming wolves and as terrible as the lightning which strikes across the desert skies in the pitch black of night like the writing finger of God. If he was arrogant, he didn't mind, for he knew states of hunger that people of less desire had never dreamed of, and he held them in contempt. She was his opposite, she could be his light. He needed her. He could not bear much longer the desperate aloneness of his life. He would break though her civilized shell and release the primal woman within. She had not given him her hand. He accepted this as a natural reticence in her and ceased his demand. They walked back to her cabin. During their walk their conversation for the first time ceased. When he opened her door for her, she went in, forbidding him entrance. He returned to his own cabin in a torment of frustration.

She had wanted to reach out to him, but she was caught in the whirlwinds of chaos. She was afraid and she wanted her serenity back. She thought of the dream of the centaur. She opened a good bottle of bordeaux, lit a piñon fire, poured herself a large goblet of the dark red wine and sat staring into the fire. After a short time, the wine, the flickering flames and the fire's warmth calmed her. She needed this to feel balanced again. The stirrings of her sexuality brought her an inner dishevelment and the beginnings of desire. She slept fitfully and awoke to the sounds of a storm that had moved down from the mountains and was crashing overhead like an assault.

She worked feverishly all day. The rain had not stopped and the lightning and its attendant raging thunder rolled across the mesas. The storms at home were impotent cries compared to such fury. By late afternoon she was weary. She had just put the tea-kettle on and set and lit the fire when Lawrence came in through the unlocked door. She realized then that she had been waiting for him. He closed the door behind him and locked it. He had a bottle of wine and the makings of supper. He didn't say a word, but went to the makeshift kitchen and put everything away. She stood in silence by the stove where the kettle was steaming. He came to her, wet with the storm, leaving great footprints across the wooden floor. In his wake were the scents of piñon wood smoke and the young green grasses of their shared yard. Her life, which she had protected before he entered, was erased when he took her face into his wet hands, touching her with the icy cold of the storm mixed with the heat of his hard mouth. She was like a solid block of unintentional resistance. She couldn't feel anything but this par-adox of cold and hot. Her mouth went slack and he covered the surrender of its parting with insistent kisses. He put one arm around the back of her neck and kissed her hard, while his free hand moved down to her rich breasts, the lovely softness of her belly and down further between the sweet firmness of her thighs, where he could feel her heat moving out to warm him. She met him at last, her arms finally coming to life, encircling only part of his broad back. He lifted her, kissing her all the while and carrying her to her celibate's bed. He lay her down, slowly undressing her. Tears were falling from the corners of her eyes and he didn't pause to wonder why. She lay finally in all her terrible beauty, round and soft, smelling the ancient smell of the Goddess in heat. He nearly tore his own clothes away while the storm outside increased, the thunder unbearably close. She watched him, knowing the inevita-bility of their meeting. Her body was alive, its smells furious with want.

He was beyond beauty to her. He was pure mind and pure animal. He and his instincts blended together against all the edicts of civilization. He moved over her body without caution or fear. He filled her past her knowledge of herself. She had never before been so held, so physically possessed. His movements shook the floor. The smooth adobe walls seemed to vibrate and she feared that they would not hold the torrential meeting of their bodies.

She was both afraid and exalted. She knew her body as a temple and he as the inevitable God-Man. When he felt the waters of her acceptance and the waves of her contractions against him had slowed, he moved her fully around and began again, his belly to her back, his hands simultaneously kneading her breasts and steadying her pelvis. She was back in her dream, in the woods. When she thought she could bear no more, his hand moved from her breast down to her clitoris, where he caressed her unceasingly until he felt the beginnings of her contractions on him again and he let the streaming burning heat of his body enter hers while their inarticulate cries rivaled the thunder.

They slept only briefly that night. They spoke only of their feelings and the sensations of their bodies. When they tired, they simply lay entwined, suffused with well-being. They reinvented kissing. Their lips traversed skin-lands with slow meticulous gestures of greeting, stopping now and again to feel the definition of a particular area of sensation, warmed by the rhythmic blending of their breaths. They murmured incoherently to each other, lips muffled against breast, neck, belly caverns—salt licks of nourishment. Neither of them spoke of time, future or past. Everything existed now. As the storm receded, they became quiet and peaceful. Dawn light brought a soft dreamless sleep to them. When they awoke, they walked into town. They shopped for food and wine, scented oils and fresh notebooks in which neither would write.

During the silent moments of their walk, Lawrence found himself surprised at the elegance and privacy this woman was able to create in her small adobe. He had imagined their clandestine lovemaking to be limited to their joint rustic cabins, uncomfortable beds and ice cold nights. He had not anticipated her artistry in creating a warm hearth with all the comforts of a true home, where they were free to experience absolute abandon. He wanted her constantly and she never tired of his desire.

That first morning was a revelation to her. She was cooking breakfast for them while he was setting the fire in the adobe fireplace. Interrupting her labors, while the piñon wood offered them fragrant heat, he lifted the blue denim hem of her skirt, caressing with his rough hands the roundness of her hips, the hard muscled thighs so used to daily swimming. She, breathless, unbuttoned his shirt and kissed his neck, biting and running her tongue along the landscapes of his chest, suckling like a child his small nipple. He kissed her forehead, eyes, the beautiful line of her collarbone. They fought each other for the sovereign rights of the explorer, until meeting at the surrendering fields of their mouths. He, so adept, beyond the simple experience of years, pushed her up and back against the sideboard, entering into her femaleness and lifting her up high against him. This was not a dream. The surging wet, the guttural cries, the smells of cooking and piñon smoke, the hot desert sun cutting through the newness of spring's relenting cold—all were breaking her old self apart. As all the old disappointed longings fell away, she clung to him like an animal lost on the mesas with no past or future, only a terrible hunger to enter and be entered, to dissolve self to self, man to woman, melting all boundaries of separateness.

What they wrote in the final days of their retreat they wrote on each other's bodies. They made love on the cold earth, the soft down of the bed, in front of piñon fires and against the farthest wall of the inn, after an evening of margaritas, their feet frozen in the cold of an unexpected spring snow. They were mad with the taste and scent of their own bodies. He had never known such hunger or such satisfaction. She reveled in his adoration of her. Often, when the madness of their lovemaking would overcome them, they would become quiet, move to the backyard and sit in the sun. He would hold her gently against his chest, smoothing back her hair from her beloved face. Their only music was the sounds of their breathing, bird songs, and the soft breeze filtering through the sage. It was in those quiet moments that they bonded deeply. All that was innocent in them, hopeful, sat in mute awe at the perfection of their silence.

When she thought of the bonds of her marriage, she remembered that Larry had not wanted her to have a child, though he knew it was her last possibility of motherhood. She had not realized how much she nearly hated him for that and how much of her own longings she had put aside in order to adapt to their safe life together. Lawrence had filled her with a hopefulness that she had been too afraid to feel. Her breasts were heavy with his touch, his suckling kisses, her belly a circumference of aliveness, dancing fires of mingling lives. They left their small adobe only for food.

Her requisite evening calls home had become monotone and devoid of interest. She sensed that Larry had finally noticed a change and had said he would fly out early and stay at the inn until she completed her work. She asked him not to, she asked him to stay at home until she returned. When he asked her why, she told him she thought she had fallen in love with a young novelist and was not sure what she was going to do. Larry was driven into incoherence with the shock. He had been so sure of her, so certain that she was incapable of acting without his counsel. He felt the best course was to remain at home and allow her to come to herself without interference. After all, she was his wife, they had a home. He continued to lunch with his women friends, some of whom he found desirable. He was certain it would all continue as it had. He would forgive her, he could do that, he was very civilized.

Lawrence made love to her at every opportunity. He told her he would sacrifice for her, would get a job and write at night. He begged her to leave "her lawyer." He refused to call him by name, or refer to him as her husband. His own knowledge of her made him her true husband. He was related to her in body, in the soul of their mutual love of literature, of the music of poetry. He was her equal in every way and he had made her body his and had given his to her. He would follow her, he would have her and he would keep her.

When she left him to return home, she made him promise to give her time to sort things out. He allowed her only a month. At the end of that time he was coming for her. They parted with pain on both sides. Their separation was tearing at their bodies, severing the fine bonds of light that had joyously danced between them. While on the plane traveling home she felt disoriented. There were no remembered actions or rules for her to turn to for answers. She was at the edge of her life looking forward into an acknowledged unknown. All she had was her desire, all he had was his. Would that be enough to carry them across the rough channels of change, through the inevitable disappointments she knew were part of love? Her marriage to Larry in its early stages had been filled with hope. What would prevent another failure if she did start over? She did not know whether she had the strength to fight Larry's rightness, his certainty about life, his forgiveness. Marriage had been her haven, her safety. Life with Lawrence would be a storm. She knew he would never forgive her if she did not leave her marriage. He would hunt her down and move her with the fierceness of his love.

Larry was waiting for her when she entered the terminal. He was unchanged. His face showed no signs of doubt as he took her bag from her. He said that he'd made reservations at her favorite restaurant for dinner and had much to tell her about what had happened in her absence. He assured her that she did not need to tell him anything about her experience until she was ready, and, if she chose to say nothing at all, he would understand. She felt herself being slowly drawn into the safety net of their marriage, where life was smooth and easy and Larry seemed so effortlessly to take care of everything. She did not know what she was going to do.

PRELIMINARIES

Shimon-Craig Van Collie

I carried that blanket with me on the night I went to the fights. Not that I was a regular fight goer, but it was a big match and my roommate, a college friend who moved to San Francisco with me the year after graduation, gave me the ticket. The blanket was an old blue wool knit that had lived in the trunk of my car during high school and college and came in handy for those late-night trysts on the local golf course or athletic field. I picked it up at the cleaners on my way to the auditorium, and no one seemed to take notice as I walked past the ticket taker and stopped at the men's room.

The main bout was yet to come, and the crowd was unsettled. I made my way through the lobby, where cigar smoke hung heavily and the talk of excited fight fans careened off the tiled floor. I presented my ticket at the door leading to the arena and stepped into a darkened portal. The din of the lobby faded into the carpeted floor and the dark blue, crushed velvet theatrical curtain hanging down the sides of the bleachers. The smells of cigar and cigarette smoke mixed with a new scent, the one of the fans' blood lust. My suit jacket and shirt suddenly clung to my skin. Above, I could see the spotlights beaming down into the pit of the arena, and I was drawn to the throaty growls coming from ahead.

A roar went up from the crowd, and everyone started rushing toward the action. I found myself standing next to a redheaded woman in an olive green, knit woolen outfit that did nothing to hide her voluptuous figure. Someone pushed me from behind and I lurched forward into her. My head came down around her shoulder and into a view of two lightly perfumed breasts that rose like brimming promises from her V-cut dress.

She turned, anger in her face, but when our eyes met, she softened, and then gasped. Instead of berating me as I expected, she asked, "Are you all right?" I straightened myself up and told her that I was.

"What's going on?" I asked.

"I don't know. I think Lawler knocked out Mazzoli."

She had green eyes, full pouty lips and a throat that made me want to lean over and bite her. Crossing her arms, she shifted her weight to her left leg, a move which thrust her ripe hips toward me and forced her breasts into even more prominent view. I assumed she was trying to display displeasure and played along.

"Aren't you having fun?"

"Not exactly." She looked down at my blanket. "What are you carrying that for?"

"No reason. I just haven't gone home yet. I'm meeting my friend here and I came from work."

"Is your friend a he?" she inquired.

"Yeah."

"Can he wait a little while?" Her eyebrows rose suggestively. When they relaxed, I noticed spidery crow's feet bracing her viridescent orbs.

"Ah, sure, I suppose."

She took my arm and we walked back into the lobby and over to a bar, where we found a booth and sat down. Our knees touched lightly under the table. She introduced herself as Vivian. We chatted, leaving out any indication about significant others in our lives. Even though I had a steady girlfriend, I wasn't about to let myself be tied down. I was talking to an exciting older woman whose toe kept pressing into my calf as we talked.

"And what about you? Are you here with a friend?" I asked.

She hesitated for a moment, turned away and then turned back to me with a serious look. "Let's just say I'm not unattached, but it's not a concern of yours, not now or in the future, okay?"

"Okay. I'm glad to hear there's a future." Again she looked away. I glanced at my watch and realized that we had been talking for twenty minutes.

"It's probably time for us to go," I said, not really wanting to leave her but also worrying that my buddy would be looking for me. For a moment, she looked disappointed, but then she asked me to walk with her on the way back. The lobby had cleared out since the main bout was about to begin. Just as we entered the corridor between the bleachers, she took my hand and pulled aside the heavy curtain on one side. She tugged me to follow her, and we slipped into the cavernous hollow beneath the seats. I followed, my heart beginning to race and my crotch beginning to tingle as the possibilities of what would happen next danced about my head.

Like two little kids playing in an old barn down the street, we walked through the darkened space. Light from the auditorium filtered through the openings under the bleachers, where we could see the back of the shoes and the lower legs of the spectators.

Vivian stopped and turned toward me, her face close to mine, her wonderful perfume filling my nostrils. There was enough light to see the sparkle in her eyes. We leaned into each other. Her lips were soft, her tongue was hot and our bodies pressed together. We kissed long and hard until the skin on my lips burned.

"Wow!" she said.

"Wow, yourself!" I held her tighter.

"I'm not going to make love to you now," she said, "although I'm tempted."

"Why do we have to wait?" I pressed my now hard bulge up against her mons and rubbed my hips slowly against hers.

"Do I look like a girl who would do something like that on the first date?" she asked.

"Uh hunh," I nodded.

She laughed and pulled herself away. "Give me your card. I'll be in touch. And bring that blanket again." She led me by the hand, back to the curtain and the light. As she walked away I admired the twitch of her buttocks, which looked not unlike two cats squirming under the sheath of her well-tailored dress.

I found my friend and tried to watch the fight, but I kept scanning the crowd looking for Vivian. Only at the very end of the bout, when we all rose to leave, did I catch a glimpse of her across the arena. She walked in front of a dark, heavyset man in a long woolen coat. In a moment, she disappeared.

That night I lay awake until well past midnight thinking about her, remembering her, smelling the faint whiff of perfume that she had left on my neck and the collar of my shirt. I was entranced, taken in by her feline aura and her feminine charm. Not knowing when, or if, she would get in touch with me drove me farther to distraction. What if she did? I wondered. Would I taste those ripe breasts? Would I plant myself between her lusty thighs? Would I kiss her long, vibrant neck as she writhed in my arms?

And what about Penny? the other little voice in my head chimed in. What about your "relationship"? Your "commitment"? Lust and morality battled each other until the early morning hours when I masturbated and fell off to sleep.

Vivian's image receded slowly on each succeeding day until a week later when a letter with no return address arrived in my mailbox. My hands trembled as I ripped it open. Inside was a fight announcement for the upcoming weekend torn out from the newspaper. One of the preliminaries was circled, with writing next to it: Bring your blanket and a condom. Make that two. Yours, V.

I arrived at the appointed time, blanket under my arm and condoms in my pocket. I saw Vivian across the lobby and we made eye contact. She motioned for me to wait while she went to the ladies' room. My chest began to tremble uncontrollably with excitement. I wondered if someone would come running up at the last second and expose me for a shameless sinner. I looked at the eyes of the other men walking to and fro. Their minds seemed miles away from anything of the sort. I took a deep breath and tried to relax.

Vivian approached with her fur coat pulled tightly around her. Cream pumps clicked joyously on the tile floor. She nodded for me to go behind the curtain. A few seconds later she followed.

"Fancy meeting you," she teased. "Do you come here often?"

"Not yet, but my hopes are high."

"And what else is high?" She reached forward to my groin,

where my cock rose to meet her touch. "Mmmm. I thought I'd wear something nice for you." She stepped away and pulled open her coat, revealing that whatever dress she had been wearing before was no longer there. Instead, she was resplendent in a black lace bra and panties, a delicate black garter belt attached to sheer black nylons. My mouth dropped and my eyes bugged out as they used all the available light in our demiworld under the bleachers to soak in her appearance. As she stepped up to me, I was overwhelmed. Our mouths met again, and my hands went to her exposed skin, which was warm and moist under the fur.

She took the blanket from under my arm and placed it on the floor directly in front of me. Slowly she dropped to her knees, pulling me with her. Our kissing continued but quickly grew more passionate to include biting, sucking and licking each other's lips, cheeks and neck.

"Quickly!" she said, unbuckling my belt and tugging at my pants. I took out one of the condoms and offered it to her. By now she had her lips on my stomach as she fished out my cock and began stroking it. I gazed up at the bleachers, where the fans were beginning to cheer the fight in progress. Their sounds drowned out ours and I felt her tongue lick the underside of my shaft. She wet my member with her spit and stroked me, rising up again to kiss me some more. I cupped her ass with my hands, kneading her flesh through her naughty panties. My tongue forced her bra away from her hardened nipples and swirled her little chestnuts in my mouth.

"Oh, God!" she moaned. Her hands left my body, and I could sense her ripping the cover off the condom, then placing it over the head of my cock and rolling it down, squeezing my balls playfully as she completed the sheathing. "C'mon, baby, c'mon baby!" The urgency in her voice provoked me. She reached down to her panties, pulled them aside and dipped her hand into her juice, smearing some of it on my cock. Then she raised her hand and held it under my nose and I inhaled her musky, salty aroma.

I reached down and dipped my own finger into her, finding her slippery and warm. I played with her inner walls and then withdrew, stroking her clitoris lightly, rolling it like a marble dipped in light oil. She closed her eyes and moaned. I placed my palm on her mons, holding her hot sex like a ripe fruit in my hand.

"Do that again!" she gasped.

"Do what?"

"The stroking. Play with my clit again."

I complied, caressing my fingers up and down over her outer labia before centering again on her button, which I stroked first gently and then, as her breathing increased and she clutched my legs and ass, harder until I felt her quiver.

"Where'd you learn to do that?!" she asked, breathless.

"You aren't the first woman I've ever met," I said cockily.

"Oh, but I want to be the last!" She buried her head in my chest and bit me hard. "Let me be that, let me be the last one!"

I leaned her back so that she lay, legs open, before me. I kissed her belly and her breasts, climbing over her, poised like a missile ready for launch. Reaching down with both hands, I ripped off one side of her panties and peeled the whisp of silk to the side, leaving her cleft visible. Vivian guided me in while I kissed her neck and felt her hair and the fur of her collar rubbing on my cheek and neck.

As the crowd started cheering, we responded with cries of our own. In fact, the noise from above formed a soundproof cloud into which we could venture, our voices safe within its boundaries as it expanded and contracted in response to the action in the ring. I grunted, pressing into her as her hips rose to meet mine. Our tongues danced and our saliva ran down her cheeks, where I rubbed my face, spreading the warm fluid over her forehead and eyes and down to her neck and upper chest. I was losing control, and I bit into the soft flesh of her breasts. She responded by raking my back with her nails, digging them into my skin.

The musk of our sweat added to the amorous, aromatic stew we were concocting. I cradled her neck in the crook of my right elbow as my left hand cupped and squeezed her smooth bucking buttocks. Occasionally I would graze the hairs on my balls, which had drawn up tight in preparation for their climactic splurge. Deep in my spine, a fireball began to grow, spreading up and forward, until it ignited, burning through my loins and up into my chest. I shouted into the fur, losing awareness of the crowd above us, not caring anymore about time, space or civilization. My body stiffened. Vivian wrapped herself around me, arms and legs locked firmly about my torso. She gasped, her breath coming in short waves, hot against my face and ear, the sound of her close yet distant as I floated in the netherworld.

"I've got to get back," she said finally, reaching up to bite my nipple. I held her head there, pushing it into my chest. We lay for another minute on the blanket and then rose, picking up the pieces of our clothing from where they had landed. She pulled her black silk dress from her bag and handed me her fur while she slipped the dress on over her head. Before I pulled on my own pants, she hugged me, raising her dress so that my warm, receding cock lay against her thigh.

"Would you like to do this again?" I asked.

She kissed me in response, playfully tonguing me and then pulling away. "I'll be in touch." She turned and skipped away, stopping at the curtain for a second to compose herself and giving me one quick look and a smile before disappearing.

The glow of our encounter lingered with me for the remainder of the night. I lay in bed this time recollecting each moment of our interlude, especially the rush of excitement I felt as Vivian opened her coat, the surge of libido when we embraced and the delirious plunge into orgasm.

I gave myself a couple of days to cool off before seeing Penny again. I invited her over for dinner. She arrived at my door with my mail in her hand, and on top of the batch of letters was Vivian's handwriting. As soon as Penny put the letters down and turned to take off her coat, I snatched the envelope and squirreled it between two books on the bookshelf.

"It feels like forever since I've seen you," Penny said, hugging me. Her slim, hard body felt familiar, but Vivian's curvaceous form was still imprinted on my cells.

We ate and then watched a video, snuggled together on the couch. To ward off the chill as the evening deepened, I went to the closet and, by chance, pulled out the blue wool blanket. We lay comfortably in each other's arms and drifted off to sleep as the final credits rolled.

In the middle of the night, Penny stirred and we both awoke.

"What a dream I just had!" she said. "I saw you with this other woman. She had this flaming red hair and you were fucking her like mad. There was a crowd of people all around, cheering wildly. I was standing behind these curtains watching, wondering what to do."

I tried not to betray the panic that was creeping up my spine. Did the blanket contain some kind of memory cells that had sloughed off onto Penny while she slept? I was glad the house was dark enough so that she couldn't see my face.

"And you know what happened next?" she asked.

My throat caught and I coughed. "No, what happened?"

"I started to get incredibly hot myself. I know you'd never do anything like that, but it just turned me on to see you plunging away inside of her. I took off my clothes and I joined the two of you and we were having a glorious time!"

I could only laugh nervously, but I was soon distracted by Penny's warm lips on mine and her hands reaching up under my shirt to stroke the hairs on my chest. As she kissed her way down my stomach to meet my rising prominence, I fantasized the two of them, together with me, and all was lost in the dark.

GLORIOUS REUNION

Hope Katz

I'm at pottery class, wedging life into a mound of soft brown clay. The aroma of warm, wet earth bathes me in a calm that comes from the push and pull as I prepare the clay for the wheel. I struggle at first to help it find its center, then close my eyes and let the rhythm take control.

It is my center that I am longing to find. The clay is but the medium. I sense if only the clay will find its center, perhaps I will, too. Then I can fill the void that has been hollow for weeks now, six of them, since last I saw him—Glen the man who won my heart a year ago.

We met at an art opening. His eyes, then the eyes of a stranger, followed me around the gallery. I felt his stare, but pushed it away. Being at an art opening, or anything that was remotely connected with artists, was hard for me then. It had been three months since my fiancé, an artist named Benjamin, called off our marriage just days before the wedding. Benjamin never told me why. He just said he couldn't go through with it. He loved me, he said, he just couldn't marry me.

The memory of that night still brings me to my knees. I remember the darkness that set in as I looked into his black-brown eyes and knew in the pit of my stomach that it was all over. I felt his fear as he paced around me, careful not to come too close or he would lose his resolve, break into a million bits.

After hearing the apartment door close behind him, I sat quite still for a long time. I don't remember thinking about anything in particular. It was as if time had stopped. The only thing that seemed to have a heartbeat was the engagement ring on my finger. It was still shiny as ever, still glittering with the promise of true love as I slipped it off my finger.

After that dream died, it was only sheer determination that made me keep living. I took a job in another city, tried to leave the pain behind. I couldn't. When the reality of the world seemed too cold and my body too hot, I would escape into a cavern of numb determination. This safe spot buffered me, hid me, helped me distance myself from the agony that permeated my soul.

When a friend invited me to the art opening, I told myself I should go. I had to snap out of it, had to get back out into the world. I could go to an art opening, I assured my reflection as I painted my lips Revlon Red. I was still breathing, after all. If I could do that, I could do anything I put my mind to. So I slipped on my black suede pumps and off I went.

Many glasses of white wine helped ease my angst as I wandered about the gallery. I felt my sense of humor returning. It struck me funny somehow that all the artists were tall, thin and had mustaches, like Benjamin.

Clinging tightly to my chardonnay, I set out to look for a painting to absorb me. I found solace looking into a surreal piece of carrot with an eye chart on it. "How clever," I thought, saying the words aloud.

From behind, the stranger with the watchful eyes, said, "Thank you. My name is Glen and that's my painting. Do you like it?" "Yes," I stammered, hardly believing the coincidence. "I like it because it has layers of meaning. You know?" He just smiled and asked for my telephone number.

I gave it to him.

On our first date we went to an Indian restaurant. We talked and talked amidst the warm aroma of curry. Hours passed like minutes. We stayed so late the manager brought us each a shot of schnapps when he asked us to leave. It was midnight. When Glen dropped me at the door, our first kiss lasted an hour. That kiss. It held the power of the wind, blowing life back into my sad heart.

Was this possible? Could I actually be so very attracted to someone else? It seemed too good to be real, too positive to be trusted. I was determined not to make another mistake. So I tested him. When we were apart I questioned his motives. What did this man want from me? Why did he show up unexpectedly at the train station, just to say have a good trip? Why on so many nights did he talk to me about anything, everything, until 3 A.M.? Why did the touch of his lips penetrate my sorrow, his hands reach me in a place no one ever touched before? Why hadn't I met him before I stopped trusting?

Still, our connection was powerful. Maybe it was also because Glen was ten years older than my twenty-eight, he seemed to have a wisdom I had not grown into. And his body, it fit around mine. He made me feel safe. Safe enough to make love to him at a time I never thought I'd have sex again. But we did. It seemed my writing and his art gave us a common ground of understanding. The plight of the artist, the frustration of the misunderstood. It was what had connected me to Benjamin. The familiarity made me connect to Glen, too.

Slowly, the dragons that haunted my dreams began to quiet. In the six months that followed the opening we spent all of our free time together. We went to galleries and art auctions, movies and concerts. No matter where we went, always the passion turned reality to fantasy; him brushing up against my blouse, barely touching my skin as we gazed at the artful use of light in a painting by Vermeer at the National Gallery; us sitting in the last row of the movie theater, kissing and petting our way through *Byron Fink*.

And after hours of concealed foreplay, there was always the candlelit bath. In the liquid tranquility, the light of two white votive candles illuminated us, helped us find peace. Helped us find each other.

On his birthday we drove to the beach and spent the weekend in bed, loving, listening to the sound of the sea outside the window. The afternoon sun beamed across the room, casting on the wall the image of our entwined bodies. Lovers silhouetted in shadows. His fingers, they danced along my body, electrifying me. As the waves caressed the sand just feet from our room, his tongue licked its way from ankle to calf drawing gentle lines of anticipation. The feel of his tongue inside me. His fingers on my lips, in my mouth, his body inside me. Then, the explosion of union. It was dusk when we collapsed into each other's arms. In those arms, my lust turned to love.

Only, the hurt child inside of me didn't trust it. Although the woman in me desperately wanted to, the little girl kept surfacing like a nagging itch. Even though the blueness of his eyes stared deeply into my soul, I was frightened. Perhaps I didn't trust myself, or perhaps the love that comes after loss is doomed. My confidence was shattered after Benjamin. I could almost see it lying in sharp-edged pieces on the floor of my spirit. Splinters of broken glass were everywhere. I went through my days on tiptoe, fearful another slice would pierce me again, reopen the wound.

My fears found proof when Glen was hesitant to commit with words. Those hot, deep kisses told me, "Yes, I love you. I won't leave. I promise." But he could never utter words of commitment. He could never verbalize how he felt. The only words he could muster were those of his own fears.

He had raging dragons, too. Divorced after eight years of marriage, he could relate to my sadness and loss. For him, though, there was guilt mixed in the batch. And his recipe proved more volatile than mine. The part of me that was afraid understood. He said he just couldn't go through another divorce. Couldn't screw up again, he said. He had to be sure, absolutely certain this time. Everything had to be perfect—perfectly safe, absolutely reliable—before he could promise his love. There could be no unanswered questions about our compatibility, no hesitation on his part. Love should never be hard work, he said.

His quest for a no-risk guarantee began to steal the spontaneity from our passion. Like a burglar canvassing our relationship, his watchful eyes seemed to be waiting for the right moment to confiscate our love.

The fear won. As weeks turned to months, he had more and more work to do, less time to see me. I knew this feeling. He was pulling away. His pull made me cling. My clinging made him pull away more. Our relationship was now an entanglement, and I didn't know how to fix it. It was the longing and the loss that helped us find a bridge to love. Now, it was the longing and the loss that was tearing down that bridge.

Then someone called to tell me Benjamin had gotten married. What? What do you mean? The voices screamed inside my head. How could this be? Was he seeing someone else when we were engaged? Was this a horrible joke? Please, someone tell me this is a bad dream. Please, someone wake me up. Please.

I stuck my fingernails into the palm of my hand and spoke into the telephone. "That's good," I said. "I hope he will be happier with her. If you speak to him, send him my best."

I placed the receiver down. My mind was racing. I was determined to keep breathing, but couldn't catch my breath. I felt trapped in a hot, black room, unable to see or feel anything. I gasped for air. Sat down on the floor and rocked myself quiet. As the hours passed, I withdrew into my sorrow. It seemed clear that everything I had done was a mistake. And this relationship with Glen, well, I was repeating patterns. I couldn't give anyone else a chance to leave me at the altar, or anywhere near it. I had to take care of myself. Had to stop the cycle. I couldn't let my heart break again. Not like that.

I called Glen to tell him I couldn't see him anymore.

He sounded sad. And he sounded relieved. "I think that's best, too," he said. He admitted he thought that we were just too different, not compatible. These words he could utter. "Maybe a writer and an artist can't live in harmony," he said. "Maybe there is just too much baggage in the way. I don't know what it is. I love you, but I have too many questions about you to continue. We aren't always on the same wavelength, and it just doesn't make sense to keep going if I'm not sure. I am sorry. I don't think I know what I want. I didn't mean to hurt you."

As I held his voice to my ear, I summoned my determination: "I'm sorry, too," I said. "And I'll always love you. You were the man who made me feel whole again, who made me smile again. I'll always be grateful for that. You were a gift. And you are the best lover I have ever had."

"I was inspired," he said, before he said goodbye.

I tried not to be terrified as I hung up the telephone. Although I had made the call, it was his rejection that sent a cannonball blasting through my center. I had failed. Again. And everything was confused. Air seemed to have been cut off, blood had stopped flowing through my body. I felt as if there was nothing left to keep me alive.

Pottery class became my temple. My mind was desperate to sort out the past. Somehow creating a vessel from clay helped. So when Glen called and said he wanted to see me again, just to talk, I suggested we meet after class. "I'd like to see you again," he said. "Really?" I said. "Yeah," he said.

Why?

But I agreed. And I promised myself I wouldn't get my hopes up. He just wants to talk, have a beer. Right? I just want to find peace. And balance.

It is the balance I am concentrating on now as I sit at the pottery wheel and feel the soft, round mound of clay rise and fall under my hands. I drip warm water onto it, making it more liquid, pliable. I drench my sponge, move it up and down along the side of the clay to remove the air pockets that could kill it. Again and again, up and down. The earth and the sponge and I work together.

I sense the clay is ready to take on a life of its own. I press my thumbs into its center to open its mouth. Deeper and deeper I go, working to expose its heart. Slowly, what was only a lifeless mound begins to grow into itself, to find its freedom. Faster and faster, the warm, wet clay whirls between my fingers. Faster and faster, it keeps time with my beating heart as the clock ticks closer and closer to five o'clock, to the time we are to meet.

I try not to think of the last weeks since we said goodbye on the telephone. One-dimensional goodbye, spoken through a plastic receiver. Pulseless. The conversation that made me want to run away and sleep, hide in my safe protective cavern. Why is escape so difficult?

It's nearly five when I wipe away the layer of clay caked on my body. I place my strong, tall, healthy vessel on a shelf to dry. Find my jacket and open the door of the classroom to look for him.

He is waiting for me outside, hiding behind a pillar, playing. Found. That black jean jacket. The way he stands, his hips loose,

relaxed in his Levi's. He is smiling that boyish grin, his blue eyes
are twinkling. The sight of him warms my heart, dries the tears,
turns my fear to longing. He still makes me hot, sticky. Was that
you I said goodbye to?

We walk toward each other. Time seems to slow. I hear my
heart pounding as he opens his arms to hug me. I find a smattering
of pale yellow paint tattooed to his neck. A kiss lands nearby. The
freckle near his ear calls my lips. His familiar clean scent makes
me want to keep going. Down, up. Inside, out.

No. I have to stay in control. Have to keep my distance. His
questions, his fears. Mine. Those are the intangible walls that
tower tall between us. The walls of heartbreak. They are made of
steel, filled with immovable, impenetrable concrete, invisible to the
people passing by. Does the passerby see the walls that keep us
apart, as we hug hello?

I pull back, feel a knot of frustration tie in my gut, tighten
around my heart. I squint as I look into his smile. I am struggling
to find his motives, to define my own. Can I hold your hand? Will
that help answer your questions? Will touching help us let go of
the fear? Make the steel dissolve and the concrete melt? If I try,
will you?

I ask his eyes, do I look as delicious to you as you do to me?
Do you want to be inside of me as much as I want you to be?
Swelling within, filling me up, making me complete. Help me create
a bond more powerful than our erected barriers. Ravish my spirit,
grab my imagination and make it spasm with delight. Rack my
heart with laughter. Lick me happy.

Impossible desire. It makes me hungry.

At a nearby bar I order tuna salad and a beer. On a stool across
from me, he eats five-star chili. His lips surround the prongs as I
want him to surround my nipple. Suck hard. Harder. Harder. Make
me quiver. Give me a bite.

We say nothing with our words. Our talk is small as we sit
facing each other on hard wooden stools. I can feel the air. It is
thick on my skin. I want to cut it with my fork. I want to wave it
away. Why can't I stop shaking? Why doesn't he love me enough
to work it out with me? Doesn't anyone love forever? My eyes are
fixed on his. I can't be the first one to blink. Won't be the one to

ask. I won't tell him how much I love him. Please, read my mind. Please, stop the hurt.

I try to stop arguing with myself, try to stop the conflict, as the waitress takes my plate. No, I don't want another Bud, but I'm still so thirsty. I watch him put down his fork, sip from his mug of dark ale. I watch him swallow. Oh, how I want his juice to flow down my throat. I want mine to drip down his. Salty, sweet liquids trickling down, warm. Hot.

The check comes. He says he will pay. It's the guy thing to do. We sit quietly for a few minutes, just staring into each other's eyes. The silence is loud as he drinks the rest of his beer. I sense he can't find anything else small to say. The vastness of the tension takes over the expression on his face, transforms his brow into a question mark. He hesitates, reaches for my hand under the table. "It's really good to see you. I missed you," he says. "You wouldn't consider, uh, our taking a bath together, would you? For, uh, old times' sake?"

My mind hesitates. My heart applauds. The link is still intact. He *does* want me. My optimism soars. My protective shell takes a break. I promise myself it is okay if there are no tomorrows. No commitments. I will still be whole. But we have this night, this moment, this second. It is ours. I feel my body start to respond. A grin is my reply.

The car can't move fast enough. Once inside his house, the dance begins. His scent fills my soul. Musky clean. We waltz around each other. Lovers wanting to prolong the inevitable. Foreplay for foreplay.

He shows me the painting he just finished as we stand in the darkened crevice of a deep blue corner of a loft that has no moonlight. We work to keep ourselves in check. I still feel the need to stay back, to protect myself. He is dangerous. He makes me vulnerable, makes me want to put up walls, then he knocks them down only to open me back up again. I am afraid to be so vulnerable. So painfully vulnerable. So painfully in love. I can't breathe. I can't *shh* the sea quiet.

Without warning, he moves toward me with a tidal wave kiss that crashes my senses to shore. Cravings explode, magnetizing us, forcing us forward toward the want. Conflict resolving conflict. Finally, total abandon.

Ripping at each other's lips, we push away the boundaries we desperately cling to in daylight. More, more. Take what you want. Take what I have. Take more. Tongues and hard, wet kisses. Find the spot where lovers go. Where lovers know. Overshirt with buttons. Buttons. Push the right ones. Unbutton the ones you can. One at a time. Open, more. Less. T-shirt. Cotton on skin. Pull it off. Skin on skin. Cold fingers find warm nipples. Hard nipples. Harder, harder. Teeth. Tongues, licking warm flesh. Warm, hot.

Deep breath. Where's the bed?

Downstairs into reality. The refrigerator is open. The dog needs to be fed. But we can grab some candles, and some wine. Two glasses. How about some brandy? Whipped cream? Pudding?— Chocolate? No, vanilla.

An ambrosia arsenal is assembled

What time is it? Who cares.

The bed. Him falling atop me. Gentle, knowing smiles. Caught in the act of opening. Touching him, touching me. Taking off his jeans. Naked him. Clothed me. Should I pull off my long skirt or let it fall around his shoulders? Cover his head? Lips on skin. Skin on lips.

He leaves me dressed. His mouth finds breast beneath body-suit. He lingers above me, his tongue talking to me with warm licks, pushing me deeper into the coolness of his black-and-white sheets. He raises himself up, smiling that gorgeous smile. His lips meet mine. I am his. Again. Oh, the joy. The recklessness of want. His nakedness, his silky, warm nakedness. Pull closer.

That body. The feel of his strong, hard, muscles against me. Delicious. My tongue lingers on his chest. Fingers find the bottle of brandy. I spill a drop and watch it dribble toward the nape of his neck, then douse him plenty and drink from his skin. Intoxicating passion.

He regains balance and arms himself with the can of whipped cream. Drawing perfect circles of whipped whiteness on my nipples, he uses his tongue like a spoon to lick them perfectly clean. Soft licks that get harder as I do. Sucking bliss. Slurp me up.

We finally find our way to the promised bath. Cleansing warmth engulfs the passion, dims the fire. Talk ensues amidst candlelight. Flickering sounds meet ebbs of light. Sips of wine cool hot thirsty throats. Tickle happy tongues.

In the water, I find his hardness. Put it in my mouth, tighter, lighter, deeper I push him in. Warm beyond simmer. Unbearable delight, just holding him there, stroking him with the tip of my tongue. I feel him get harder and harder. I find the spot that makes his back arch, stay for a second longer than he can stand. Then I put him whole into my mouth, sucking harder, faster, more. Yes. Swallowing. Yes, oh yes.

We rest, legs entwined. Our bodies take time-out in respective corners of the big porcelain bowl. Leg around leg. Toes find fingers. The glow of candles dims our need for words. Dancing light finds his dimples. His blue eyes twinkle in the shine. He gives me a nasty grin. We soak and breathe, the spell only slightly broken by the serenity of the bath. But this isn't serene and this isn't ordinary. This is heaven.

Soon, the distance of bodies is too great a barrier. Unchained, I move inside the circle of his legs. Between his thighs I rest mine. His arms blanket my body. Engulfed. All arms and legs and soon, I turn to find his mouth. There we find solitude, kissing with our hearts. Lovers lost and found again.

Passion turns from tidal wave to typhoon. We grab towels to remove dampness, then find our way back to the bed, snuggle beneath crisp sheets. There is nothing cuddly about this, though. This is fire, hotter than memory recalls. The Zen of passion.

Biting need flows like blood through ventricles. Fast. Pulsating. Involuntary. His mouth finds mine. In an instant he has mounted me. Touching, gravitating to the place he found effortlessly for the past year. It has been lost for what feels like forever. Tonight, it is reclaimed.

"What do you want?" I ask.

"You know," he says.

I do.

I move from beneath him to let his mouth find the place where few are invited, fewer are welcome. Lips on lips. Heated sweat boils and steams. The whistle of a ready teapot. Is that me? More, he groans holding tight beneath me. My arms are climbing the headboard, fingernails claw at dark red wallpaper. Pulling intensity, need personified. Trust from lust. Taking what only lovers can, taking what no other can touch. Inside. Deep inside. Buried treasures unearthed. Pain or pleasure?

Pleasure. How many ways can you please a lover?

Passion turns molehill to Everest. Taller. Higher. Waiting is impossible. He mounts me again, sliding himself inside masterfully. Home.

Come with me, someone breathes.

But just before we do, in my ear he whispers, "I love you."

Does he mean it? Can we try again? Can we kiss each other healthy? Can we love away the fear? Can we be brave in daylight, too?

Maybe.

Maybe not.

For as I lie in his arms, I smell his love and, still, I sense his hesitation. As the sweat dries, the dawn sparks a light in me. It is a dreamy place where relationships are born, a rocky place where they are tested. Commitment is a messy business that has no patience for ambivalence. True love does not just begin and end. It is a gift that needs to be nurtured with time, care, patience. There is nothing safe and neat about it.

When there are questions, that is when the real work starts. And that is when the real love begins. Just as he cannot be blamed for the sins of Benjamin, I cannot be expected to provide a safe and sure harbor from the unpredictable world. Love does not come with a no-risk guarantee. I cannot give him that.

What I can give him is my promise to love him with everything I am, to never give up, and always to be his friend. I can give him the gift of my undying loyalty, uncompromising faith, and unconditional love. If that is not enough for him, neither am I.

I know somehow in the place where truth lives, that I am not enough for him. Or perhaps, I am too much.

So I push back the covers, reach one last time for his lips and look long into his eyes. If this is to be the last kiss, the final touch, I want to remember exactly what color his eyes are.

Ocean blue. Hazy and opalescent, they hold all the fury and

magic of the sea. In those eyes I see the beautiful spirit of a man who does not trust either of us enough. Who is still holding on to the hopes and fears of a boy. Who has locked himself away in a protective cavern of his own, a place where no one can hurt him, where no one can reach him.

It seems the only gift left to give him is the gift of goodbye. So I gather my clothes and that sheer determination and I find my way to his door. Then I shut it, gently.

The morning air blankets me, and a quiet settles into the center I have learned tonight to fill with myself. As I make my way home I think somewhere between hello and goodbye and orgasm, I grew up.

Glorious!

THE ACCIDENT

Dina Vered

My September stint filling in for my newspaper's Jerusalem correspondent was over and I had three days left before returning to the Paris bureau. The *hamsin*, the hot desert wind, was making everyone a little crazy, so I decided to escape to the Galilee.

Driving my air-conditioned Renault in the scorched Judean desert north of Jericho, I felt free from press conferences, free from my demanding editor, free from newspaper deadlines. Since arriving in Israel, I'd been writing nonstop, covering political conflicts, conflicts which had gone on for centuries. The longer I stayed in the Middle East, the less I knew. All I knew now, was that I needed a vacation.

Peering in the rearview mirror, I noticed new blond sun streaks in my hair. The mirror also showed an open road—no cars or cops—so I teased the speedometer up to 130, then 150 kilometers. How many miles to a kilometer? To hell with the mathmaticas—there was no speed limit anyway. By driving fast, I'd reach Tiberius in time for an evening swim in the Sea of Galilee.

Ahead was a confusing crossroads. Keeping my eyes on the road, I blindly rummaged through my purse for the map. Unable to feel it, I looked down. But just when I spotted the map, my Renault jerked left and crossed the white dividing line. I hit the brakes; but instead of slowing, my car swerved even farther into the left lane.

Adrenalin shot through me. On this deserted road, a truck was barreling toward me, just seconds away. Yanking my steering wheel right, I stepped on the gas and screeched an escape to the dirt shoulder of the road.

But my Renault kept going, diving over the shoulder into a deep ravine. When the car flipped over and landed on a boulder, I knew it was delivering me to my death.

Stillness. Was this death or its audition? I panicked about the gas tank exploding. I panicked about burning in a fiery fury. Panic? If I was panicking, I must be alive. I snapped open my seat belt and like a movie stuntwoman leapt out of the car, tearing my dress as I fell to the dirt below.

Shocked and helpless, I stayed on the ground and curled into a ball, waiting for the blast. But nothing happened. I looked up. I was stuck in an abyss with a Renault perched on a boulder like a crippled bird. I crawled up an embankment onto the road. I waited and waited. But there were no cars. Except for that killer truck, the road was unused. It was dark and this was the West Bank, near the minefields and barbed wire along the Jordanian border. I was alone, in no man's land.

Echoing in the distance, I heard "Allahu akhbar," Allah is great, the *muzzein* calling the faithful to the mosque. Finally, I spotted headlights and waved a pickup truck to a stop. Seven Arab workmen in black and white *keffiyahs* climbed out. They stared at me, a blonde in a flimsy, torn cotton mini. I was severely underdressed.

I told them what had happened, but the men clearly didn't understand English. When I pointed below to my captive car, they began chattering animatedly in Arabic. They took a rope and a crowbar from the truck and climbed into the ravine. The men tied the car's bumper and pulled it. But the Renault just dripped its black sticky juices onto the desert dirt. The car clearly was not going anywhere, but the men kept pulling, trying to get it off the boulder. I was getting frustrated. I wanted to get somewhere safe.

A Peugeot stopped, and out stepped a strapping, bearded Israeli in typical kibbutznik clothes: denim shorts, sandals, and a Chicago Bulls T-shirt. "Beseder?" he asked.

I nodded yes, knowing it meant "okay" in Hebrew. "Do you speak English?" I asked, hoping he'd offer me a ride out. But he ignored me and, instead, silently surveyed the Arab men pulling on my car. "Wait here," the Israeli ordered curtly and scrambled down the embankment. A lone Israeli with seven Arabs in a remote ravine.

When the Israeli started yelling in Arabic to the men, I realized he was no kibbutznik, but probably a fanatical Jewish settler. The situation looked explosive. I stepped to the edge of the dark ravine. "What the hell are you doing?" I shouted angrily to the abrasive bastard. "They're trying to help me and you're chasing them away!" Ignoring me, the Israeli made his way up to my car and grabbed my suitcase from the seat.

After a few minutes, the Arabs filed back into the truck and the Israeli swaggered toward me and handed me the suitcase. I took out a sweater and covered my torn dress, as he held the car door open. "They need to get back home quickly—there's a curfew in Jericho," he explained in perfect BBC English. "There's rioting and stone throwing and . . . shooting."

Rioting? Shooting? Maybe this Israeli with the steely exterior wasn't such a bastard. If he hadn't driven by, I'd have had to spend the night under curfew in an Arab village.

As we drove off, he turned on the radio news. "What's happening?" I asked.

"The army's moving into Jericho," he said, translating the Hebrew. "It's bloody. Four soldiers killed, five Palestinians wounded." My newswoman's antennae started waving. Luckily, I was off-duty.

The news over, he began to interrogate me. "What are you doing here alone?" he said as if I were a naughty child. "It's dangerous, driving this road."

"It was the shortest route. I'm a reporter and was taking a few days off to explore the Galilee before flying back to . . ."

"I'm driving you to the Bet She'an police station," he said, cutting me off. "You'll report the accident and Hertz will tow the car."

"I'm Alana Greenstein," I said, breaking the silence. I studied his strong profile, the brown eyes with the long, long lashes. "And you?"

"Joseph," he answered, "Joseph Hassan." His eyes fixed on the road ahead. "So where should I drop you off?"

"Any hotel near the lake."

"Aren't you meeting someone?"

When I told him I was traveling alone, he turned toward me, exploring me with sudden interest. Then with Israeli bluntness, he asked, "Are you married?"

As I shook my head no, I noticed his pleasure. But something about the way he looked at me stopped me from asking the same question. "So why does a kibbutznik speak English with a Brit accent?" My reporter side was kicking in.

"I'm not a kibbutznik," he said firmly. "I've been living in London for a few years and just returned last month."

"So why'd you leave Israel for so long?"

"Too many hot heads on all sides of the borders . . . too much blindness and madness that will never stop, not in my lifetime. I wandered around Europe, had a studio in London. But I was unlucky selling my paintings."

"Why'd you come back?"

"Family business," he said hesitantly, then added, "and intense nostalgia. No matter how long I traveled, I wasn't at home. So this time, I'm staying here."

Joseph was a man of many parts. He intrigued me—mentally and physically. "Where'd you learn such good Arabic?" I asked.

"All around," he said in a tone that warned: no more journalistic probing. This well-travelled, multilingual Israeli was no simple painter. My journalist's instinct told me he was in army intelligence, probably Shin Bet. I had to stop the questions.

At the Bet She'an police station, no one spoke English, so Joseph gave the accident report in Hebrew. Then he called Hertz and explained where they could find the car. He told me he'd stretched the truth: blaming the accident on faulty brakes and omitting the part about my kamikaze driving.

An hour later, Joseph pulled up to an outdoor café overlooking the Sea of Galilee. When we ordered, he insisted I try the local delicacy, St. Peter's fish. The tensions of the accident began to ease with the help of the Carmel wine and lapping of the lake's waves.

With each sip, I drank in more of Joseph's striking features. His skin, a mahogany glow, was dramatically framed by his black beard, thick wavy black hair and straight white teeth.

I pointed to the twinkling lights around the lake. "Kibbutzim?" I asked. Joseph nodded and pointed to the mountains in the distance. "The Golan Heights," he announced. They were a boulderous backdrop, a harsh reminder of spent bullets and seared Syrian tanks.

"The Middle East," I sighed. "So intricate, so complicated . . ."

"It's a deadly puzzle," he added darkly.

A successful journalist, I could easily get the unsuspecting to open their souls. But like a well-trained intelligence officer, he was constructing boundaries I couldn't cross, so I let him guide the conversation. Joseph's exquisite mind captivated me as he talked knowingly about subjects from French films to Indian food to Japanese art. I sat fascinated as he told me about his favorite artists—about Gauguin's childhood in Lima, Caravaggio's mischievous exploits in Malta.

Joseph told me he was about to teach art in a high school in Haifa because he couldn't stomach the business of selling his paintings anymore. "I'm going to teach classes on perception," he explained. "So many of us see only what we want to see." Again, I suspected his story had stretchmarks, a convenient cover.

When he poured the last glasses of wine, Joseph told me why he had decided to leave London. "Whenever I painted, I found myself looking out my studio window at the heath, thinking about my family and friends here," he said slowly. "I was feeling cut off from my source, from this," he said, making a sweeping gesture over the lake. "That's why I came home. This land is in my blood. Transfusions don't work. I know, I tried."

The wine bottle emptied, our dinner finished, Joseph looked at me across the table. "I'm glad I stopped on the road so our two worlds could meet." This was a special man from a complicated land, and I wanted him. I didn't know who Joseph really was, and I knew he couldn't tell me. But the fire inside him made other men seem half-alive. This was an Israeli Zorba, a man with passion.

When a Michael Jackson song came on the stereo, I groaned. Joseph asked why and I explained that we had grown up in the same neighborhood, in the same psychiatric supermarket—Lost Angeles. Joseph was curious about my life there. "People agonize about their diets and aerobics classes, whine about their car phones and plastic surgeons." I leaned toward him. "What I like about you Israelis is you don't whine about insignificant things. You're much deeper."

"Don't mistake our neuroses for depth," Joseph answered darkly. "Not all Israelis are the same. Just because we share the same land doesn't mean we share the same emotions." He got up abruptly. "Let's go. I've got to find you a hotel."

We drove from hotel to hotel. Tiberius was full. He headed out of town, down a wooded dirt road to a secluded cluster of cabins huddled by the lake. "Wait here," he said, parking near a horse stable. "The manager's an old friend. He'll arrange something."

He reappeared, grinning. His friend had an empty cabin. We walked to the cabin and he put my suitcase on the big double bed. Then he took my hand and led me back into the night. We walked to the lake shore, the *hamsin* blowing off the Golan Heights.

He slipped off his sandals and waded deep into the water, wave-lets nipping at his shorts. I followed him in, feeling the delicious waters of the Galilee. I edged in farther and farther, lifting my white dress. Together in the lake, we were feeling without touching, speaking without words. Scudding clouds and wind-ripped palms, the air sweet with scents of flaming hibiscus. Perfect.

Joseph drew me close, strong and determined. The water splashed as he clasped my head, raising it to receive his urgent kiss. Our lips met—this felt rare and real and right. I felt his tongue outline my lips, then explore my mouth.

His fingers traced the contours of my breasts, then his hands cupped them, warming them through the wet cotton. He kissed me harder and deeper, pressing me so close, our wet bodies were one. I felt his penis grow harder, bulging against me as we rocked in an embrace. I felt the warmth of his hand as it edged up my leg. I was about to feel this man inside me.

But suddenly, Joseph pulled away and led me gently toward the rocky shore. As we wordlessly splashed our way back, I sa-vored the next scene: making love in the double bed.

When we stood on the cabin's porch, Joseph hesitated. "I want to stay with you tonight, Alana," he said giving me a penetrating look, "but I must return to Haifa. Tomorrow, I won't leave you."

The next morning, I waited on the beach, trying to read. My stomach was growling for breakfast, but I didn't move. Each time the gravel crunched, I searched the road expectantly. Finally, I spotted his Peugeot. "My family delayed me," Joseph explained uneasily. "Sometimes the ropes of tradition bind too tight."

When I asked what he meant, he explained that he was temporarily staying with his parents. He told me that they expected him, the only son, to carry on family traditions. With difficulty, Joseph told me the only time he'd ever seen his elderly father cry was when he announced his engagement to an Irish woman. When he broke it off, his close-knit family acted like a death sentence had been lifted.

With empathy, I told him that my parents also celebrated when my brother broke his engagement to a *shiksa*. So many Jewish parents believe that when a child intermarries, it's like breaking a link in a two-thousand-year-old chain.

Joseph's friend, the manager, came out leading two Arab stallions. We spent the morning galloping through the gentle hills of the Galilee up to the Mount of Beatitudes, for a sweeping view of the lake. When we returned, his friend refused to let us pay for the horses or the cabin.

As we drove off in the Peugeot, Joseph pointed to a stack of CDs and told me to choose. Eric Clapton, Milton Nascimento from Brasil, the Les Têtes Brûles from Cameroon . . . I asked him why there were no Israeli singers. "I don't like them," he replied curtly. Joseph had so many conflicting parts: he could be compassionate, understanding, and intolerant.

We swam in the Jordan and hiked in Tel Dan. We visited the sea grottos of Rosh HaNikra on the Lebanese border. We stopped at a cafe in a Druze village in the Golan Heights. Again, Joseph knew the owner. Even though we ordered only coffee, the owner insisted we feast on hummos, tahina and tabouli. When we left, he refused to accept money.

That evening, we drove to Jerusalem. The steep mountains rimmed the beguiling Valley of Sorek, where Delilah had won Samson's heart. The valley was home for bohemian Israelis—writers and artists.

Joseph had arranged a perfect love nest for my final two days in Israel: a 180-year-old stone house with stunning Arab architecture. It belonged to a sculptor friend who was traveling in Italy. In the living room, with its graceful arches and vaulted ceilings, Joseph sat at the black piano and played Mozart like a professional. I rested on the couch listening and dreaming, wishing this were our home.

When he finished, Joseph got up and gently kissed me, then disappeared into the kitchen. A few moments later, he came out—naked and strikingly handsome. Black hair marched up his broad chest. He was carrying a jar of honey and stood over my head. He dripped long lazy lines of honey into my mouth, and slowly unbuttoned my blouse as he snaked the thick golden syrup down my stomach. He straddled me, and his tongue slowly traced the sweet trail. Then he buried his head between my legs and I felt his tongue tease my clitoris, circling faster, edging me to climax. He stopped, then slower and slower, bringing me down, then up again.

As I savored the wild ride of the senses, I dipped my fingers into the jar and painted his penis with the sticky liquid. As I massaged it harder and faster, I felt his tongue do the same to my clitoris. I moved his penis into my mouth. Sweet and thick, I felt it growing. As I sucked it harder, hungrily, his deep moans appeared to be the countdown to explosion. Then suddenly, he pulled himself up.

Joseph led me to the bedroom and gently laid me on my back. As he crouched over my stomach, I looked up into his eyes, eyes that had seen so much. Then he closed them and burrowed his penis deep inside me, and very slowly moved in and out. Our bodies were undulating as we kissed. I felt as if our very souls were connected.

His pianist's fingers pressed firmly on my clitoris, in crazy, creamy circles. Allegro, adagio, presto, his fingers played me. My every nerve on edge, he pushed me to the precipice. Then he paused. Then again stacatto, thrusting me higher, much higher.

We were breathing in harmony, in flowing rhythm, moving to greater and greater pleasures. The intensity of our passion was much more than exquisite sensual adventure. Our bodies were speaking in movement.

Joseph's face was straining as he pushed inside me. He was on fire. A wildman, he moved harder and harder, urgently, almost violently. Then he pushed my legs behind my head, opening me up wide and entered deep, deep into me.

It was too much. I screamed, unable to hold back. All thinking stopped as waves of orgasm overpowered my mind. My body kept jerking, as we launched off, exploding in unison.

We clung together, our bodies glued with sweat and honey.

I felt him stroking my hair. I looked at him and started translating what my body had just said. "I don't want to leave you. I don't want to lose you . . ." He put his fingers on my lips and silenced them. His face told me he was struggling with his feelings.

Jerusalem's magical light smiled on us as we spent the day in the garden. Still and hot, it was filled with a tangle of jasmine and lilies of the valley. Joseph was sketching, but wouldn't show me his work. We tried prolonging the day. We both knew I was leaving the next afternoon, back to Paris and more assignments. I was always on the road, a bedouin roaming the world's airports, passport bulging with visas. When intimacy with a man became a possibility, my editor would order me onto another jet plane, another city, another hotel.

On our final night, we showered together. Joseph tenderly soaped each of my breasts. Each leg, each arm. He made me feel soft, a sensuous female. He looked at me and I smiled—I was naked and wet and I loved it. Stripped of my briefcase and beeper, I felt happy. Joseph made me want to miss my plane.

He twisted the long gold chain I always wore and quizzically held up the locket. It was a gift from my grandfather to my grandmother, I explained. I showed him the line from the Song of Solomon inscribed inside the locket. Joseph translated the Hebrew words: "My beloved is mine, and I am his . . ."

The phrase was perfect. I lifted off the necklace. "It's what I feel for you. Keep it. Whenever you see the necklace, I'll be with you." I tried placing it over his head, but he refused to take it.

At thirty-four, I'd spent too many years searching for love, had frequent flier romances with a United Nations of men. But I was no longer enjoying the quest. Between the adventures and the affairs came deep loneliness. My diaries were filled with pages of yearning. They read like an echoing void.

Joseph led me out of the shower, dripping, to the bed. We made wet, gentle love, bodies speaking slowly, savoring the sensations. He kissed every contour. Hungrily, we explored each other. Joseph's greatest joy was giving me pleasure. He played my body, gently touching it like he'd been given a music score to my most sensitive secret spots, the paths to my pleasure.

I'd never been with a man like Joseph Hassan. Suddenly it all became clear—I'd be stupid to leave him. Stupid to escape on a jet plane. "I'm canceling my flight," I blurted out. "I'll ask for a leave. I want to stay with you."

Joseph stiffened and sat upright. "Some boundaries can never be crossed," he said, looking troubled. "I live in a world you'd never fit in. I'd never make you happy, not here," he said, looking straight through my eyes. "Love like ours must have a beginning, a middle and an end. Take that plane tomorrow, Alana."

I took the necklace off again and placed it over his head. "Keep the necklace," I said, unable to look at him. "Keep it and remember my love."

He cuddled me in his arms. I felt his tears against my face. At first I thought they were mine, and soon they were.

Aroused by the golden shafts of dawn, I reached over for Joseph. His side of the bed was empty. Groggily, I surveyed the room. I shuffled into the living room. I found his sketchpad under the jar of honey on the piano. Inside was the drawing he'd made in the garden. Joseph really was an artist. He'd seen inside me, capturing the Alana I'd hidden from myself.

Then a note slipped out. I tensed as I read it:

Alana, the words of the Song of Solomon are true: "My beloved is mine and I am his." But it continues, "until the day breaks and the shadows flee away . . ."

Well, the day has broken and with a crying heart, I've fled

away, back to my world. The more I know you, the more I want
to cut the ropes of tradition, but I can't. I made that decision
when I returned to Israel.

My Lady Pirate, my love will always travel with you. Each
time I see your necklace, I'll remember our love.

I read his note again. And again. Maybe I was too direct. Maybe
the instant intimacy scared him. Maybe my talk of love came too
soon.

I couldn't lose him like this. I telephoned Information in Haifa.
No listing for Joseph Hassan. I searched my mind for clues. How
do you trace someone in army intelligence? I called the army
spokesman in the government press office. No luck. I called every
high school in Haifa—Joseph Hassan wasn't teaching art anywhere. I'd find him and no matter what his world was, I'd share it
if he'd let me.

I telephoned the Paris bureau and asked for a few more days.
No dice. They needed me for a page-one story. I'd give Joseph
time to think and cool off. He'd contact me. He had my card. He'd
miss me.

After three weeks of silence, I realized I wasn't going to hear
from Joseph. I tried to forget him, but after another two weeks, I
felt even emptier. The echoing void grew unbearable. I had to return to Israel.

I rented another Hertz car and traveled the same road. Past
Jericho, past the ravine where we'd accidentally met. As I approached the Sea of Galilee, I felt strangely elated. After many
wrong turns, I finally found the cabins. I waited until the manager
finally showed up. He was my only link to Joseph.

"I'm looking for your friend, Joseph Hassan," I told the squat
man with the dark mustache. "He brought me here five weeks
ago."

"Joseph?" The manager looked confused.

"You gave us your horses."

His face lit up. "Oh, Yusef Hassan. He's from my village—
Shvar'am."

"Where's the village?"

"Near Haifa," the manager answered. "Drive on the road to the north." He carefully wrote the directions—in Arabic.

"An *Arab* village?" I asked the manager. He nodded.

I was stunned. So that's why Joseph, or Yusef, disappeared. He wasn't in army intelligence. He was an Israeli, but an Israeli Arab. No wonder he didn't tell me—he knew I'd be afraid to love him.

It took over an hour to reach Shvar'am. The village tumbled over the hills terraced with gnarled, twisted old olive trees. The clanking of sheep's bells greeted me. I drove past men washing their feet outside the mosque.

There it was, a white stone house cut into the crest of a hill. Yusef's home, his world of tradition. Outside, an old man in a flowing white *keffiyah* was puffing on a waterpipe. "*Salaam aleikum,*" I said in halting Arabic. "Yusef Hassan?"

"Welcome," he said, graciously ushering me into the courtyard. A woman, her faced lined and worn, was crouched over a kerosene stove, plucking feathers from a goose. She smiled, offered me a stool and hurried into the house.

"I am the father of Yusef," said the old man proudly, as he sat beside me. "You wait. He comes from teaching soon."

The old woman came out of the house and offered me a tray of pastries. She was followed by a delicate-looking teenager, with almond-shaped brown eyes and black hair. The girl poured me a demitasse of thick Turkish coffee.

"She's Nabila," said Yusef's father with a great grin. "And tonight feast for all the village. Feast for Nabila and Yusef. You welcome."

As the girl bent to refill my cup, I sucked in my breath. A necklace fell out of her bodice. My necklace. She caught my gaze and smiled sweetly as she played with the long gold chain.

NIGHTHAWKS

FROM A PAINTING BY EDWARD HOPPER

Erik Jendresen

The smoke kept coming out of her mouth. Just kept coming while she talked and the counterboy nodded. While he clamped a clean ashtray over the one she used—while she smiled and told him that she only smoked three cigarettes a day and this was her last, so he needn't give her another ashtray—the smoke kept coming out of her mouth like the words.

When there was no more smoke, she glanced at the man beside her, then brought the cigarette to her mouth with her hand flat, fingers straight and spread except for the two that held the cigarette. She drew on it casually, then parted her lips and let the smoke come out again—all by itself. She closed her eyes and then inhaled through her nose and the smoke followed. Three cigarettes a day and each one counted. This time she blew the smoke out—turning her head slightly—like you blow on a dandelion or an ember, steadily . . .

Two cars drove by, took the corner one after another. I felt the headlights through the glass and watched the gleam move along around the stainless steel coffee urns and the varnished mahogany counter edge and the low window ledge of tile, yellow and sea green.

The boy changed ashtrays for her again like he thought it would get him somewhere; she smiled at him but frowned slightly when she stubbed out her cigarette, the last. All gone.

The man beside her said, "Is that yesterday's last or the first of three?"

She smiled and said, "Neither."

"You're cheating," he said.

She nodded slowly and lifted a matchbook from the counter. She looked at it because it was something to do.

The counterboy did the shell trick with the ashtrays again and cleaned out the dirty one. He caught me watching the two of them. He knew what I was doing.

Watching them like a hawk. All of us nighthawks here at this time, so late. I will be up tonight until the planet spins back into the light. Here on the second stool from the left with my back to the window on Greenwich Avenue. I'll follow the woman with the red hair and the red dress and the man with the fedora and the long sharp nose, follow them into their night.

She likes him because he walked into the place and sat next to her without hesitating. Likes him because he drinks coffee late and because he's the cat that swallowed the canary.

They got up to leave then, an act so clearly understood, so *tacit* that it should have clued me, but I missed its meaning only to feel it later on. The half-dollar did the coin wobble on the countertop. The counterboy nodded, and the woman lifted the black cloth coat from the last stool beside her and they passed behind me and out.

Arm in arm they walk like an old-fashioned couple, till he takes his hand out of his pocket and lets it hang and her hand slides down the length of his arm and grasps it.

The rented room is half a block from here; up three flights, and they are in. The door closes and he flicks the lock.

But I didn't watch this, I just saw it. I pushed my thick white cup to the inside edge of the counter and the counterboy who wasn't a boy at all—he must have been forty—he took it and filled it from the urn. His reflection was a thin white line on the polished stainless. He slid the cup back at me—

"Some guys . . ." he said.

But it was too hot to drink. I stared at the black shiny surface and the tiny steam fissures . . .

She leans forward now, hands on the thick-painted white windowsill, feet spread slightly on the hardwood, head down, and the air pushes the curtains framing the open sash and her hair hanging in simple long waves. Eyes closed she listens to the New York nightvoices asking, answering, bitching and wailing, moving all over down there. Feels the air on her arms and the back of her neck and down her spine, and thinking about it, shivers. Opens her eyes and sees her small breasts, her spread thighs, and him, sitting on the bed edge, in his pants still, suspenders shrugged off, barefoot, elbows on knees, hair shining, looking at what she is showing him and . . . remembering.

My fingers tightened around the handle of my cup. I had not known that it was like this. I had thought they only just . . . when did she lose her clothes? I had not seen her take them off. Or did he take them off? Where are they? Over there, by the door: the red dress and stockings, the brassiere . . . Pay attention, I told myself, because he is remembering.

It's safe for him now; he can remember because he is with her—not like the other times, the all-the-times that he could not let himself think about her because of what the memories did to him, the way his mind would tense, cringing from the pain of missing her.

There were also the times when he wanted to hurt, to see if he really felt what he feared to feel—this man who lived by his wits. When those times came he would sit, staring at nothing, alone—he had to be alone—and try to remember Chicago—Chi like a loaded .38 at his temple. But he could never pull the trigger on the memory, so he would wince and lift himself from some chair and smoke a cigarette and think about anything.

Like the marriage that she is trying to make work on account of she should.

But now. Now Chicago is in the room with them. And San Francisco and the little harbor town across the bay where they ate breakfast. And all the other places that he had forgotten because he couldn't hold on to them. She smiles at him, upside down, looking up from under her arm, her hair hanging down to touch the floor there by the window, and he smiles back at her.

He moves behind her now, and her lips part when his hand snakes around her side and presses into her belly. The other hand slides up her spine to the back of her neck, back of her head, pushing it down so that he knows she will see the hand on her belly move between her legs and

"Oh . . ."

The hand that has loved her and known her like her own—finger sliding into the slipperiness between the warm lips—starts their hearts racing, her breath coming in short exhalations whimpering pleasure and relief in every breath. And the fleshy place behind his knuckle is moving in her time, pressing—

Her body gasps. And the hand moves, the finger draws out wet from the lips between her legs and up her belly leaving a long musk moist trail between her breasts to the hollow at the base of her—

"Love," breathes in her ear and she shivers.

—throat, to her chin, lower lip, and she takes the finger into her mouth, in her teeth, and the touch of her tongue makes him laugh there at her ear.

Tasting herself on his fingertip, she pushes against the windowsill, feels his cock behind the rough wool trouser fabric pressing into her ass.

"Fuck me," she says not before his other hand pulls down the zipper and flicks out the button and the trousers fall in wrinkles down to his ankles.

I brought the thick cup to my lips, but the coffee was warm. The counterboy watched me over the edge of a newspaper folded to the races at Aqueduct. Maybe he'd give me another. I closed my eyes and rubbed them—an instant only—

Inside. From behind he's inside of her. Her feet are planted firmly apart now. Deep inside, he is a part of her own wet pink flesh. Sliding back . . .

She knows that when you touch yourself it isn't like when another touches you because you can feel both the touching and the being touched, but with him it's like fucking herself, she can feel him so fully. He loves her like she would love herself—

"Ah . . . don't . . . stop . . . don't . . . stop—"

His hands on her hips, holding her still, sometimes moving her, he touches her so deep—well, it's a place hidden so far up inside of her that it is the unreachable epicenter of her self and the secret *of her femaleness and it has only to be touched—by him—to send her, all of her, there. She is going there now, not out of her body, but in. Her eyes half-closed like the eyes of memory. He grows inside of her, or she tightens around him, the sensation is the same.*

The fresh coffee stung my lip and burned the tip of my tongue, dammit all. Sure, he'd refilled it, but I wasn't paying attention. It was getting late and I noticed my hand tremble as it came away from the cup.

For her, the giddy spinning convulsions of orgasm never mattered when she was with him because it is and always has been and always will be love which stimulates her with every sliding frictive instant—every frozen moment filled full of him. And she always came with him, and it had never been an end, but the moment that signaled the beginning of the next time they would love—it had always been this way because she had come the first time he touched her: long ago in a dark room at her place, back from the theater before they said goodnight. Kissing, she thought that she trembled, but it was he. He trembled when they kissed, though his hand was certain and firm between her legs through the fabric of her skirt, his middle finger moving—the length of it pressing flat—not penetrating—against the curve of her cunt—the fleshy part behind the knuckle massaging her with such unconscious knowledge that she gasped at the miracle of it. She came in an instant; he held her so tight.

My hand closed in a nervous fist on the varnished countertop. A squad car prowled up Greenwich Avenue.

He pulls back, slides out from her. He glistens in the moonlight at the window, and she stands. He turns her and they kiss, his wet cock pressing up against her soft belly. Her hands explore the surface of his back, lean and tough, and down to his ass as she sinks to her knees and his penis points the way up her body, between her breasts; then she takes it in her hand, the unpainted fingernails of her middle finger and thumb just meeting, pulls her head back and fills her mouth with it. The black-and-white car creeps slowly by on the street below while she concentrates with animal-like preoccupation on the head of his cock. Her full, so red lips pull back as her head moves in trancelike motion and her hand follows, slipping moistly along the length of it.

The first time he remembers—an icy day when they were alone in the big quiet house, the radiators ticking and pinging, warm and dry, her baby asleep. What had started on the couch with only their hands touching, fingers exploring fingers, became a standing kiss that would not end. Then another room. And she had reached down and felt him below his thin leather belt and had pushed him gently back and down into the overstuffed embroidered chair and had gone to work with her lips and tongue and that hand . . .

The one that had picked up the matchbook. I should have known. It began to make sense to me then, the way he came into the place and sat beside her and the high-tension familiarity of it and—the matchbook—it was old and worn, wasn't it? Sure it was. And all this while I thought they only—

But he is still remembering. She is on her knees on the hardwood floor, his cock in her mouth, in and out, his head thrown back, breathing fast—he is remembering that first time—how when he came she swallowed him whole like that was what she did it for—give it to me, let me drink it, she had seemed to say, because I love you and I want everything of you.

She pulls back suddenly, unsheathing him wet, and shakes her head side to side to side; her auburn hair whips across her mouth and clings to her lips and his hand is on her cheek, sliding back under the hair sticking to her mouth and pulling it back behind her ear, his hand behind her head, pulling her up to his need to kiss her. So she stands and rubs the length of her body against the length of his clean wet cock and he runs his tongue up under her lips. Lifts her, a hand under each spread thigh, and slides her down onto him, transfixes her smoothly, and carries her like that—high, her hands on his shoulders, his mouth at her neck—to the wall by the bed. Her ankles cross behind him, her thighs ride on his hips.

Like at his place, that night back from the train station, walking in and dumping the bags and pressing her, fucking her, high up against the front door before she even had the chance to look around.

His body holds her there, nothing else, hard against the wall and his hands take hers and raise them high and apart like Mary Magdalen crucified. Palm to palm.

There was something about their hands that I did not want to

know, but I was long past controlling myself. I pushed the hat back
from my forehead, felt the sweatband stick, and tugged a paper
napkin from the shiny dispenser. The counterboy started watching
me then.

"Tell me everything," she whispers.

*"It's like creation," he breathes. "Like a plow rutting through
the dewiest darkest soil of the earth. And you and I are the same,
we're the male and female that split from the one, and we're des-
tined to live apart and come together, and come together when the
Sun and the Earth tell us to." He kisses her against the wall. "Did
you know that?"*

*She nods and unlocks her ankles and lowers her legs and he
lifts her up and off of him. She puts her hands against his chest
and pushes him back to the bed, gives him a shove and his legs
buckle and he falls back on the knobby white bedspread. She stands
there at the edge of the bed and he can see the hair between her
legs is wet, actually glistening with pendant drops of dew that will
taste like sweat-salt. As she puts one knee on the bed, then the
other, straddling him, taking his straining erection in her hand,
he remembers the clean musk fresh taste of her—*

*Fist around his cock, she lowers herself over the end and off
again, on . . . off . . . on, rubbing him against her clitoris, using
him with childlike indulgence, then in—all the way—to touch that
place . . .*

I swung quarter round on the stool and got up, nerves quivering with caffeine, and pushed through the yellow door with the
window in it—bathroom in the back. I closed the door and found
the light switch that also started up a ceiling ventilator fuzzy with
dark gray dust moss. The palms of my hands cooled against the
white tiles.

Back at my stool, my coffee cup was gone. I gave the counterboy the sign and he filled a fresh one. I would have it with a cigarette, see, because they weren't going to stop and I had to see it
through.

"Waiting for someone?" he said. He couldn't hide the suspicion,
well, the uneasiness in his voice.

"Sort of."

Right where I left them. He's on his back and she's riding him fast. From her waist up she could be dancing—but a primitive, lazy-necked, closed-eyed, smiling dance like they dance in the islands . . .

There is an island in the dream they share—well, a sort of place with a terrace of terra-cotta tiles and a low brick-latticed railing facing on a western sea vista because the sun is always setting when they think about it. There are tall cool drinks in their hands and an almost grown daughter of hers—all of this in a memory of the future—

She falls forward suddenly in giddy exhaustion, her hands landing deep in the mattress on either side of his head, her hair falling into his face, strands of it sticking to the sweat on her brow. She stares into his blue eyes. And he knows that she sees everything there is about him. Every thought and feeling and purpose, everything that's genuine and everything that's false, all the guilt and all the innocence.

"I love you . . . for the right reasons," she said to him once, long ago by the captured candlelight of a cut-glass globe on a restaurant table in Philadelphia. And he cannot forget it. Because he has been loved before by women who needed to love him or women who saw only the romance of his desperate life and his tenderness and his youthful masculinity and wanted him to love them. But to be loved by a woman such as she . . . this uncompromising Southern-born, Boston-bred female who understands things that most people never think of . . . he does not need more than that—more than her love—or so he tells himself when he is alone and without her because he has to be and cannot bring himself to entertain other women in his bed or his thoughts.

But she knows all this, too. She knows too much. And he lifts himself deep into her. She opens her eyes and smiles down at him. He pulls her to him and rolls over on top of her, pulls himself out of her and kisses her breasts, massages her nipples, one after the other, between the tip of his tongue and the roof of his mouth. Down her flat belly . . . yes, he remembers the taste and the florid wetness that makes his lips and chin shine as he licks and tickles the lips of her cunt and presses his tongue up against her clitoris. His eyes look up from under his brows at her stomach rising and falling

in uneven breaths, and quivering now, she is gasping, making
mmm *sounds.*

I struck a match and set fire to the end of a dry cigarette. The
tobacco sparked and crackled when I drew on it. It even tasted
dry. It had been hours now, and I knew that the old counterboy
was worried. He would have talked to me if he wasn't. He thought
I was in my own world and it was a dangerous place to be. But it
wasn't my world at all. He must have been a simple man.

She is coming so close now, and he grins there between her legs.
What could please him more than moving this woman he loves?
If every day he could bring her down there, grasp her by the soul
and guide her to that long moment of involuntary ecstasy and all
the little temblors that his touch played into her, bring her daily
to that place inside of themselves. All despair ends there, vanishes
in the lifetime they live together on nights like this—mornings and
late afternoons past.

"I love you so much," she says like the very first time. It always
sounds the same and it always means as much. And he moves
slowly up from inside her thighs and lays his body down with care
along the length of her—

Plunges his cock as deep as it will go. And she inhales his own
breath through her smile as all of her strength brings itself to bear,
and she tightens herself around him and over him. His arms
around her back pull her to him, almost inside him.

Now.

The ash fell from my cigarette and broke on the shining countertop. The old cigarette was still between my fingers but there
was nothing left of it.

"Are you . . . okay, mister?"

I looked up from behind my hand. Did I say something?

Her eyes are closed so tight. She is holding the feeling with all
her might. It's the beginning, remember.

"Are you all right?" he says, so close to her face. She opens her
eyes, glistening with delight. "Hmm" comes from the back of her
throat, a one-syllable laugh because he always says that. Then
her mouth opens in a soundless "ah" as he pushes himself in again
and his pelvis presses hard against hers, then away, then once

more as he comes liberally, smoothly with a fast hot breath—a shuddering contraction of every muscle in his long shining body—and keeps moving in ever easier smooth strokes. Buries his face in the hair next to hers and breathes the heat they have made and the smell that still clings to a blouse of hers that he keeps in his closet back home.

I moved the ashtray away with the back of my hand, likewise the ash that rolled, breaking up as it neared the edge of the counter. I blew the rest of it away like you blow on a candle, and wiped the ash off the side of my—

And that's when he looks at her hand. Lying palm up by her head. While he moves slowly, tenderly still inside of her, he kisses her lips and the eyelids she closes for him, and takes her hand in his and looks at it. She smiles up at him and they roll onto their sides while he looks at the too familiar pattern of lines—life, heart, love . . .

"Do you want some breakfast?"

The light had changed. Like a child, sometimes the night grows into day before you know it. I wasn't hungry, I even wondered if I ever would be. But I knew it would make him feel better if I said yes, so I nodded. They would be eating together soon now, this man and this woman whose palms matched, lines mapping the same course, changing as the other changed, promising that they would meet again and always on nights when the hawks watch the doves . . .

"Forget it," I said to the counterboy. Because maybe they'd come back and I never wanted to see them again, though I knew that I was stuck with them. The memory of them. They knew about memories. Sometimes they're all you've got.

11:30 P.M.—
SATURDAY NIGHT

Marsha Powers

She unlocked the front door and they stepped inside. Her living room was reduced to an eerie grayish blur of odd shapes and forms. She had left the nightlight on because she didn't want to come home to a dark empty house. It wasn't living alone, per se, that bothered her. She just didn't like sleeping alone—at least not every night. Could he sense that? She wondered.

Possibly he thought she was on the prowl, like a cat in heat. After all they had just met. A few hours ago they were virtual strangers. The very idea of asking an attractive man home for a drink excited her at the party. So she did it.

Since her divorce, she had buried herself in her work as a commodities trader for one of the biggest firms in town, and busied herself with the details of decorating and furnishing her new home. She suddenly became aware that she was driving herself so hard because she was unfulfilled. A long list of important clients and attractive plant stands did not fill her needs. The time had come to make contact with men again.

She'd been avoiding the dreaded necessity of dating. She felt dating was akin to being on audition, trying out for the role of the girl who is brought home to mother, the demure, sweet, potential babymaker. With the divorce she relinquished that role. Now she was looking for a series of one-night stands, her leading man changed at her bidding.

She flipped on the overhead lights, dropped her keys on the hall table and walked across the plush carpet to the well-stocked mirrored bar.

"Please come in," she said with an alluring tone.

He followed her inside and stood stiffly, not totally at ease. He quickly assessed his surroundings: airy, albeit a bit fancy, clean and well-maintained. He noted the flowery framed prints on the walls. She likes flowers, he thought and stored the information in his mental likes/doesn't like, file. The women he dated were always impressed with his thoughtfulness.

"What would you like to drink?" she asked and looked directly into his eyes. Hers were pale blue, his were deep brown. Hers reminded him of bleached denim. He decided that she had pretty eyes. He filed that too, women liked to be complimented on their eyes. Windows to the soul and all that.

"Wine," he answered. If they went to bed he didn't want to battle the effects of hard liquor depleting his energy.

"Make yourself comfortable." She fluffed the pillows on the silk-covered sofa. She had ordered it especially for the room. She loved its rich peach color, accented in white and deep navy-blue piping. The matching loveseat and chair were arranged in a semicircle, to give the effect of space.

While she poured wine into crystal goblets, he moved around the room. The temperature was stiffling. Why do women have to keep the thermostat at sauna levels? he wondered. Tugging at his collar he said, "You have a lovely home."

"Thank you." She smiled. "Feel free to look around."

He was surprised that he felt relaxed among all the finery. Due to his size he usually felt like a bull in a china shop around precious objets d'art. Somehow she had accommodated for that. He was impressed.

He gravitated to her entertainment center like a little boy in a toy store. The state-of-the-art equipment covered most of the north wall; a high-tech CD player was housed in an expensive walnut cabinet, next to a wide-screen TV. Her CDs were shelved in a rolling drawer under a dust cover.

She noted that he stepped carefully, as if he feared soiling her carpeting. The carpet was a soft virgin wool, an impractical off-white. She loved the way it contrasted with the navy-and-peach couch, and she enjoyed the feel of the luxurious pile beneath her bare feet.

Her extensive library of leatherbound books attracted his attention. He believed looking at a woman's books was a way of cutting through the icing to the cake below. Scanning the titles, and recognizing several, he was pleased to see that they shared some of the same favorite authors. He saw a copy of Erica Jong's *Fear of Flying*. A term from the book tripped into his mind, "the zipless fuck." He recalled it meant strangers having a passionate, impersonal encounter. Suddenly, he wondered if that was what she had intended for him. Was he going to be her zipless fuck?

"How about some cheese and crackers?"

"Yes, that sounds nice," he answered.

Normally he wasn't a nosy guy. Then again, she seemed proud of the place and had invited him to look around; the least he could do was give it the nickel tour.

He studied her paintings and realized that he didn't have anything hanging on the walls of his home. In fact, his walls were bare. He meant to do more personalizing, but there didn't seem to be much point. He had lived there for ten years, but it still had the appearance of temporary quarters. He regarded his bachelorhood as a way station, the time between college and real life. He hadn't meant to stay single so long, but getting the stores started and devoting himself to their success had been his main priority.

He told himself, and anyone who asked, that he hadn't found the right woman yet. The thought had occurred to him that he had found the right woman, in fact, probably more than once, but because he was too self-absorbed and preoccupied he had lost her.

He had had a lot to deal with, he rationalized. His career-ending injury and early retirement from football had thrown his future into a turmoil. Opening the stores was his salvation. Otherwise, he might have hit the bottle, or worse. He had seen it happen to a lot of guys.

Standing at the bar, she noticed him looking at her Renoir and

Monet reproductions. She hoped he didn't think she was pretentious, or so shallow as to pretend the prints were originals.

"Did you do the interior decoration? It's beautiful."

"Yes," she answered smiling at his awed tone. "Thanks."

His compliment sounded sincere, but she wondered if he was the kind of man who felt that while decorating was an acceptable job for a woman, the male-dominated business of buying and selling commodities was not. Her ex-husband had been threatened and jealous of her success. She knew men used the ability to make money as a measurement of intelligence and masculinity. Women who made large sums of money jarred their scoring system.

"I have an eclectic collection of CDs to choose from, if you'd like," she called out as she walked into the kitchen.

In a few minutes she heard one of her favorite albums, Willie Nelson's *Stardust*. "We seem to have the same musical taste," he said over the music.

"I think he sold over a million copies of that album. It appears that we're in a large group," she answered. It wasn't that she was insulted by his pointing out their similarities in taste, she thought; she just didn't expect they would have any in common. At the party he said he had been a professional ball player until his career-ending injury and subsequent retirement. He told her he owned and operated a chain of sports equipment stores. What she knew about sports couldn't fill a thimble, she mused. Jocks were not her forte.

"Your wine," she said as she handed him the glass. He took it and followed her to the sofa. She sat on one side and he sat on the other facing her.

"As far as cocktail parties go—Marie's was really very enjoyable," she said, before she sipped her wine.

"Have you known her long?" he asked stretching out his legs to get comfortable. He wanted to take off his shoes and loosen his belt, but most of all he wanted to tug off his tie. He'd been wearing it since 6 o'clock and the damn thing felt like a noose. He almost missed her answer.

"Yes, we went to school together," she said nodding.

"Hunter?" He hoped he remembered correctly.

"Yes," she said, smiling broadly.

Her gums were pink and healthy, he noted. Then his eyes focused on her blue hair ribbon. If he knew how she would react, he would have untied it and kissed her on the neck.

He was staring at her hair. Was there something wrong? she wondered. She pushed her shiny brown hair over her shoulders and then asked him, "Would you mind if I change the music?"

"No, not at all," he said agreeably. He watched her cross the room. The fabric of her dress clung to her as she walked. He wondered if women picked out dresses that clung on purpose? Did the manufacturers design them that way? Like a planned defect?

He loved looking at women. He loved their differences. And their similarities. His eyes stayed on her as she moved.

Her smooth legs were well-formed, not spectacular, but she did have tight calf muscles and nice ankles. She still had her high heels on. He wondered if she was going to keep them on in bed? Was she into kinky sex? The idea sort of turned him on. He liked high heels. The women who worked in his stores wore athletic shoes. He missed high heels. The sound they made on the floor. The way they made a woman's ass higher when she walked.

It was her swaying ass that had first attracted him at the party. He liked the way she walked. He wondered if she was doing it on purpose or if it was her natural walk? He found his eyes seeking her as she mingled with the other guests. He had asked Marie for an introduction.

"I hope you like jazz," she said as she sat down again.

"I do," he said leaning back into the sofa enjoying the music. She moved closer.

They talked easily about books, and movies. She said she wanted to see *Jurassic Park* as soon as it got to town. "I loved the book," she said and then smiled.

"It's a date, we'll go together. That is, of course, if you want to?" He hesitated and looked at her.

"I'd like that," she said, shocked that she meant it.

They chatted about work and the schools they attended. Traded stories about their background and families. While the whole time they were each thinking about having sex.

He told her he was an only child. She said he was probably spoiled. He said he wasn't, but that he'd like to be. He smiled when he said that.

She told him a funny story about her older brother. He heard affection in her voice when she spoke of her family.

He asked her if she had ever been married? Her eyes cast down, and she said, "I'm recently divorced . . . In fact, that was why I was at the party. Marie thought it was time for me to get out and meet new people. Socialize."

"Was Marie right?" he asked softly.

"Yes," she answered quickly. "I'm glad I went."

"Me too," he said as he debated kissing her. "I'd like to kiss you, may I?"

Sensing that he was unsure, she moved closer and let him caress her. He held her firmly, without aggression. It felt good to have a man's arms around her, to have her arms around a man. Intuition told her he was strong, but now he was gentle with her. Would he be a slow, tender lover? Or fervent, full of heated passion? In the best of worlds, he could be both. She told herself not to expect too much. The first time with someone could be awkward and frustrating. Then again, she corrected herself, it could be exhilarating and wonderful.

He tilted her face up and kissed her lips. His mouth tasted faintly of wine. She wondered if her mouth did too.

Running his tongue along her mouth, he outlined her lips, softly at first, then with purpose. She felt herself moisten as she imagined his tongue on her flesh, parting her, licking her. Softly, then with purpose.

Her fingers fanned across his back. Pushing herself into him. Pulling him to her. She was aware of her need to feel the warmth of his body against her own. He gently caressed her. Holding her close, continuing the kiss, till she was breathless. She closed her eyes and let herself be filled with the heady sensation. She felt she was parched with longing, and then suddenly, she was being quenched by the mere touch of a man.

It didn't matter that he was a stranger. That made it more exciting. Not knowing his next move. That was why she asked him home. To be made love to in a way she couldn't anticipate. To explore her sexuality and not be expected to perform in an accepted fashion. Toward the end of her marriage, lovemaking with her ex felt preprogrammed and predictable. There was nothing predictable about this man.

Feeling her relax in his arms, he continued to kiss her. She seemed almost hungry for his lips. Trying to recall if she had said how long she had been divorced, he replayed pieces of their conversation in his head. It was obvious she had gone without sex for a while. A jolt of pure happiness surged through him. Meeting a horny divorcée at a party wasn't exactly like winning the lottery, but it came close.

With each kiss she loosened her muscles, relying on his strong shoulders to keep them upright. He liked that. She may make a good living, he told himself, but she needed a man. He could tell by the way she was clutching him, and holding on for all she was worth.

He knew he could push her down on the sofa and undress her, but he didn't want to rush and chance ruining the moment.

He was content to hold her and kiss her and hear her purr in his arms. For now. Feelings, scents, and senses collided in his brain and body at high speed. No one cohesive thought registered; instead, he felt a barrage of pleasure and excitement. He knew he could sleep with her. And he knew he would enjoy it. She responded to his touch and gave back in equal measure. He wondered if she would be an imaginative and able lover. He wanted to find out.

His hands mapped her body, sending off impulses of newly explored flesh through his fingers with a vibration of discovery and conquest. Each inch of her was an adventure.

She was trim, not quite skinny. Subtle curves and graceful arches, like a ballerina. Far from an hourglass figure, but pleasing all the same. And she had a soft, throaty, sexy voice.

He had had to strain at the party to hear everything she was saying. He recalled that she didn't throw her head back and roar with laughter at his jokes, or use any profanity when they talked. She was a real lady, in the best sense of the word. There was nothing showy or obvious about her.

Up close, his nostrils detected a flowery fragrance. Some

women doused themselves in perfume, not her. Trying to associate the scent, he settled on roses. If they slept together, he decided he'd send her some. Usually, a small bouquet was a sure way of getting asked back for seconds.

She reclined on the sofa in a supine position opening her arms to him. He covered her body and began kissing her throat and the nape of her neck. She allowed herself to be swept away in the moment, aware of the pleasure. Breathing in his aftershave and musky male scent, she melded her body to his and let out a soft groan of sensual delight.

Her pulse was racing. He could feel it pounding under his tongue. He let his tongue trace the pale blue vein that ran along her throat to her chest. She offered herself up to him, and he began unbuttoning her dress. He heard his own heartbeat hammering in his head as he kissed her exposed warm pink skin.

Seeing her seminude body beneath him, his brain absorbed a series of random images. Flat stomach, full, round breasts, with a hint of nipple pushing through her lace bra. He figured her for a runner, or a work-out junkie.

A vision of her naked and sweating invaded his gaze. He felt himself respond to his mind's image.

Leaning down he covered her breasts with his mouth. Teasing her nipples with his tongue, flicking them till they responded. She moaned and arched her back. He shifted to obtain a direct contact position. He was hard and straining against his pants. He bent his head and sucked on her breasts again. Lifting his head he saw his saliva glistening on her erect nipples. She clung to him, breathing in short gasps, as she rubbed herself against his hardness.

Years slipped away. Suddenly, he was a teenager again. Hormones rampaging through him, consumed with the ache of his erection. Necking, groping, so turned-on he was totally absorbed with lust, as he dry-humped his girlfriend on her parents' sofa, while they slept upstairs. He remembered the frenzy, the almost, but not quite, unbearable pain of being denied. Then he recalled how excited he would become. Getting so close, and being held at bay. His penis felt like it would explode.

He thought he had lost that level of excitement, as he gained entry to the many women who had followed his high school sweetheart. His labored breathing and heightened arousal brought it all back. Instantly, he experienced an exquisite flood of memory.

He kissed her deeply. Exploring her mouth. Allowing his tongue to thrust where he could not. He pushed his hardness toward her, and clamped his hand on the crotch of her panty hose. She opened her legs wider and put her hands over his, pressing him to her. She was wet and getting wetter. Using his fingers and palm he rubbed and massaged her hot mound. Testing, experimenting, watching her face, learning what excited her, what made her quiver.

He ran his free hand over her breasts, cupped them, gently squeezing, watching her moan in delight. He forgot his need, succumbing to hers. He wanted to give her the thrill of an explosive orgasm, and he wanted to watch her while she had it. Her eyes were tightly closed, her mouth was open. The taut skin on her throat and jaw was strained as she gulped air into her lungs.

Abandoning, surrendering, she floated into the pleasure, seeking the joy, allowing herself to be enclosed in the rapture. She felt the jolts of her orgasm. Radiating from her center, spreading through her innermost being. Guttural, animalistic grunts and groans emanated from her chest, as the waves of orgasm rolled and pitched inside her.

Finally, she lay back and tried to compose herself. She grinned. She would have stretched like a cat, if he wasn't still on top of her.

A great sense of relief filled him. He was concerned that he wouldn't be able to stall his own orgasm long enough for her to have one first. Now she had, so he could stop worrying and get on with his own needs.

He stood and took her hand. She followed him willingly to the bedroom. Sure, he thought, she would probably follow him to the edge of her balcony for another head-banger like the last one.

Upon entering the bedroom he enclosed her in his arms and kissed her. It was their first kiss standing up. He noticed that she was shorter than he estimated. He guessed five-feet four. That was great. He felt tall. And strong, and needed, and wanted, and able. A good combination. He released her and began to undress.

His eyes fastened on her. Hunger and sexual arousal filled his gaze. Standing half-dressed, she realized her power over him. Instead of feeling shy and insecure about her nudity, she felt bold and brazen. Thank goodness she had spent time at the gym in preparation for just such an event. She began going to the gym the day her ex-husband moved out. Then she threw out her old nighties and lingerie and spent a small fortune on push-up bras, garter belts, lacy hose, and high heels.

She wrapped her arms around his waist and crushed him to her body in one long, slow, sloppy kiss.

He recoiled from her embrace. Concern that it would be over in a matter of minutes surfaced over his desire. He didn't want their lovemaking to be a series of fumbling grunts and embarrassed apologies.

"Uhh . . . I need a minute to cool down," he pleaded.

"Don't," she said.

Then she kissed him with a passion he would never have guessed she possessed. Her tongue surged deeply into his mouth. Her teeth gently bit into his lower lip. With a wild and urgent need her hands gripped his body, molding herself to him. His breath was harsh and rasping in his throat, as he clutched her hips to his.

Silently, she eased him to the edge of the bed, lightly forcing his shoulders down with just the merest touch of her fingertips, till he was sitting facing her.

She remained standing in the diffused light from the living room, coupled with the moonlight that shone in through the bedroom window. Reaching behind her she untied her satin hair ribbon, letting it fall in a wavy arch to the floor. Her long shining hair cascaded over her shoulders; she shook it out with both hands, aware of his eyes upon her every vixenlike motion.

Posing in front of him, she slowly removed her dress. The creamy blue silk fell from her shoulders. Gradually she slid the dress off till her breasts stood naked before his eyes. With a toss of her hand she threw the dress at him, and a whiff of her perfume sailed across the room.

He tried to reach for her, but she spun away from his grasp. Her eyes met his, with a silent message. But he was too intent on her body to look her in the eyes.

Teasingly she lowered her pantyhose, letting them fall around her ankles. Then she daintily stepped out of them. She was naked except for her filmy bikini lace panties.

Moving to the edge of the bed she reached for his hand. He gave it to her, trancelike, totally mesmerized by her movements. Taking his hand, she slid his fingers under her panties, placing them on her velvety soft opening. His eyes reacted in instant understanding, and so did his fingers as they plunged into her warm milky lips. He groaned with the excruciating excitement that raced through his body.

Suddenly she pulled away. He looked at her dumbstruck and pained. Then he reached for her again.

Slipping beyond his reach she moved behind him. Her hands glided over his shoulders and unbuttoned his shirt. She pressed her naked body on his back in a catlike motion as her hot probing tongue licked his neck and earlobes.

"Please," he said in a strangled voice, "I can't hold off much longer."

"Sssh," she whispered, "we have all night."

Finally she removed his shirt. She flung it across the room and danced around in front of him dangling her breasts in his face. His eyes were fixed on her jiggling rosy-erect nipples.

She reached down to his slacks and opened the belt. While unbuttoning the waistband, she kissed him with promises of ecstasy. Her tongue rolled in and out of his mouth, while her teeth gently chewed and bit as she sucked his lower lip into her mouth. Again, he groaned and reached for her, again she resisted his grasp.

Sliding down along his legs she tugged his pants off, purposely grazing his legs with her breasts. His stiffness strained against his briefs. She lightly stroked it with her fingers through the cotton material.

"Please—I want you . . ." he begged.

Grabbing the elastic band of his briefs she set him free. His hardness sprang out red and swollen. "It's so big and thick," she said in awe as she gripped the shaft tightly in her hand. "I'm going to love having you inside me. To feel you filling me." She blew a stream of hot breath on the throbbing head.

He gritted his teeth, but a small droplet of semen leaked out. It glistened in the light. She bent over and gently rubbed it off.

A deep low growl forced itself out of his mouth. "I want you," he said in an agonized voice. He knew she would eventually submit. In an odd way he was enjoying her game.

She delicately placed both her hands on his muscular chest and pushed till he was lying on his back. Slithering, she crawled up the length of his body. His eyes were fastened on her as she positioned herself over him.

She reached behind him to the nightstand and produced a condom. "Shall I?"

"Please, hurry."

She quietly tore the package and carefully took the condom between her fingers. Then she slowly rolled it over his erection, her palm and fingers caressing his shaft. He groaned. The warmth of her hand and her skilled fingers sent a jolt of pleasure through his genitals.

Very gradually and deliberately, she straddled him. He slid in her and felt enveloped in heat and softness. She sat atop his hips, melding herself into him.

She straightened her back and locked her legs around him. Then she forced her inner muscles to tighten and contract on his throbbing erection. Milking him in heavenly softness.

"Yes!" he screamed out loud. His hands shot out and clutched her hips to his own. The tremors of his ejaculation jerked his body in a spasm of sublime release. His buttocks tightened as he thrust deep inside her, filling her with his heat. His juices rushed out in a torrent. Within seconds he was completely spent.

Instantly he realized she hadn't climaxed, and he felt guilty. "I'm sorry," he said quietly. "I tried to make it last, but you had me so excited I couldn't control myself."

He looked so sheepish and humiliated, she giggled.

"I wanted to give you pleasure," she whispered.

"I have never had an experience like that."

"Well, we'll see what we can do about that next time."

She slithered along his side and stopped at his hip. Raising herself to her knees, she took her long brown hair and wrapped it into a bun at the nape of her neck.

The moonlight bathed her naked body, giving her breasts a

silvery glow. He waited to see what she was going to do next. When she asked him home earlier he had thought he might have a nice one-night stand. He never figured he would be having one of most memorable nights of his life.

Gently stroking his organ, she removed the wrinkled condom. Positioning herself so he could see, she slowly slid a fresh condom on his stiffening cock. Using her tongue and fingers she managed a perfect fit.

Her lips caressed his shaft lovingly. He raised his head so he could watch as she slid his shaft in and out of her mouth, enjoying the sight and the sensation equally.

Holding her lips around the base of his stiffening member, she began to stroke him. She synchronized the rhythm of her mouth and hands to the semi bump-and-grind dance she performed with her ass, which he saw reflected in the mirrored closet. He could almost hear the music.

She cupped his balls, kneading them between her long graceful fingers. His penis immediately responded.

Instantly, he wanted to enter her again, but she wouldn't remove her mouth. He reached for her repeatedly, and still, she didn't stop. Nipping, sucking, and tongue whipping the head of his cock till he was once again in a frenzy of excitement.

"Please! I can't take it . . . !" he warned. The intense pressure and release took him by surprise. He groaned and buckled as he erupted, spurting his juices in exuberance and sublime satisfaction. The thick sperm enveloped his organ in the confines of the condom, wrapping him in his own warmth. When he was soft and there wasn't an ounce left to be pumped from him, she lay contented next to his sweating body.

"Once again I apologize," he said with deep sincerity.

"Don't," she whispered. Then she lightly placed her hand over his mouth to silence him. "The next time you'll last all night."

"Next time!" He laughed. "I hate to break this to you but I'm no kid. I can't promise you a next time."

"Don't be so sure," she said slyly. She ran her hand along the curly black hairs on his chest. They were beaded with sweat droplets, catching the light like tiny prisms.

"How about a shower?" He asked as he kissed her ear.

"I thought you'd never ask." Teasing him, she playfully cupped his balls in her hand and squeezed lightly.

His voice got husky: "I'm asking." He kissed her lips with renewed hunger and longing.

She released him and stretched her arms high over her head, twisting her torso to show off her nudity. Then she turned and smiled a sly grin. Parading into the bath she managed what she thought was a pretty good wiggle. "I'm ready any time you are."

"I don't think I'll be ready for anything." He feigned exhaustion by slumping his broad shoulders back onto the pillows and letting his arms hang uselessly at his sides. "I'm drained."

"I'll tend to your tired body. I have a few tricks up my sleeve," she called back to him as she entered the bathroom.

"You don't have any sleeves. You're bare-ass and beautiful. But no sleeves," he called back.

"That's what you think. Come in here and see." Sitting on the edge of her ceramic bathtub, she placed her right foot on the rim, toe pointed. He stood in the doorway watching. "Why don't you try this sleeve on for fit?" Very seductively she inserted her finger into the swollen red lips of her dripping vagina.

Slowly pushing her finger in and out, circling the petallike folds with her fingers. She opened her legs wider and gasped.

She had never masturbated in front of anyone in her life, yet she felt no embarrassment. Scooping her round breasts in her hands, she crushed them together bringing her mouth to them. Then she licked her button-hard nipples.

Raising her head she met his eyes. His deep brown orbs were fastened to her, watching every movement.

She began caressing herself, rubbing her hands along her finely formed body. Breathing in gulps, as her finger moved purposefully.

Unconsciously he licked his lips and a sweat necklace formed on his forehead. He was amazed at what he was seeing. In fact, he was totally spellbound.

The woman he had pegged as the perfect lady, someone he figured would be too modest to walk around nude in her own home, was putting on a sex show for him, lasciviously pleasuring herself in front of his eyes.

He watched her perform the way a man watches a woman behind a hidden camera. The sounds and sights she offered burned into his brain, scorching his flesh with desire.

She saw his cock bounce and strain forward. That turned her on more. Within moments she was moaning, lost in a sexual fog of gratification. Her eyes glazed over with libidinous delight.

Stretching out as far as she could with her legs open and poised, she inserted two fingers into herself. They both heard the small sucking sounds as she pumped. Pearly white cum trickled along her thigh like opalescent tear drops. Her eyes tightly closed and her jaw clenched. Then she threw her head back and moaned in pleasure as her body quaked in a powerful spasmodic climax.

Her musky nectar dripped from her finger. She held it up for him to see. He swallowed; his throat was raw from his own ragged breathing.

"Nice and warm in here. You're invited to come inside." She smiled wickedly, her bright blue eyes taunting him. She lifted her leg with her hand and opened her secret, most private part for his eyes.

His eyes riveted to her. His chest expanded like a bellows as he inhaled her scent. He didn't want her to stop.

She leaned over and caressed her legs, knowing that with each movement she seemed to be inviting his touch. His deep brown eyes recorded each motion.

Seductively, she ran her finger over one nipple and then the other, until her pink buds practically begged for suckling. Then she licked her own finger slowly, sucking it in her mouth as if it were his cock.

Watching him, smiling cattishly, she opened her legs. Gesturing with her hips in a lusty fashion, she whispered, "It's all for you."

He sank to his knees in front of her. Burying his face in her breasts, he sucked and kissed, as his hands traced every delicious sensation she offered him.

She put her arms around his neck and kissed him with a passion that almost singed his lips. Her tongue found his earlobe. Tracing it with deep breaths she whispered, "Fuck me." He lifted her from the bathtub and carried her back to the bed.

Her legs straddled his hips as he laid her down. He watched

her smooth another condom over his enlarged and erect penis. She was immensely pleased that she had been able to bring him to such passion. Immediately he was inside her, grunting as he ground himself deeper and deeper. She tightened her muscles around him and bucked like a wild horse under her rider. This time he stayed hard until she was breathless and exhausted.

He rolled over and slept. She wondered if she would see him again? And then she wondered if she wanted to? The sex was exhilarating and somewhat empowering. Men did this all the time, she thought. Meet a stranger, bring them home and sleep with them. It was interesting as an experience, but she wasn't sure she wanted to repeat it.

They fell asleep in each other's arms as the dawn's light shone through her curtains. The next day he sent her three dozen roses with his phone number scribbled on the card. She tucked the card into her lingerie drawer.

ESPRESSO AND . . .

Rob Scott

It is a café from the mid-sixties, or from a movie about the mid-sixties, located in a storefront off of a narrow one-way street that is little more than an alley. The furnishings are sparse, small square wooden tables with thick varnished surfaces, matted paintings by local artists on the walls, complete with ludicrously high price tags. The vegetarian and whole-foods menu specials are written in pastel chalk on several strategically placed blackboards, the No Smoking warnings and fire alarm boxes show bright red against the whitewashed walls, with a few voluminous ferns and spider plants hanging in discrete corners. I've just come from the unemployment office, where I have been told yet again that there are no jobs in the area for a Ph.D. in Comparative Literature. They want me to try job training, prepare myself to become a data-entry clerk or a paralegal. I always come here, to this restaurant, when I am depressed, because they have the hottest vegetarian chili in the state, and the staff doesn't hurry you out when you finish. My chili is gone, I'm on my second cup of espresso, and now I sit alone rereading the want ads. Hope springs eternal. The door opens, garish sunlight pours in from the street, and dark blue overalls pass by just barely within my peripheral vision. I glance up and am struck by the way she moves, the way she holds her arms folded across her stomach as she walks, and the look in her eyes, as if she were flying blind, by radar, or by instinct. Now she is seated at the next table, wearing glasses, perusing an architecture magazine. Fifteen minutes later, my third cup of espresso is empty, the want ads have been read with nothing to show, her salad is gone. Our eyes have met at least twice, over our reading, over our coffee cups (she takes hers black, I notice), but we have not spoken. The thirtysomething yuppie couple at the corner table are deep in conversation about their evening's plans.

"But I've already seen that movie . . ."

"I haven't. We never do anything I like."

"We went bowling with your brother last week, didn't we?"

It sounds like a bad sitcom script. The elderly woman at the table by the street window has eyes only for the waiter. After several frantic waves, she finally calls out, "Excuse me, could I have my check . . . now, please?" He puts down the dishes he was going to take into the back and pulls out his pad, heading in her direction as he does the addition. My neighbor asks him as he passes, "Your restrooms?" He nods over his shoulder, back toward the narrow corridor leading to the kitchen.

She hesitantly gets up, looks over at me for a second and smiles; then she heads back that way, and I get up and follow ten steps behind her. I cannot see her face but I know she knows I am following her. Her walk changes, to one of confident provocation, of self-possession. As we pass the stainless-steel countertop where the coffeepots are kept, she can see my reflection behind her and she slows ever so slightly. At the doors of the restrooms she lets me catch up to her, smiles again and looks at the doors. There are two, plain wood, unlabeled, both ajar. Behind them are small single bathrooms, white ceramic-tiled, decorated with old advertising posters for soaps, toothpaste, hair tonics and lotions. There is a toilet and a sink in each, back to back, separated only by a floor-to-ceiling partition, which I know (but does she?) is perforated by a grill at the top. She seems to be offering me my choice of doors. As I move to take the left, she slips through the right-hand entrance. I see her smile once more; then the door closes and I hear the click and the snap of the bolt.

I go into the one I have chosen and also lock it. There is a mirror on the wall over the sink, next to the washable board on which customers are allowed to write their graffiti in felt-tip marker. I notice that I am flushed and that my heart is beating rather faster than usual. Through the grill I can hear the sound of buckles and a zipper, the rustle of denim and cotton being removed, then the plastic-on-porcelain clink of a toilet seat and the musical sound of her urinating. But then there is more. The rustling of paper is followed by a softer rustling, a movement of flesh against flesh, a moist sound, then a soft purring sound, a softer gasping breath, a low moan, and I know her secret. I smile as I unzip and take myself in hand, urinating loudly and laughing softly to myself. Her voice comes to me through the grill: "Don't forget to turn off the water when you're done," and she giggles—a pleasant, laughing voice and even more pleasant giggle. I have no answer, but I climb up on the toilet seat to wait for another chance. She must know, because she asks, "What are you doing?" I answer truthfully, that I am standing on the toilet seat with my cock in my hand awaiting further instructions. I hear her climbing too, and suddenly through the grill we are face to face, but barely. We can see each other from the bridge of the nose up. She is as flushed as I, but her eyes are smiling.

"Hi," she says quietly.

"Hi," I answer.

"Did you hear me come?" she asks.

"Yes, I did," I answer.

"What did you think?"

"I liked it. You really seemed to enjoy yourself."

"Would you mind returning the favor? I'd like to hear you come too."

"I'd be glad to, but I'll need help."

"What kind of help?"

"Tell me a story. Tell me what you were thinking about when you came."

She giggles again. I like the sound. "Are you hard?" she asks.

"Very. What were you visualizing before?"

"You. Standing there naked in the middle of the café, holding your cock in one hand and the want ads in the other, glancing over them at me. And I was naked too, sitting at the table in the middle of the restaurant, eating my sandwich with one hand, rubbing my clitoris with the other. And no one around us was paying any attention. And actually, I started thinking about it out there."

"Oh, my. Umm, could you make yourself come again? I think it would help me." I was now beginning to pump my cock at a regular rhythm, and I could feel the usual buildup of heat and tension that meant I had just a couple of minutes.

"I could if *you* tell *me* a story—tell me what you were hoping I was thinking about." She is whispering now.

"Umm, I'll try . . . if you'll pardon the . . . irregular breathing . . . Umm, I guess I was hoping . . . for something similar, although maybe . . . it would then continue . . . Oh, you sound wet."

"I am . . . go on with the story."

"Umm, sure . . . well, after sitting there . . . masturbating in the middle of the café . . . you walk over to my table . . . and rip the want ads out of my hands . . . push me down in my chair . . . kneel on the floor, half under the table, and take me in your mouth. While you suck me, one of your hands . . . is on my balls, squeezing and just holding them, the other is . . . on your own nipple, doing the same thing. I've got my hands . . . in your hair, touching your ears, your neck . . . How are you doing?"

"I'm getting . . . close . . . You?"

"Almost . . . Do you want a countdown?"

"No, just time it . . . so that . . . when you come in the . . . story, that's when you really do . . . I'll be there too."

I could hear the toilet tank rocking in rhythm as she pushed and pulled at herself, the wetness of her flesh making splashing and smacking sounds.

"Okay, umm . . . so you're under the table sucking my cock . . . and I'm playing with your hair and face . . . then you look up . . . at me . . . and stand up . . . and climb onto the table's edge . . . and push my plate back . . . then you pull my head into your pussy. I flick my tongue in and out . . . up and down, using it like . . . a finger . . . between and around all your different . . . layers . . . over and over . . . for several minutes . . . nibbling you . . . and you keep . . . playing with your nipples . . . pulling them, twisting them, pinching . . . and I've got your clit between . . . my teeth . . . and you've come twice already . . . and then finally you push my head back . . . and slide down off the table onto my cock, just like that . . . and you throw your arms around my neck . . . and kiss me . . . Oh God, I'm going to come . . . Oh, that's it . . . Up and down, squeeze me tight . . . oh yes, your tongue is in my mouth, your legs are around my waist . . . I've got a hand on your left breast, I'm kneading it . . . the other is on your right ass cheek . . . Oh god . . . I'm coming . . . Are you coming?"

"Y-y-yyes . . . Yes! Oh, yes . . . yes . . ."

A pause. Eye to eye, we smile again. I wipe off the wall, straighten myself up. I hear her doing the same. The clink of dishes from the other side of the door reminds us that this is a public place. She says, "Give me two minutes head start." I hear her flush; then her door opens and shuts. I run water, flush, smooth my hair, and exit. She is gone. None of the other customers look at me, but none of them are the same as those who were there before. On my table, my want ads are gone, replaced by her architecture magazine. With her address label on the back. I pay my bill and leave, smiling.

PART THREE

The Perfect Match

In my letter inviting authors to submit stories for this project,
I requested that real-life heterosexual couples write *separate*
individual renditions of their sexual relationship or independent
descriptions of a sexual experience they shared (à la *The Alexan-
dria Quartet*). I was hoping that these paired stories would clarify
even further the differences between the erotic writings of men
and those of women. To this end, I have selected stories from three
couples which not only illustrate the differences in male and female
perspectives but also show how disparate successful sexual relationships can be.

Susan and Max were close friends for six years before initiating
a sexual relationship. They've been married two years now, work
together, and spend very little time apart. While this degree of
togetherness might feel claustrophobic to some couples, it adds to
the intensity of Max and Susan's sexual relationship. "Because we
spend so much time together," says Susan, "we're always being
very physically affectionate. Therefore, at the end of the day, or
in the morning, or whenever it is that we actually have intercourse,
it's the culmination of basically twenty-four hours of foreplay,
which for me as a woman is great." This sense of intimacy and
joyful sexual expression is obvious in their stories.

Within this tightly intimate relationship, Max and Susan compliment each other in a way that intensifies their lovemaking. Max is a voyeur while Susan is an exhibitionist. "I've always been an exhibitionist," remarks Susan. "I don't run around exposing myself with a raincoat on, but I do like to show off both physically and verbally. Before I met Max, my boyfriends would get intimidated by the way I freely talked about sex or by the way I dressed, but Max is such a voyeur, that he loves it."

"I love to watch Susan or smell her as she walks by," Max told me. "It tells me that something exciting is going to happen before too long. And I love the fact that Susan is a strong woman who loves sex. It's the woman's strength that becomes the powerful aphrodisiac for me." So, while other men might find Susan's strong sexuality a turnoff, for Max it's a definite enhancement.

A particularly exciting sexual experience, which occurred not long before Max and Susan received my letter of invitation, forms the basis for their tales and provides me with what I was looking for: male and female viewpoints in response to the same material. Some of the differences you'll notice include Susan's emphasis on the details of the story of Purim and on her *feelings* during the sexual encounter. In typical male style, Max develops his own fantasy in reaction to Susan's rendition of the biblical version.

The second couple merge their stories into one through letters written to each other while the woman is on a business trip. Khafre and Patrice have been married for thirteen years. Khafre wrote his part of the story first. It is built on his strong but unpursued attraction to dominance and submission. "It's the way my nature is," says Khafre. "I'm a salesman and I love to go to San Francisco because it's so much freer. There are a lot of people there who are involved in the things that go on in my head and I like being around it. Because my wife is not into it, it's really an unexpressed part of my life."

Whereas most women might have considerable difficulty dealing with a partner whose sexual fantasies, and hopes for real experience, fall along the lines of dominance and submission, Patrice seems quite open to the idea. "While the story is pretty much based on Khafre's fantasies," says Patrice, "I've kind of tied into them. I don't practice it, but it has become a part of me in terms of fantasy. Khafre has brought all this stuff home, sexual equipment and things, and it intrigues me. I think there's a possibility that at some point in the future I might practice it, but I haven't worked my way to where I can actually do it now." So, in this perfect match, Patrice is open to Khafre's sexual proclivities and Khafre is willing to wait.

For both Patrice and Khafre the erotic component in the story concerns power. And, although for different reasons, both view the power as held by the submissive person. "The woman holds the power," contends Khafre, "because if she says no, the man has to respond. If he doesn't, he could lose the relationship. And since there aren't many women who would agree to this lifestyle, it's quite a risk."

"I think the power lies in being the recipient of such intense desire and passion," says Patrice. "It's not the submission that's the turn-on, but the interest or passion expressed by the dominant partner." And while it is the fantasy and not the reality of the sexual relationship that drives their story, I must admit, until I interviewed them, I thought their story was true.

Michael and Deena have been married over five years. He is thirty-six; she is fifty-six. Not the perfect match from a stereotypical point of view, but, as you can see from their stories, in the deepest aspects of their souls, they fit together perfectly.

For Deena and Michael, eros has a profoundly spiritual element. "For me," says Deena, "our sexual relationship has a quality of personal or spiritual revelation that has to do with the deep bonding between us. I think it's our vulnerability, or willingness to be vulnerable to each other, that makes the sex so exciting. It has a draw, an excitement—the sense that there's a real danger, yet it's perfectly safe."

For Michael, the spiritual aspects of his lovemaking with Deena are a direct outgrowth of twenty years of Buddhist practice. "The Buddhist practice of just sitting still on the one hand and making love on the other," he explains, "is two sides of the same coin. Both involve going deeper into a kind of nakedness of the spirit, an undefendedness and a willingness not to impose order on things but to delight in them as they present themselves. I take this experience and knowledge with me into every aspect of my relationship with Deena."

For both Deena and Michael, the erotic content of the stories is based on memories of early childhood. For Deena, it is a sense of shyness. For Michael, it is a sense of innocence and openness, a whole universe of mystery. But within this perfect match, we clearly see typical male and female approaches to the eroticism. In both stories, Deena is being seduced while Michael is the seducer. According to Deena, "I'm aware that my shyness is seductive so I'm aware of drawing him toward me in my writing just as I am aware of his pursuing me in his writing. I think this is all part of the dance." And while Deena's story emphasizes the relationship, Michael dwells on more graphic detail. "I was much more drawn to the explicit details of the lovemaking," says Michael. "The explicitness is not where the erotic power is for Deena; it seems to be more in the interaction than in the visual."

Does reading these stories help you perceive the underlying erotic thread of your relationship? Does it help you pinpoint the unique essence of your bond? While the stories in this section typically reflect male and female styles, these opposing approaches to the erotic do not detract from the couples' sexual relationships. Instead, the differences are complementary, leading to a more complete whole once the two parts actually merge.

ESTHER

Susan Block

Everyone has a desire, an aspect of their sexual nature that touches not just their erotic encounters but almost every inch of their existence. Mine is exhibitionism. Not that I flash strangers in public—please! It's just that this simple wish to be seen (or heard) has been a motivating force in my life, probably since I emerged from my mother's womb, kicking and screaming for attention, calming down only when I was satisfied that all eyes and ears present were upon me.

For years, I drove myself and several boyfriends nearly crazy with my shameless passion for erotic attention, until I found my husband, Max. Max looks at me from every angle. He is my director, my reflector, my dog, my butler, my little prince, my great king. He's the curator of my exhibition.

For over two years now, Max and I haven't been apart for more than an hour or two at a time. We are beyond "codependent"; we're obsessed with each other. He looks at me, and I look at him looking at me. Often, while I put on makeup, talk on the phone, write at my computer or sit on the toilet taking a pee, I look up and find, to my ceaseless wonder and supreme delight, Max watching, smiling, sometimes masturbating. I love this to the core of my baby girly girl/old wise woman soul. It keeps me in a constant state of wet heat. It makes me feel powerful and secure; I think that finally, maybe, just maybe, I'm getting sufficient erotic attention . . .

So . . . it's the first night of Hanukkah, the Jewish "festival of lights." I never liked Hanukkah much, always thought it was a weak version of Christmas, never was very inspired by the main Hanukkah story of the Maccabees, a biblical gang of hotshot Hebrew thugs who narrowly won an unimportant battle with some imperialist Greeks just before being slaughtered in the course of a long bloody war.

So we put Hanukkah on hold and devote the early part of the evening to making one of our videos, "Power & Surrender," starring me, shot by Max. I play dress-up in pearl white stockings, push-up bra, garters, regal robe, high heels, exotic makeup, lots of rings and chains around my wrists, my waist, my throat, my ankles. All this metal weighs me down, and I move slowly, languidly, wielding my soft red deerskin whip, posing and proclaiming from our big brass four-poster bed. This bed is my stage, my boudoir bully pulpit, a sensual soapbox. I expound into the microphone, my blood boiling in more ways than one. I have my period tonight.

Max makes love to me through his video camera. The lens is his tongue kissing me, his hands caressing me, his firm rod penetrating my softness. I watch Max watching me, his large, strong, sexy physique anchored behind the tripod as his imagination runs wild over every curve and crevice of my body with his long hard lens.

We finish making the video for the public, but keep the camera on for our private pleasure, and I strip for it, for Max, slowly peeling off my stockings, shaking my breasts loose from my bra, sliding my hand between my legs, curling around in the electrical cords and bedsheets. I watch myself being watched in the video monitors, through my husband's watchful eyes. I see him stroking the oblong bulge in his shorts. He lets his shorts drop, up pops a profound erection, and he points it at me like a living telephoto lens. I explode into giggles, jumping up and down on the bed like an excited child. My husband, the voyeur. How I love him.

"C'mon," he says, turning off the camera, and zipping up his shorts. "Let's light the Hanukkah candles." Max converted several years ago. He says he prefers the down-to-earth approach of Judaism to the constricting Catholicism he grew up with as a little prince in Italy (Mom was an Italian princess; Dad a Czechoslovakian prince). But I think the driving force of his conversion is his potent attraction to the shrewd sensuality of Jewish women.

On holidays (and there are so *many* Jewish ones), I like to seduce my husband into an erotic evening laced with Bible-style fantasies. We don't feel the least bit blasphemous about this. Actually, according to Jewish law, it's a "mitzvah" (good deed) to have sex with your spouse on certain holidays. Sex can be a form of worship, a fulfillment of God's will, an affirmation of God's glory. And the Bible, especially the Old Testament, is filled with springboards to sexual fantasy. The Song of Songs is pure erotic poetry, much better than *The Joy of Sex*. Genesis also features some hot sex scenes—incest, adultery, polygamy, fornication, masturbation, drunken debauchery, lots of seductive maidens and horny shepherds (not to mention horny sheep!).

But my favorite is the Book of Esther. Queen Esther is the ultimate shrewdly sensual Jewess, a heroic exhibitionist who saves her people from genocide. All the little girls in my Hebrew school wanted to be her. I remember dressing up in a regal robe and playing Esther in a Hebrew school play when I was eight. It was one of the heights of my prepubescent exhibitionism.

At this point in our evening, I've already stripped off my lingerie (except my panties with minipad—don't want to bleed all over the place, not yet), but I put my regal robe back on before we light the candles and say the Hebrew prayers. I feel like an excited little girl in a queen costume, my juices mingling between my thighs, as I recite the litany of my ancestors. *Baruch atah adonai.* My husband looks so handsome in the candlelight. *Elohenu melech haolom.* He is my prince, my king. *Ashair kidishanu bimitzvotav.* He looks like an angel. *Vitzivanu lihadlik nair.* Actually, he looks like Jack Nicholson. *Shel Hanukkah.* A devilish angel-king, my husband, my someone to watch over me.

Since the more Hanukkah-appropriate Maccabees fought violence with violence and Esther fought it with sex, I decide to tell Max the story of Esther. We toss the wires and microphones out of the bed and get under the covers, our arms and legs wrapped around each other, and I read to him from our paperback Bible, embellishing Esther's story with little legends I remember from Hebrew school.

The tale begins with a great feast, the culminating weeklong banquet in a festival that's lasted 180 days ("Wow, and we think when we have an all-night bash, we're being decadent," Max exclaims). King Ahasuerus, who rules 127 provinces from India to Ethiopia, is the man behind this mother of all parties, filled with lots of eating and drinking, carousing and cavorting, as the best Old Testament parties are. *And on the seventh day, the king, merry with wine,* calls for his wife, Vashti, *with her royal crown, in order to show the people and the princes her beauty.*

"In Hebrew school," I explain to Max, "I learned that 'with her royal crown' really means 'wearing nothing *but* her royal crown.' "

"Ahah," says Max, thoughtfully rolling my nipple between his thumb and forefinger. "Queen Vashti is a little exhibitionist."

"No," I correct him. "The king *wants* her to be. He thinks showing off his naked wife to all his friends and subjects is the perfect capper to six months' worth of merrymaking."

"I agree." He wets his finger, circles my very erect nipple.

"Mmmmyeah. But Vashti doesn't. She refuses to parade her naked self before the king and his royal party animals, so the king has her kicked out of the palace. Some translations say she's killed." Max and I agree that execution is a rather drastic punishment for refusal to submit to domestic sexual harassment, but we can't conjure much sympathy for Vashti, the mother of all party poopers, obviously with no zest for exhibitionism.

"Mind if I suck on your nipple while you continue the story?"

"Not at all." I position the Bible around his head as it rests on my breast. My body shivers as he nibbles. I think about the many sexual "favors" I perform for my perpetually horny husband that so often wind up pleasuring me as much as him. I wonder if he'd ever call me into a party of men and ask me to dance naked . . .

"*Then the king's servants said, 'Let beautiful young virgins be sought out for the king,*' " I read.

"Virgins! Ooh, let's do a virginity check . . ." He slides his left hand under my panties, between my legs. "Oops, I think I broke

the virgin's hymen," he laughs, showing off his bloody, sexy fingertips.

"I am unclean, O Lord." I know he loves it, biblical prohibition
and all.

"I love it," he says, licking his fingers lustily.

"I love you, my darling vampire boy. Do you want to hear the
rest of the story?" I so adore teasing him into a lather like this,
going back and forth between hot sex and cool conversation.

"Of course." He nestles his head against my breast; his fingers
slip back into my panties, gently fondling my tingling netherlips.

So I tell him about the great Babylonian beauty contest where
all the hottest virgins in Ahasuerus's kingdom compete for the
chance to be queen. Mordecai the Jew enters with his cousin Esther, but warns her to keep her Jewishness to herself. "Even in
these days before Ivan Boesky, it was not cool," I add. "It's never
totally cool to be Jewish. Non-Jews are almost always suspicious
of Jews."

"Everybody's suspicious of everybody these days," Max reminds me, and I go back to the Bible, reading of Esther's extraordinary charm, her "comeliness," her shrewd sensuality. King
Ahasuerus is dazzled by her and gives her a prime position in the
royal harem.

Then Esther *goes in unto* the king. "You know what that
means," I tease, "and she gives the king the best head he's
ever had."

"That's in the Bible?" Max, my excited student, sits up in bed.

"If you read between the lines. I mean, King Ahasuerus falls
madly in love with Esther after just one night, so I figure it must
have been a *hot* night. Anyway, he crowns her queen, and holds
another big banquet with lots of eating and drinking in her honor."

"And she parades around wearing nothing but her crown!"

"I would think so," I say. "I mean, that's Ahasuerus's fetish,
and he adores her, so she must be an exhibitionist. I can just see
her belly dancing naked on a pedestal high above those crowds of
drunken revelers drooling at her beauty—"

"I can just see you as Queen Esther," Max croons in his melt-
ingly mellow baritone voice, caressing my body with both his hands
as if he is molding it into a statue.

At this point, we could easily start devouring each other, but I go on with the story: "All this time, Mordecai hangs around outside the harem"—"Can you blame him?" asks Max—"and he discovers two eunuchs ('Biblical post-op transsexual slaves,' I explain) plotting to kill the king. He passes this on to Esther, who passes it on to the king, who has the eunuchs hanged and has the incident entered in his Book of Chronicles. Then Ahasuerus promotes one of his princes, Haman ('a Hitler wannabe,' I say) to be his main man. All the people bow down to Haman, except Mordecai, who's Jewish and doesn't bow down to anybody except God. Haman vows to kill not just Mordecai, but all the Jews, and, since he's now the king's pet, he uses the royal seal to decree that all princes in all provinces prepare *to destroy, to slay, to annihilate all Jews, young and old, women and children, in one day, the thirteenth day of the month of Adar, and to plunder their goods.*"

"Oh, this story isn't so sexy anymore," he pouts, my little boy.

"Life isn't just a barrel of orgasms, darling. Don't worry. It'll get sexy again." I pull off his briefs and comfort his semihard cock. Since Max was born in Italy, he's uncircumcised (shh . . . don't tell the rabbis!). When he's soft like this, I love to play games with his foreskin, which he calls his *cappucino* ("little hood"), pulling it up and down, sticking my finger inside the silky folds. Of course, when I do that, it doesn't stay soft long . . .

"The old ethnic cleansing routine," I muse, stroking his cock with one hand, holding the Bible with the other. "Mordecai roams outside the harem wailing, until one of Esther's eunuchs comes out. He gives the eunuch the bad news and tells him to tell Esther it's up to her to change Ahasuerus's mind. Esther's hesitant; according to law, anyone who approaches the king in his inner court without being invited is put to death, unless the king holds out his golden scepter. Mordecai reminds her that the lives of all Jews, including hers, have already been condemned. Besides, he adds, perhaps she was blessed with her 'comeliness' for a nobler purpose than just keeping a horny king happy. So she decides to give it a try."

"Yay Esther!!" Max's cock is hard as a rock. I lean over and tell *it* the next part: "So Esther goes to Ahasuerus, and the guards are about to take her away to be hung when the king sees it's her and holds out *his golden scepter*." I examine Max's golden cock. I lick up the shaft, tasting it, twirling my tongue around the luscious head, his hand gently rubbing my hair. I suck his cock, the golden scepter of my king, the wand of life—my life.

"Mmmm . . ." groans Max, "No wonder he holds out his golden scepter. Does she suck it like that?"

"It says she *touches the tip of the scepter.*"

"That's pretty hot."

"So are you, my king." I kiss the tip, and go back to the Bible. "So, the king falls in love with Esther all over again. He says he'll give her anything she wants. But Esther doesn't spring the big request right away. She's coy, she's cunning, she's cool."

"She knows how to turn a man on and on and on . . ."

"Mmmyeah . . . She says she wants to give a private dinner for the king and Haman. Ahasuerus is so excited he calls for Haman right away so dinner may begin. Esther entertains like a great geisha, and when the king is drunk, well-fed—and probably well-fucked—he asks Esther again what she wants. He'll do anything for her, he'll give her half his kingdom—"

"I'll give you my *whole* kingdom if you suck my cock some more."

"Such a deal!" I put down the Bible, pull back my hair and swallow him up. I fantasize that I am Esther, expertly sucking the king's cock, keeping him on the aching edge of orgasm, as he begs me to let him come, offering me anything I want. I want so much. I want him to give me life itself, and he does. He gives me everything.

But I don't let him come. I go on with the story: "So, Esther asks the king and Haman to come back tomorrow for another dinner. Esther's so cool. She plays her potentate like an instrument, and he departs in a state of erotic agitation. On *his* way home, Haman runs into Mordecai, who still won't bow down to him. Haman's so mad he can't wait until the thirteenth of Adar. He builds a gallows in his own front yard, and gets up early to see about obtaining Ahasuerus's okay to hang Mordecai that day. But that night, Ahasuerus, still in heat over Esther's teasing, can't sleep, reads the entry in his Book of Chronicles about Mordecai saving his life, and decides to honor him.

"When Haman walks in, hell-bent on getting Ahasuerus to sign

234   *Susan Block*

off on hanging Mordecai, Ahasuerus, being king, speaks first: '*What shall be done to the man whom the king delights to honor?*' Haman, assuming Ahasuerus means him, suggests that such a man be given the king's robes to wear and the king's horse to ride while one of the king's princes rides before him through town proclaiming his honor. Ahasuerus loves the idea, and commands Haman to do just that . . . for Mordecai the Jew. Haman's totally humiliated ('He feels worse than a newly castrated eunuch!' I say), but he obeys— he has to, he's a company man. And he's *still* hopeful about attending Esther's evening soiree."

"Little does he know he's about to get his pompous princely cock cut off . . ." Max strokes his own still-hard member protectively.

"Esther throws the dinner party of her life, with lots of wine and sex and sweetmeats, which has the king down on his royal knees *again* begging her to tell him what she wants."

"I surrender, Queen, I'll do anything for you! I'll eat your hot little pussy!" Max uncrosses my legs, holds a thigh in each hand, and dives between them. He gnaws at my pad and panties like a dog in heat, then yanks them off. I scream with gleeful outrage as he thrusts his tongue deep inside my cunt, smearing his face with the blood of my affliction and the juice of my affection.

I wrap my legs around his head, close my eyes, and let him suck me into a state of semibliss. But I don't want to come before the end of the story. "Do you want me to finish?" I ask.

He looks up, licking his lips, my blood-faced angel. "Oh, definitely. But I'm going to keep eating you while you talk."

Sounds reasonable, and so deliciously decadent. I open the Bible and take ten minutes to find my place. "Let's see . . . the king . . . mmmm . . . the king asks Esther what she wants . . . mmmyeah . . . that's sooo nice . . . she wants . . . oooohhh Goooddd . . . she wants him to suck her clit—"

Max stops. "No," he says, "that's not in the Bible."

"Right," I agree breathlessly. "But something tells me the king is not licking Esther's pussy while she tells him what she wants."

"I don't know; she's a powerful woman. She could tell a man to do anything anytime." He resumes sucking me slowly, sensually. I feel an entire Bible story raging within my loins, the armies of menstrual pain battling the armies of sexual pleasure for control of the temple, my body. At first, it's a close contest, but pleasure overtakes pain, and I feel myself opening up to ecstasy. I breathe deep into Max's mouth, and pick up the Bible in an erotic trance. No one is here but the two of us, yet I feel as if the king's great feast is going on all around us. All the princes are watching as I lie in the royal bed, my legs spread wide, my sex blood red, gushing with arousal. I imagine two eunuchs holding my legs apart so the king can eat me before his guests. All the princes are stroking their scepters, drinking their goblets of wine, watching and listening as I writhe and recite their story.

" '*What is your petition, Queen Esther?*' the king begs the beautiful Jewess, '*It shall be granted you. Even to the half of my kingdom, it shall be fulfilled,*' " I read, enunciating as best I can as ripples of pleasure and pain whirl through my pelvis and stream up my spine. "Then, simply and succinctly, Esther asks for her life and the life of her people."

"And he grants her that, of course." Max stops eating me. "It's amazing," he says, "the power of a sexual woman." I snap out of the trance, fathoming how downright heroic this ancient, unpolitically correct, exhibitionist foremother of mine turned out to be.

I cross my legs again, and Max frowns, but I *must* finish the story. "When Ahasuerus asks Esther *who* would destroy her people, she points to Haman. Shocked, the king steps out for some air. Now Haman gets down on *his* knees to beg forgiveness from Esther" ("What a woman!" Max whistles) "and the king walks back in on them and bellows: '*Will he even assault the queen in my presence?*' and Haman is taken away by eunuchs who hang him on the very gallows he prepared for Mordecai" ("Wow," says Max, "that's like having dinner in the White House, then being taken out and shot by post-op transsexuals!") "The king gives Haman's property to Esther, makes Mordecai his new right-hand man, revokes the Jewish genocide edict, and the thirteenth day of Adar becomes a day of *gladness, feasting and holiday-making,* as it still is. That's the holiday of Purim, when all the girls dress up as Esther and flirt shamelessly with all the boys." I shut the Bible, looking up, eying my lover flirtatiously.

"Thank you for the bedtime story, Queen Esther," he purrs and turns out the reading lamp, so our only light is the flickering Hanukkah candles. "Now I'm going to put my queen to sleep." He kisses me, and I taste my own blood mixed with love juices and the wonderful, intoxicating scent of his breath. "I'm the king," he whispers, "and I'm having a feast for my queen." He caresses my neck, my cheeks, my forehead. "The feasting hall is filled with people—men and women, young and old." He takes both my ears in his strong fingers and massages them, turning Esther's story inside out: "My queen is on her bed, dressed in white, gold and red; white for her innocence, gold for her royal splendor, red for the blood of her womanhood." My ears are filled with ecstasy. He rubs and pulls the hard cartilage, the soft lobes, his fingers probe deep inside. "Four eunuchs, also in white, gold and red, lift up the four corners of my queen's bed and bring her into the feasting hall." If there is such a thing as an *eargasm*, I'm having one. "As the guests hear my queen entering, they begin to masturbate and fondle each other." He stops rubbing my ears and strokes his cock, rubbing it between my legs, pushing the head up against my pulsating clit. "The eunuchs set down the bed in a roped-off area in the middle of the hall. Men and women jump up from their tables, spilling wine and food, jockeying for positions near the bed."

"I'm pretending to be asleep," I murmur, filling out Max's voyeurist fantasy with my exhibitionist viewpoint, as I slide his golden scepter between my liquid lower lips. "Slowly, I rise, sitting up in bed. I see that I'm surrounded by hordes of people celebrating, salivating, masturbating openly. I see my king on his throne, watching me. I feel safe. I feel wild. I lift up my veils to show myself, saving my most sacred private parts for last." I pull Max down so his chest presses against my breasts. I caress his arms, his shoulders, his back. I love to kiss and bite his shoulders, so strong but tender, as they surrender to my teeth.

"Everyone wants you," he whispers, holding my ass cheeks in his hands as he pushes deeper inside of me. "Guards have to stop the people from climbing over the ropes and into your bed. Then the king claps his hands—"

"Oh, my king, I love my king!" I wrap my legs around him, his soft skin, his hard muscular ass pumping into my impassioned flesh.

"You point to various men and women in the crowd," he continues, "inviting the chosen few to line up before you and tell you how they would service the queen." He pulls himself up on his hands, still inside me, and I reach up to bite his hard, salty nipples.

"And what would you do to service your queen, young man?" I ask in a haughty whisper.

"Um, I would kiss the queen's feet . . . suck her toes . . . worship her body . . . while she whips me with her red leather whip . . ."

"Ooh, sounds good." I smack his beautiful butt with my hand (who has time to find the whip?). "And you, Prince, what would *you* do?"

"I would fuck my queen in the ass, spank her with my cane . . ."

"Oh, you nasty prince!" Max is deep inside me now, the head of his cock gently pushing up against that spot on the ceiling of my hothouse vaginal chamber. He licks his finger and rubs my clit into a plump and juicy frenzy. I feel my body ascending to a higher plateau, tension releasing from my stomach, gathering in my ass muscles. I exhale deeply, allowing myself to experience a little preorgasmic whoosh of dreamy pleasure, then another, then I inhale, holding back for bigger, better things.

"You pick fifteen men and women," he breathes into my ear, "all hard, wet and hot. The four eunuchs lift your bed, take you into a room with crystal glass walls, and the chosen fifteen follow you in. One glass wall looks out onto the square where the whole city is watching you. Another glass wall faces the banquet hall so the king and the guests can watch you as they smoke and eat and drink."

In my head, I'm being sucked and fucked, feasted upon and fornicated a hundred different ways before thousands of strangers. In reality, I'm making quiet, private love to my husband, in the missionary position, my favorite position for having self-shattering, leg-stiffening orgasms. I feel one of these coming on. I try to float above it as long as I can . . . cool . . . like Esther . . .

"And there's a video camera filming you—"

"Video camera?" God, don't confuse me when I'm about to come . . .

"This is a very modern palace. It's our palace. I'm going to build it for you someday. And there are several video monitors in the banquet hall so everyone can get a good look. Plus, the show is

playing on TV sets everywhere in all the cities and villages
throughout the entire kingdom, so all the tribes and clans may
partake in the beauty and knowledge and ecstasy of the queen."

He stops moving for a moment, and I feel the orgasmic tides
gathering to a point within me, a point of no return, a point of
departure for points unknown. He reaches under me and lightly
squeezes my ass. The point explodes into a storm of points and
lines and squiggles and stars—"Oh God! Oh God! Oh my God! My
God! My God! God! God! God!"—a flood of blood, a festival of feasting and fornication, a sacrifice, a body prayer, a song of songs.

My husband, Prince Maximillian Rudolph Charles Giovanni
Leblovic di Lobkowicz di Filangieri, is fucking me. He and all his
princely Gentile ancestors are fucking the little Jewish queen.
What grace, what madness. He humps me like an athletic animal,
a barbaric conqueror, a prince, a king, an angel, a boy, a wild,
bucking, snorting horse. He pumps me, gripping one of the brass
bedposts, as I continue coming all over his cock. I slap his rear. He
spanks my clit. I stroke his balls. He fucks me harder.

"*Look* at your hot little queen," I hiss to make him come, "sucking cock, her ass up high, getting fucked—"

He fires. "Oh Goooooooooooooddddddddddhhhhhhhhh!!!!!!!!!"
Baruch atah adonai. He collapses on top of me, his spirit rising.
Elohenu melech haolom. I don't know when he rolls off of me,
sometime after we fall asleep. *Shehehiyanu vikiyamanu vihiggi-
yanu lazman hazeh*. We are blessed indeed, blessed with life.

In the morning, blood trickles down my legs. The sheets look
like ancient hieroglyphics, or maybe a Jackson Pollock painting. I
consider doing an art exhibit ("Period Paintings"!), then feel a familiar spasm splintering my belly, stick a towel between my thighs,
and hobble into the bathroom with the Bible.

I sit on the toilet, letting my blood drip down into the porcelain
bowl, attempting to reread the Book of Esther, but too crampy to
concentrate, too plagued by my own pain to believe in silly old
stories about the power of love conquering the violence of life.
Then I look up, and there's my husband, watching me. He smiles
and shrugs, still watching, beaming the beneficent glow of a well-
fucked king. Pain surrenders to love. Tears fill our eyes. We kiss.
Amen.

SUSAN

Maximillian R. Lobkowicz

I'm a very young, what they call "middle-aged man." Actually, I'm a little boy, especially when it comes to sex. It's my third marriage. I have four kids, I'm a grandfather, and I'm forever horny, running around and about my life in search of adventure, sexual adventure.

Now, I know you might have heard, or been told, that little boys are supposed to grow up and settle down. They should get married, have children, buy a house, have a career, get a stock portfolio, retire and die. There's more: We have to be creative, contribute to the community and the future of our children and grandchildren.

So what happens if you're born, the future looks bright, you get married, life's okay, but every year it gets worse? You wonder if it's true that, after a while, love withers away. Man's only true power tool gets greased once in a while, but for the most part, it stays wrapped up in a cotton cloth, lying dormant except for a little necessary maintenance. Life gets even worse—joyless. The mind becomes obsessed with all kinds of sex it isn't having, the body starts its decline into sickness. I can do without anything except sex, because sex is what drives my spirit.

All right, you don't have to agree with me. Certainly, I can't argue with you. If you've given up on sex, I feel bad for you, but

I support your right to be miserable, eat yourself into oblivion, or just die a slow death from depression.

My second marriage lasted four years. Mercy! What a hellhole of misery. A human disaster. I turned to food; I didn't blow up to the proportions some people do, but I was plump, frustrated, sexually on ice. At least, I managed to maintain some sort of relationship with my beloved, eternally hard "friend" who suffered so much from the lack of sexual activity.

There I was, on the way to the other side of life with a grin on my face and my friend in hand. We were like buddies with AIDS, dying every moment we took another breath. Was this the meaning of my life? A little boy with no love, and no possibility of sex, is not a very happy little boy. Unhappy little boys create misery in their own lives and in those around them. I was miserable, but I was loyal. I didn't even have the courage to cheat.

But I was determined, obsessed by my need for sex. I masturbated *a lot*. Like a nineteen-year-old. In the car, the shower, under the covers. Every second I was alone I had sex with myself.

Then, ever so slowly, I realized I was in love. Not with my wife, whom I had at this point separated from so I could have more freedom to masturbate. I was in love with a friend, the most beautiful and sexual woman I'd ever met. A darling, brilliant girly-girl with a sex drive that could wipe out whole armies and bring blissful peace to the universe.

When I was a boy, I used to dream about a beautiful mystery girl I could love and trust forever. I discovered that mystery girl embodied in this dear old friend. I had never approached her as a sexual playmate for fear she might reject me, and I'd lose her as a friend. But I wanted her, oh, how I wanted her. I would see her at parties in her little miniskirts, low-cut dresses, supertight jeans, high heels, garter belts, blue eyes, blond hair that changed through the years depending on the style. I would get these little notes from her signed with hugs and kisses and other telltale signs that she might, in fact, have an interest in me.

One day, I decided to surrender to her, to stop being just a man and become the little boy I've always been inside, give up all the nonsense in my head about the million obstacles that could stand in my way. We kissed, I touched her hand, inhaled her aromas, looked into her eyes and my misery was over. I was born again.

So it's the first night of Hanukkah. I'm married now to the pretty little blue-eyed girl in a miniskirt, my mystery girl. Her name is Susan. Her lips are full, red; her face sculpted like the most magnificent piece the masters have ever made. Her little body is a wondrously delicate creation that ensnares the look of every man who lays eyes on her. She is the centerpiece of my life. Since we've been together, we've never been apart. I drink, sleep, eat and market my little girl. I thrive on her beauty, intelligence, and that seductive sexual allure that I love to watch both men and women discover in her.

Tonight I'm filming her. She's lacy and racy. My eyes follow her through the monitor, and I'm amazed. I find new excitement, rediscover old passions in the corners of her body. I'm tense as I film. I'm excited. Sure, those are the lips I've kissed 200,000 times by now. Those wet lips that suck my cock with the gentleness of an older woman seducing a young boy, and the strength of an S&M queen dominating the crass barbarian who wants to overpower her. Fuck the film—I'm so turned on! Those lips that I used to wonder about, fantasize about, now excite me every time I watch her speak, drink or eat. Those are exciting lips, I think, as the camera pulls back. Now I know—I don't wonder—I *know* about those lips. So does the little kid in my pants. My crotch heats up with excitement as the camera moves down her neck, along her collarbone, around her shoulder, over her breast, down along her ribs.

I watch her body move, her hands exploring, her eyes imploring her audience, her voice serenading my ears through the headphones. I'm hot. I'm always hot around her. I want to stop filming. I want to grab her in my arms, kiss her, slide between her legs with my tongue. I want to tear off her stockings, rip off her panties, and I want the camera to keep rolling. I don't want to give up the memory of what I am seeing and feeling.

This is becoming a religious experience. We are alone. We turn off the camera and turn on the fireplace. (Here in California, you don't build fires; you turn them on.) We light the Hanukkah candles. Susan prays. I just stand there. I have an erection. With each word, it gets harder, warmer. I can't understand what she is saying. (I don't speak Hebrew.) I watch her lips, I hear her beautiful voice speaking to all these people in history.

I don't want to seem too disrespectful in the middle of this religious moment and I don't want to rush anything, but I'm dying to get in bed to start our holiday of sex. I feel like a little boy who can't wait for the chance to get his hands under the girl's blouse, to touch her exquisitely formed breasts, her hard nipples, to hold her in my arms, run my hands along her back, to slide my fingers between her silky, bloody panties (it's that time of month), her wet lips parting as I explore the entrance to the forbidden cave of my childhood. It's dark and musky inside, a wonderful place to escape the world and feel the pleasures and warmth of love, sex and discovery of my own passion for my beautiful wife, my mate, my Hanukkah date. I'm a happy dog in the dark bedside corner of my great love.

The years of waiting while we were standing there in prayer are over. Now we're in bed. She looks even more beautiful in bed. I feel her heat. I smell her sex. She's going to tell me a story—oh boy. Susan tells great sexy stories about her erotic fantasies. She has them all the time. No matter what else is going on, the two of us always make love. We use everything and anything to make love—a conversation, a salesman's glance, a friend's advance, a holiday. Life with Susan is paradise.

This is a religious story, an amazing Bible story. Is this the story of Hanukkah? No, this is the story of Purim, the story of a beautiful Jewish queen: Esther. It's wild.

I'm ready, I've *been* ready. But Susan can always make her little boy even more excited than he already is. I now find myself going back in time to what must certainly be a distant relative of Susan's, an exhibitionist queen, with a pervert of a husband who is king of one of the largest empires in his time, and he wants to show her off to all his kingdom. Hot shit deluxe! I'm sucked in. This king is a man after my own heart, a man that is truly in love. No veils for this guy.

I listen to my wife read the Bible, closing my eyes, picturing myself as the king, watching from my throne as the queen's bed-bearers bring her into the great dining hall. She is splendid in her white, gold and red robes. Her eyes search the room for those who will be her handpicked lovers for this festival of pleasure. I instantly redecorate the palace, modernize it with electronics, video cameras, rainmaking machines, TV monitors in every room. I build my Jewish queen the most beautiful public bedroom: she is surrounded by glass, marble, sound machines, roofs that open, gold, silver, gems and massive velvet curtains that cover the window that faces upon the public square and the great dining hall.

I want the whole kingdom to watch her with me, share her, delight in her, worship her, fuck her . . . I want every man and woman to know that such love exists for all of us, if only we have the courage to explore.

I watch her as the men and women of the kingdom parade before her, whispering their desires in her ear. She chooses her lovers one by one. Her beautiful bejeweled hands reach out, touching the men's erect cocks, the women's hard nipples. As they are chosen, they kneel down before her, tasting her wet lips, sucking her toes, reaching inside her robes to fondle her breasts.

I know what each feels. I smile, stroking my cock, so warm, and growing with each stroke. She looks delicious. Her eyes meet mine, and we smile. She has picked ten men and five women. Some are young, some old, some crippled, all beautiful and handsome. She has chosen them based on their desires and fantasies. She is stroking herself in her bed. She is truly my princess, my Jewish goddess. There is no better woman, none more exotic, none smarter. She enchants all those who meet her eyes. She is my seductress.

I watch her as the bedbearers lift her up again. In the great hall, people are masturbating, wine is overflowing, food is everywhere. Everyone is in a state of ecstasy. Outside the walls in the public square people have come from all over the kingdom to view their splendid queen.

As I listen to Susan telling Esther's story, I explore her warm thighs. My fingers reach deep inside her wet pink lips, and I lick them like the nectar of a sweet peach. She tastes delicious, so sweet and warm, a little bloody. I want to slide down between her legs and have her drown me in her warm river of Queen Suzy juice. I want to bottle her, package her. This story she is telling has me wild. I close my eyes, lay my head against her breasts. Her aroma fills my nostrils. I feel peaceful. I have a raging hard-on. I'm in heat. I want to fuck her. I may not make it to the end of the story.

Susan's voice takes me back to the palace: erotic festivities have begun, and I am about to witness the rapture of my wife, my darling baby girl. I want my princess/queen to have everything. I want her to give pleasure to the world, one by one, cock by cock. The old pervert king and the hot young prince have many things in common, but the thing we cherish most is our Queen Susan, the most beautiful of women, the most sexual, the smartest, the hottest. We know that women like our queen make the world better.

I hear Susan's distant voice calling me. I rise from my throne, and my guests follow me into the public bedroom. We sit at the queen's table. There is wine and food. Golden cocks (scepters?) are placed at the center for the women. The velvet curtains are drawn both on the great hall side and onto the public square. There is music and cheering. The queen lies strapped to her bed in golden chains. She is on her stomach, her buttocks in the air, her veils pulled just above her waist. Her hips are moving.

Her sex servants ask the first man to step forward. He must first be undressed and washed in the golden bidet which is brought next to the queen's bed. Her eyes are intense; the man's cock is hard, pointing towards the sky. Her servants wash him, soap his crotch and delicately clean him. Then he is dried, and a golden hand-wrought sheath is placed over his erect cock. Chains are pulled around his balls and waist, and he is given the queen's favorite deerskin whip. It is a deep burgundy red, like her blood, with a golden handle.

My queen struggles to her hands and knees, her beautiful ass high in the air. Her sex servants pull her silky panties down to her knees and the young man steps forward. I can see my queen's hips move slightly. She loves to be whipped ever so gently across her beautiful ass. She loves for men to see her like that.

The young man takes a step back. His eyes meet mine. I nod. He moves his arm back and delivers the first stroke. Susan groans with joy. The whip is soft and gentle. It feels good striking her delicate pussywillow skin. Again, he raises his arm and delivers a blow across her beautiful buttocks. Again and again, he lets the whip fall across her ass, between her open pink pussy lips. Her body is moving like a wild lion caught in a trap. The lit candles at the foot of her bed cast a warm glow over her pink pussy lips.

Outside, people are watching, drinking and fucking, their bodies smeared with food, blood and cum. The dining hall is an orgy palace. The queen's brother watches, stroking himself with each stroke of the whip on his sister's ass. My queen is wild, twisting and turning in her chains.

My head remains on her breast . . . my mind flashing through time . . . where am I?

The servants summon a beautiful young woman from the waiting area of the queen's lovers. She moves across the bed between the queen's legs, licking her, driving her tongue deep inside the queen, as the young man continues to whip her. The servants remove the sheath from the young man and unchain the queen. She takes the young man's cock and slides it between her red lips. He disappears inside of her, his ass tightens, and in seconds, he explodes, screaming out to God for mercy. He has felt the lips of his queen over his staff. He falls to his knees, as the young girl moves over her queen.

Me, I'm watching, my head on my queen's breasts. What is real no longer matters. It's all there, every frame, every second being captured by my imagination and the reality of Susan's story.

I hear Susan tell of this beautiful queen who saved her people, gave joy to her world: Esther. I slip back through my mind to my queen's public bedroom. She is exquisite, and she is now being fucked in every delicious opening of her body. She smiles at me, her king. The guests are happy.

Now there are five young men. They are spread-eagled and chained to steel posts in a semicircle around her bed. Their cocks are all hard. Female sex servants move from one to the other, licking and caressing those steel-hard shafts, preparing them for my queen.

She slides off her bed like a snake. The sex servants stand behind the men with cowhide whips, stiff and hard, like razors when they hit their target. The queen prowls along the floor like a lioness, in front of her boys. Suddenly, she moves toward the first boy. His cock disappears inside her hot mouth.

Now the sex servants start to whip their prisoners as my queen moves down the line, devouring them one by one. Within minutes they have all spilled their seed between my queen's lips; none could resist. Cum covers my beautiful maiden, dripping over her lips, her chin, her breasts, her stomach, her thighs, her feet. She smiles at her king and, with her hand, motions him to her.

I cannot resist. I am enchanted by my mistress, enthralled by her beauty, her wild sex. I lean over, I cover her with my shadow. I am every man and boy who has ever fucked her. I am all the men that wish to fuck her. I am her pimp, her prince, her king. I'm in charge of marketing. My life's purpose is to show her off to millions of men and women. That's my passion. That's my business.

I pump deep into her pretty pink pussy. It's the most powerful pink hole in the universe. I start to spin, falling deeper and deeper inside. I slide between her legs, tasting her pleasures, drinking her oceans, sucking her nectars. She is the woman of my life, how many lives—I'm not sure.

Happy Hanukkah . . . Oh God, I love you, my goddess . . .

THE LANGUAGE
OF DESIRE

Khafre and Patrice

K,

What would become of us if anyone could guess our most secret desires?

If I had known eighteen years ago, what I know now about your desires and my own, would I have run from the crowded conference room where I first felt the intensity of your gaze roaming freely over my body, your dark eyes seeming to possess a sinister wisdom all their own?

Or would I have run to you, quicker and with much more ease and comfort than our coming together has ever produced?

As I fly thirty thousand feet above ground en route to New York, a city where no one will know anything about my desires or about you, I feel alone, and yet know that I am not, because of the common language we have come to share in our deepest, most private selves.

As this plane glides through the air, I write these words trying to create a language of desire, a language I can share with you once I again place myself at your mercy, lay myself beneath your punishing hands, my wrists and ankles bound, in our ritual of possession.

* * *

I am continuing this letter from my hotel room in New York City. The sun is shining here. It is unusually warm for this time of year. When I close my eyes I see your body curl into itself while the cool blue fingers of winter stroke you in your lonely bed.

It is soothing to write these words. They help ease my loneliness for you here in this city of nervous energy. These words are mere fragments of desire, pieces of myself I can spread on the page as easily as I will spread my legs for you at your command, once I return home.

I remember the first time you shaved me. I stood naked on the gray tiled floor, my only adornment the black leather slave collar around my neck. My toes lightly caressed the floor's sleek coolness beneath them.

The scent of my pussy rose from between my legs. Its deep musk aroused me. As your power always arouses me.

You made me stand with my wrists behind my back; you had them loosely tied with nylon cord.

My nipples stood in the charged air, the very tips long and dark from all the years of your suckling.

Your left hand stroked the inside of my thighs while your right hand surely, steadily moved the razor over my pubis, removing the dark tangle of hair of which I had always been so proud.

I was even more proud to be offering myself to you, to sacrifice this bounty of womanhood, my strength and power, for your strength and power, in an even exchange of power for power.

And when your tongue entered me, you made me hold still, so still. You said you would swat my bare behind if I disobeyed. And the light flicks of your tongue over those lips and inside them, the deep searching for the answer to the question in your eyes, caused me such exquisite pain that you showed me no mercy as my moans grew wild and my hips thrust out of control against your face until you found what you were searching for in the tart liquid wetting your face.

And then you sat on the floor and turned me over your knees and laid the palm of your hand on my buttocks over and over, the licks falling like rain, and I became a child again, the wild child chased, the one to be tied down, panties around my ankles, and your hand struck my ass until the sun burned there, until the wild child left my body and came back again, red-faced, red-assed, safe and loved in your arms.

Is it politically incorrect for me to kneel between your legs and take your cock into my mouth? Is it the knees that make it incorrect? But it is those bent knees on the hardwood floor that I love as much as the sleek silk of your flesh beneath and around my tongue. I love the feel of my submission, the way I am split open with your power. I find myself yearning for your touch, your power, your cock inside my mouth.

I love to wake you in the morning with my tongue between your legs, softly slurping you awake. And for those times when we are both home from traveling, no telephone, no children, nowhere to go but inside each other's arms, it is then that we set our ground rules for our evening play.

They would have us believe it is not possible to delve this deeply into our innermost desires, to expose the rough-edged faces we would otherwise show no one. I am glad our almost twenty years have found us growing sexually together, exploring the difficult topography of the worlds of sexuality.

I look forward to whatever awaits me upon my return to your playroom.

Patrice

P,

Your absence brings back memories. Before I met you I had just ended a long-term relationship, and that ending left me knowing one thing: I could only live life my way.

I was resigned to spending my life alone. Past relationships had proven it would be difficult to find a woman who would submit completely to a man with a strong need to dominate.

I remember the night when you came to my place for dinner after we'd been seeing each other for two months. I had wrestled all day with my past, with the way I had always compromised what I wanted in a relationship.

I decided I would tell you my wishes, and either our relationship would end that night with the truth or be the start of something much deeper.

You asked me what was bothering me, since I barely touched my food.

I told you I wanted something from you. I handed you that long black velvet box. It contained what I wanted.

You seemed shocked and excited. I knew you didn't know what to make of our relationship since sex, up to then, hadn't been a part of it. But I could tell you were drawn to me, that you liked my strength and power, as well as my beard and shaven head.

Open it, I commanded you. It wasn't what you expected, not a pearl necklace or a diamond bracelet. No, that set of gold handcuffs and the leather collar weren't anything you'd ever imagined.

You asked me why I gave them to you.

I admitted that I had kept us from being intimate, that I wanted you, but had decided that the next time I chose to be with someone, it would be totally consistent with the way I felt inside. I told you I'd like to share my life with you as the facilitator of your pleasure, as well as your pain. With me as the punisher and you as the punished.

You asked what it was I wanted from you.

And I said, your surrender.

You asked me what I wanted you to do.

And I told you to take off your clothes. I still remember the feel of the dark blue dress and how beautifully it fit your slender hips and buttocks. It was nice to see it come off and reveal your stocking-clad legs, garters, bra, and panties. I remember the sweat on my nose and forehead.

I told you to take everything off. Once you were naked, I asked you to put on the collar and handcuffs. I could barely control myself. My body was electrified as I looked at you standing before me, your deep rich skin, your hair pulled back. The only thing on your body besides my gifts was the flickering light of the candle which sat on the table.

You were exquisite.

I lifted you into my arms and took you into the bathroom and filled the tub.

I ordered you into the tub. I told you how beautiful you were and you smiled. We were both silent as I washed your body with scented soap and a soft sponge. The warm water and the wine you'd had at dinner relaxed you. Your body yielded to each of my probing caresses and I explored every recess over and over as if I were learning to play a song by heart.

I dried you off with a thick towel. Your body was flushed. Your breasts and vulva were swollen with warmth. I put a leash on your collar and led you to the back bedroom where I placed you face-down on the cushioned table.

I fastened your ankles to the lower corners of the table and fastened your wrists to the top of the table.

You asked what I was going to do next.

I said I was going to give you pain and pleasure, to push you beyond your sexual limits.

I rubbed massage oil along your back and shoulders, down the length of your arms, massaged your hands, and always watched your body's response.

Your head nodded and you drooled with each of my caresses. Then I massaged your feet and when my hands moved up the backs of your legs, you couldn't help but moan your approval. I kneaded your protruding buttocks with great love and affection, then SWAT!

You screamed and struggled against the restraints. SWAT!

You screamed for me to stop. SWAT!

I told you to give yourself to me and that this was a part of the giving. You stopped struggling as the heat grew with each swat of my hand on your buttocks. Finally, I stopped.

I helped you to your feet and you walked unsteadily behind me to a chair. I bent you over the chair so that your behind was in the air. I secured your ankles to the legs of the chair and stretched your arms until I could attach your wrists to the chair as well.

I stood beside you and looked at you while you looked up at me. I began to caress you, one hand squeezing your breasts, gently rolling and pulling your nipples, while the other hand caressed your round behind and entered your vulva in search of moisture.

Your breathing increased when I found your spring of life. And it flowed over my fingers.

I told you to give it to me. Your breathing became moaning. Your moans became a plea for me to fuck you.

I stripped and walked slowly behind you, my erection passing

near your face. You told me I was beautiful. You told me you
needed my cock inside you.

I kneeled and opened your ass cheeks and sucked the fluid flowing between your thighs. A deep moan came from within you. I
stood and watched you slump over the chair, nearly spent. I entered your body over and over, filling you completely until your
writhing quickened and your moans became incoherent chanting.

I joined the chant with my own cries of pleasure until you
screamed my name. That scream triggered our mutual release.

After I untied you, I carried you in my arms and placed you
for the first time in my bed.

I put my arms around you and laid your head on my chest. It
was then that I asked you to marry me, and I waited with anticipation for your weary, but delighted yes.

Khafre

K,

Three days left. You should be here in this violent city. And
though you have forbidden me to touch myself in your absence,
my fingers cannot help but lie like agitated birds near the dark
place there, between my legs. My back longs to arch, my legs to
thrash below these chaste cotton sheets. I run my fingers along
my body's sweeps and hollows, and it trembles like the live thing
it is beneath my curious hands.

On what part of my body does your touch not bring pleasure?

Because of you I have become a sexual adventurer, an eager
explorer of the many-faceted pleasures that await us all.

I love sex, the stink and flavor of its dark wildness, the way it
makes my body deepen, ripen, swell.

Remember the night you first entered me from behind? Your
fingers moved over and around my clitoris, then thrust inside my
pussy as if your fingers were five slender cocks, though I rode them
as if they were one.

And your slippery cock nudged my anus tentatively at first,
then pushed through that ring of fire until it found another home
there. And you moaned in my ear and buried your face in my neck
to still your eagerness to thrust. But I offered my ass to you, as I

have offered myself to you so many times since. And we rode the crest of our desire together, moaning, plunging, thrusting, until we reached that deep spot, the very core of our souls, and found the howl that lies inside each of us.

What woman does not want to find herself to be the object of intense desire?

The thrill of being desired is for me the ultimate intoxicant. When you initiated me into the loving ways of erotic power exchange I felt I was at the height of my sexual powers.

I reveled in the textures of silky stockings on my legs, the bite of garter straps on my thighs, the pinch of the underwire cups of lacy brassieres securing my breasts for your viewing pleasure.

The look on your face was my gift, the wanting there, the desire. And then you slipped the black velvet hood over my head and laced it. You tied my hands behind my back. In the darkness within the hood, my trust in you deepened. I was as vulnerable as I could ever be. This was our most intimate moment. The only thing real to me was your touch and the sound of your voice, murmuring, soothing, moaning.

You punished me for moving, for not being able to keep my hips from dancing as you stroked my pussy, nibbled my nipples. And dance my hips did, first in the air, then over your knees as I wiggled my ass, then ground my mound into the cruelty of your legs while you spanked me for all my transgressions, my rigidity and fear until I sobbed incoherently and you masterfully brought me back to myself, safe once more in your arms.

There are days now when I walk the streets of this city, barecrotched, feeling the air on my pussy, the freedom, knowing that soon you will be wanting me, holding me, stroking me there.

I cannot wait to caress you in the airport. To smell you. I know I am ready to travel the deep terrain of our loving for all the years to come, on whatever path our journey together shall take us.

I am devoted to your pleasure, as you are devoted to mine.

I have cast aside the thick veil of repression and exposed my true self to the sun.

In Submission,
P

P,

It is Friday afternoon, and I've been at the office making arrangements for your return. This is a very special weekend. The hotel room will be ready; the white orchids you love will be there.

I look forward to this celebration of twenty years of marriage to the one woman who, over the years, has been a lover, mother, and best friend.

I have asked you to belong to me in the most literal sense: the giver of pleasure, the provider of pain, the fulfiller of fantasies, and the slave of eros. In return, you received my undying adoration and commitment.

When we were newlyweds, we were inseparable. Discovering how to please each other sexually became our primary focus until the flame of our desire could ignite from a simple thing like a whisper or a gaze.

You were without a doubt the most sensuous person alive. You desired all sensations, the more extreme the better. And there was nothing I enjoyed more than providing those extreme sensations for you.

I loved watching the nectar flow from between your legs after one of the many spankings I gave you. I loved watching you collapse with exhausted bliss from the multiple orgasms I sparked in you.

The sex became an obsession, and the pain and punishment an addiction. We were no sooner satisfied than one of us wanted more.

Then we had the children, and both of us careers, so finding time and privacy for intimacy became difficult. But you were always able to let me know when we needed to spend more time together, especially when you'd pretend to burn my dinner.

"Well, maybe I just need a little spanking," you'd say and smile.

And yes, spanking will be part of our ritual this weekend.

I've arranged for us to have adjoining rooms at the hotel, just like last year, so we can have some privacy for preparing ourselves for our evening together.

I can see how you looked then. There was soft music playing in the background. When I entered your room you were still in the bathroom. I took a deep breath and checked my appearance in the mirror.

I was nude except for a Kente cloth necktie and my skin glistened from oil and perspiration.

The door opened slowly. I always notice your scent first. You were nude except for a white wedding veil that cascaded down your back and covered half your face. I could see your smile beneath the veil.

You were, and are, magnificent.

We walked toward each other until we were face to face.

I held both of my hands around the base of my testicles. My penis protruded toward you and I said, "I am here for your pleasure, to give my life to you, to be your counterweight in life, directing you back to yourself. This is my pledge to you on my manhood, but you must come freely."

Your eyes never left mine. You slowly raised your veil and revealed your beautiful large, brown eyes and moist lips. You slid to your knees before me and held your breasts in your palms. You raised your breasts and eyes. Your lips parted.

You said, "There is a special place inside of me, a place where I can rest. You make me feel safe and beautiful. Submitting to you is the easiest thing in the world for me to do."

You placed your lips around my penis and sucked it like you'd been taught so long ago, wet, fast, and deep. You sensed the core of myself rising. You removed your lips from me and raised your eyes again to meet mine while continuing to stroke me with your fingers.

You said, "I do," and I erupted over your moving hand, the sides of your cheek, and onto your breasts.

I know now that no matter what the future brings, you'll be there with me. And I chuckle to myself thinking how lucky we are.

Khafre

SHY

Deena Metzger

You asked, and so I will tell you. I am shyer than I was. The truth is that each day I become shyer. This marriage is the cause. I didn't expect it. It was not the territory I expected to enter when we took our vows.

"How does it happen?" you ask. You ask because you want to hear this. You want me to whisper it into your ear as we make love. You lean toward me, the candlelight on your cheek, your young eyes shining. You move your hand through my silver hair; then you trace the contours of my one breast and run your fingers along the tender narrow ridge of the scar so that my flat chest shivers and the nipple puckers on the other side as I begin to tell you what seems unbearably clear: I am too young and shy for what is about to occur.

"How do you know you are too shy?" you ask.

"Because I am shyer than I was yesterday."

"Why?" you ask.

"Because each day I am younger than I was before. Once I was a woman and now I am a girl."

"Why?" you ask.

"Because you see me," I say. "Because you want to see me.

Because you want to see more deeply inside of me than anyone has ever seen before. You want that."

"How do you know?" you ask. You always want that. Something more. "Open to me," you say, "the way a girl opens, the way a flower just wet with the morning unbinds its white petals to the sun."

"I don't know how," I say.

I was not always this way. I was brazen once. I was buxom and called myself a wench. I was securely bold, impudent and rude. I primped and flirted like a brash milkmaid. Or I wore black leather belts which drew together at the waist like medieval bodices and pulled the blood-colored satin blouse down to display plump breasts. I was safely audacious in knee-high boots with four-inch heels, in narrow velvet or leather skirts slit to the hip or hemmed mid-thigh, wasp-waisted corsets, heavy hoop earrings, bangles, gypsy castanets, delicate gold chains dangled about my hips, a jewel shining in my navel above the black lace underpants cut in a cruel V to a narrow waist. I had so many faces painted with red or white lipstick or enhanced lashes or a dark beauty spot carefully placed near the corner of my eye. I disguised myself as a hussy, a tart, or a trollop, and occasionally as a harem dancer or Scheherazade.

"How did it feel?" you ask.

"I felt alone," I say.

Your hand moves down toward my belly. "Petals," you say. "Move gently," you say, "so they won't bruise." The white cloth of my panties is soft and thin and white. There is the scent of almond blossoms in the room.

"Tell me how it was," you insist. "But tell me how it was before the blood red lips and the black leather, before Salome and the harem dancer."

"There were always veils," I say. "Before everything, there were veils."

"Tell me about the veils," you say.

"From the beginning?" I ask.

"From the beginning," you repeat.

"When I was a girl . . ."

"A girl?"

"A young girl."

"Was it long ago?"

"Very long ago. Forty-five years ago."

"How young?" you ask. "How young were you?"

"Ten," I say.

"How was it when you were ten?"

"I danced," I say. "With veils. I put cloth, any cloth, under my eyes. I darkened my eyes with kohl. I took off my clothes and wrapped myself in cloth. I didn't have breasts yet. My mound of Ishtar was bare and white. I could see it glow like a moon through the gauzy cloth as I danced with the chiffon draped about my hair and affixed across my face under my eyes.

"Who were you?" you ask.

"I was a priestess from Lebanon," I say. "I was from Syria. Or Egypt or Greece. I lived in the temple. I danced for the Goddess. I covered my forehead with necklaces and beads. I was learning my work."

You smile tenderly at me. You stare sadly into my eyes. You wait for me to speak again.

"At ten, I was hidden, and also I was very shy."

"Show me," you say.

"I can't show you," I say. "You know more than you should ever know. I am too young now," I say.

"How young are you?" you ask.

"Younger than you. I am twenty years younger than you are now."

"Yes," you agree, "you are younger than I am. I can see it now. Show me how young you have become." Your hands stray toward my belly.

"I can't," I say.

You put the music on the tape recorder. A thin mideastern flute fills the room, plaintive and sweet. Breeze in the almond air. Horn calls of goats. Olives and oil.

I press the white cloth down toward the pubic bone so that my belly rises smooth as if I were a child.

The oil drips down on my belly and fills the little cup which marks the omphalos, the entrance to the other world. I want to dance with you. I place oil on your belly. I fill your larger cup. I want to see your hips move alongside mine. I want to see them rise up to the invisible gods called into the room by the drum and flute. My hips roll and yours roll beside them. They make a sign of infinity. The two infinities connect. I put a date into the cleft between my legs and then slip it into your mouth.

How long has it taken us to enter this country together? I know this desert. I learned its territory when I was a child.

You are Aries. You are the wild ram. I run my hands through the wool of your hair and pull the tight curls with my fingers but I am careful not to spill the oil too soon. I dream of placing a thin white wick in the cups of oil on our bellies and setting them alight.

Dance, my love.

"Tell me everything," you say. "Tell me how it was when you were a child."

"About the veils?"

"Before the veils," you say.

"There was nothing before the veils," I say.

You smile patiently. Your mouth moves down to my nipple, which hardens as it did when I was a young girl. "How young?" you ask.

"Before the veils," you say.

When you were coming to see me for the first time, I was afraid and regretted that I had given you my address, that I hadn't worn black leather, that I wasn't armored, that I didn't have a pearl-handled knife in my garter so that I could protect myself by impersonating the woman I thought you wanted to find. You had sent a letter to me which had intrigued me and made me afraid. You referred to my work, to the novels and poetry I had written, to the image of the Holy Prostitute I had embellished again and again. You asked if I knew her sacred dance. She is the peacemaker, I had written, but maybe I feared war. The houri danced a lonely dance of hours in my mind.

You had telephoned when I least expected to hear from you. The man I had played with through correspondence revealed that he had a voice. I suspected the voice belonged to a body with legs and hands and mouth. I gave you directions to my house only when I was distracted momentarily from my intent to put you off. That night I slept in my clothes and dreamed you were an axe murderer. In the morning, I thought of wearing black leather but was afraid of turning you on.

You arrived in an old car, wearing clothes without any pretensions and looking deceptively sweet. In the middle of a conversation about Buddhism and the revolution in Nicaragua, you put your hand on my knee and asked to be my lover. The silver bells around the waist of the priestess of Ishtar jangled in my mind while the ten-year-old I had been stared at herself in the mirror and placed a silk chiffon scarf under her eyes.

For a moment I forgot I had only one breast and was twenty years older than you. I wondered how it would be to take this young boy to bed?

You returned three months later. I had planned a seduction, platters of fruits and cheeses, wines and other delights. You were so young, you wanted none of my artifice. You said, "I would like to look into your eyes for a long time." You would have liked us to strip our faces away.

You took off your clothes as if clothes were an impediment to undressing. You gave my attire no more attention than you pay to garments on racks in clothing stores. You pulled me to you and kissed me on the lips, your tongue in my mouth, slow and exploring. Then we moved apart and we looked in each other's eyes for a long time. An hour perhaps. Or longer. An entire day, perhaps. Afterward I was undressed and I didn't know how it had occurred.

"Tell me," you ask again, so patient with your knowing and so relentless, "about the young girl you were. Before the black leather and the red satin, before the silver bells and the silk veils."

"I was never a young girl," I insist.

"You were a child," you assert. "You were a child. I remember," you say. "I can feel her under my fingertips," you whisper as you slide your hands along my body.

Now after seven years with you, I am just beginning to imagine the possibilities of nakedness. Now after seven years, I am becoming the young girl at the core of every woman. Now for the first time in my life, I am the Kore, the one without a name who is just learning to dance.

"Spread your legs," you say. The music echoes your request.

The white cotton folds damply between the parting of my labia. I turn toward you, my hips still moving as you bend over me, the rhythm in your fingers and your breathing. Infinity in the hips. Eternity. The past and the future running like opposing currents in a blue river.

The oil runs down onto the cotton cloth, which you pull down slowly, and then I am naked before you except for the veil of history and memory across my face. You take the veil between your fingers and draw the silk down slowly, and my eyes open to your eyes staring at me, watching every gesture.

"How shy are you?" you ask.

"Very shy," I answer.

"How shy, tell me. Tell me as you open your legs. Show me the secret shyness."

I watch you rise. I reach for your sex. I hold it as I would hold anything, now, to steady my life.

I do not know what is about to happen. I am a young girl. I have heard stories of the dances of the hours. It is dawn. We are about to dance dawn. There is a sea of night within me and the light is about to enter. A single blade of light. A ray from the sun, pink and throbbing. Your finger enters me. Without thinking I open my mouth. A small bird not even singing yet. I want something. Something to enter my body. Something to see in the dark. A light.

"When I was five I had a lover," I say. "If a five-year-old could have a lover, I had a lover. Sandy was also five. We held hands, treated each other with exquisite tenderness and spoke about our marriage. We spoke to each other with the trust five-year-olds can have for each other. The war came. His father was moved to another base. I never saw him again."

"Come to me, my love," you say. "You will see him again. But you must go back. You must be that girl again. Open your legs farther. Go back farther. Open farther. How sweet you are. How young.

"You are my bride," you say. "This is our marriage. You are wearing white. I am your first and only love," you say. "You are a young girl. You are innocent as a child."

Now in the bed, I am five again. Now I wear white cotton

panties. Now I am enflamed for the first time. Now my body is hairless and no one has ever seen me before.

Now I undress myself from all the artifices and wiles that have ever covered my body. You look in my eyes as you enter me. I open them wide, as wide as my mouth and the entrance between my legs. I let you into my eyes. We travel back in time.

"I don't know," I whisper, or I moan, or I shout. We run exploring with each other, leaping over rocks, climbing the mountainous path, rolling in the fields. I watch your face; I see it reshape itself. The man falls away. This smile belongs to a young boy. I can see that you also have never made love before. You are so surprised. You are exultant.

"I can see you," you whisper, as you enter me even more deeply. I let you see everything. Everything. After all, we are children and innocence spills over us in a white ecstasy of rams and ewes, of white milk, of moons and the first day of almond blossoms. It is dawn, my love, my sweet love, my dear young lover. We have married again and the sun is rising once more on our wedding.

HIDDENNESS AND DESIRE

Michael Ortiz Hill

And so now, lover, I try writing you about hiddenness and desire even as I feel the deviousness with which I would incite your desire with my words. For after seven years you are still the beloved and after seven years there is still nothing I enjoy more than to see you naked in your pleasure and to let you know that I receive the gift of it with gratitude.

When I was five years old, I remember my surprise at seeing the long slit revealed when my girlfriend next door lifted her dress for me and pulled down her white cotton panties to her knees. It was not the "lack of a penis" I saw, like the Freudians say, but rather something like a fruit split from above the little pink bud of a clit to between the legs and up toward the small of her back— halved like a peach, yet whole and containing an invisible center. The five-year-old has his own desires to touch, to see, to open up and, I believe, without even being able to form the concept, he desires to "know" that invisible center.

Now, thirty years later, while I make love with you and you give me that long split that halves your body and offer it up to my mouth or fingers or cock, I find it both strange and natural that the persistent naiveté of the five-year-old remains unchanged. The desire to "know" your nakedness, the strange alchemy of tenderness and passion, caress and request, is the only thing that has really changed—becoming at once more articulate and refined and also more deeply mysterious. For it seems that the further I go into our loving, the less I understand what it would mean to "know" you.

First, of course, there is the pleasure of just seeing, of looking at you. The simple grace of watching you sleep, partaking somewhat of the child's curiosity but with an elegant slowness of having been long married to a beautiful woman. Looking, without being seen looking, is an unmediated pleasure. Poised next to you, not wanting to wake you so I can take in fully your dark body on the white sheets, your one breast folding over the edge of the old mastectomy scar, the Modigliani curve between waist and hips, when you lie on your side, the enticement of stray pubic hair showing from where your underwear almost meets the crease of your thighs. This is a private pleasure, deep, sexy and full of gratitude—somewhat different from the sly humor of when I watch you dress, pretending I am reading, and you dress for me pretending you are oblivious to my watching.

And then there is the wild complexity of watching you grow shy and radiant as you try to take in my delight at the beauty of who you are—including my delight at the courage of your vulnerability.

For example, there was that humid afternoon in San Juan. You always prefer to make love around midnight but I was so hungry for the solace of your body that I blindfolded you and with great mock poetic flourish whispered in your ear about the rising of the moon, breeze blowing in the window from the phosphorescent surf and the sweet sounds of the little green coqui frogs, no bigger than my thumb, chirping from under the mango trees, like the songs of a thousand nightbirds. And then I covered your body with a white linen sheet from head to toe and then slowly, very slowly, pulled the length of it over the length of you and recited your beauty centimeter by centimeter. I would caress you with my eyes and then with my words, letting you know what I was seeing, where my eyes were dwelling or delving and, also with my hand and mouth, oiling your body, taking your nipple under my tongue just for the pleasure of seeing it hard and telling you that I saw it.

By the time I pulled the sheet over the thin brown hair between your legs, you were writhing, even whimpering a little and when I knew you couldn't take any more, I asked you for the gift: "Please lover, spread your legs for me so I can see you" and when you did, trembling, I said, "Please now open the lips of your pussy with your hands so I can taste you with my mouth."

These gifts we pass between us are so terrifying that I know they are sacred, that they proceed from that "invisible center" that is so mysterious and compelling. My tongue savoring your taste as I carry for a few moments the contralto of your pleasure when I push the tip of it under the hood of your foreskin. Or because you were blindfolded, helping you find my limp cock so you could take it into your mouth, and me squirming as it grows hard when you run your fingers along the length of it. Or my one finger and then another slipping inside and under the rim of your pleasure to that soft place where I draw small circles that make you wet enough to receive me. Every little gesture is like an ideogram that is radiant with meaning and yet never other or more than itself, like what the Buddhists call a *mudra*, a simple opening of the hand "like a flower opening in the void."

Taking you from behind in San Juan was such a *mudra*. They say that this is how Lilith, the first woman, liked it. Because she was really an animal from the waist down, and unwilling to be tamed by Adam, she preferred to make love with the beasts. It was with Eve that sexuality was humanized, say the rabbis, because with her the sacred circle of fucking face-to-face replaced the wild bestial hungers of Lilith. I often thought, "Why choose between the way of Lilith and the way of Eve?"

Why is it that it so often seems that this moment of asking is where we touch the mystery, the unspeakable vulnerability? I said, "Turn over, sweetie," and then said, "Lift up your ass just a bit," and as you did so, the full triangle, your musky little nest of darkness and beauty, was given to me and I accepted the gift of it and entered you as Lilith would be entered.

That's always such an extraordinary moment, isn't it? The request for the gift and you giving it with the blessed gesture of tilting your ass up to receive me. I always like to enter you slowly enough that you unfold with my penetration and I unfold inside of you. But there is always a point when your hunger becomes so alive that it awakens my own and I realize with surprise that my cock is also a gift that you are taking inside of you. That day my fierceness got so tangled up in your pleasure, some sort of animal of light mounted me when you turned me on my back and, straddling me, you mashed your wet pussy against my hardness in such a way that I didn't know your wildness from my own. I tell the truth when I say that in those final few thrusts when your orgasm overwhelmed the two of us I felt like a woman suddenly inseminated with the seeds of her lover's ecstasy.

What is it that happened, lover, and what are the words that can sing of it? Who was the woman and who was the man? Who penetrated and who was penetrated? Who was the god, the animal, the human being, and what was this dance that they did that afternoon in Puerto Rico? All I know is that after you came you gathered my pleasure like someone who lives only for beauty, like a woman who gathers an armful of wildflowers just to take them to the edge of a cliff and toss them into the sea.

"The ocean likes wildflowers," you said as you took my cock into your mouth and ran your tongue under my foreskin. I could hear the crashing of the surf outside our cabana and had not a glimmer of what you meant when you ran your fingernails down the stem of me to the very root, sucking fast and then slowly. How merciful your mouth has become over the years—and also how merciless. It demands only everything, offering reprieve and then taking it away. My hands clung to the bed like the very earth when I came in your mouth. White petals flying everywhere, the air full of white petals—and then only the susurration of the surf carrying me off to sleep.

You always claim that I attribute too much to the child that I remember I was, so I always feel perfectly at ease in claiming the preposterous. I think when I was five years old I heard the far echo of this sacrament of marriage when my girlfriend let me look between her legs and my desire to know what was "inside" was ignited. Those who forget what childhood is—who forget their own childhood—would prefer that a five-year-old be innocent of desire. They forget that desire itself is innocent—is, in fact, the essence of innocence. What amazes me is that in opening up her legs for me that little girl opened the door that leads to the deepest mystery that people can share. I found at that moment the beginning of a very long thread that would lead me through a maze of laughter and heartbreak and complexity and pleasure. When I was five I couldn't even begin to imagine where this desire would lead me. Now as a man I can imagine it even less. The hair of your pussy— wispy, thinning—barely hides the soft contours of that split fruit I beheld for the first time so many years ago. And my desire to touch its invisible center has not diminished in the least.

How we terrified one another the first few years we were together—so starkly did we each carry the fear of being loved. Like that time we made love on the rug in front of the fire. We had shared a bottle of red wine—as usual me drinking the greater portion (and a bit dizzy because of it). I was, I thought, in a kind of "Beethoven mood"—my cock charged with thunder and lightning—the bow of a stringed instrument that would slice through the worlds and astonish you with its virtuosity. There was a violence of passion that night, a reaching out for love through a fear that I thought I could hide from both you and myself. I wanted to sweep you up—I *insisted* on sweeping you up—and moved inside and out of you with fury until something pierced open and we came to orgasm at the same time.

After fucking I was drifting off into my familiar opium dream when you perkily said you knew what it was like for a young boy to make love with his first woman. Feeling every day of the twenty years' age difference between us—feeling, in fact like a young boy with his first woman—I was rendered helpless by your description of the earnestness, the desire to please, the terrible vulnerability scarcely disguised with a kind of gallantry and the hope that she'd be kind enough to shelter his fantasy that he knew what he was doing. Aside from your description being more precise than I myself could have crafted, you also held up for me a mirror of the fifteen-year-old boy in me who has approached every woman and now his wife with that same complex pathos of fear and the desire not to be so afraid. When I saw him in that moment my heart broke and I cried freely, feeling no protection from this kind of loving.

When I was fifteen, my future seemed so simple. I would be a

Catholic priest, a monk, perhaps a Trappist—but in the meanwhile, I was lost in the dark night of sexual need that would not go away. Like legions of Catholic boys before me, I relied on the venerable and time-tested ways of "mortifying my flesh" in order to see God—sleeping on cement floors, taking cold showers, testing the limits of sleeplessness, tying string around my scrotum. I was also rather clever in devising new ways of expunging desire from my body—meditating on dog shit before I went to school in the morning, for example. Strangely enough, all this had the approximate effect of pouring kerosene on a fire that was already out of control. Within weeks I was staggering around in a delirium of erotic appetite. And so my older sister, whom I lived with in a shack in an orange grove in Southern California (in her great kindness and without consulting me), contrived that a friend of hers would seduce me—either, I suppose to siphon off some of my obvious turmoil or to thicken the plot.

My first lover was plump and exquisitely sensitive and, at the ripe age of twenty-three, a young boy's fantasy of the "mature older woman." When she took my penis in her hand and guided it into her, I began trembling so much that my teeth chattered madly. When she asked me if I'd ever made love before, I wanted to say yes and to pull, like a rabbit out of a hat, some facsimile of expertise and casualness. Instead I stuttered the obvious to my great humiliation and then looked away unable to bear her delight at initiating me. It's fortunate that when you're fifteen, desire is more intelligent than fear and can outmaneuver it, can even outmaneuver embarrassment if your first lover is tender enough and skillful enough in her tenderness. That night I made love until three in the morning with the same sweet and frightened fury that would eventually find its resting place in our marriage bed. After I came I sucked her to orgasm, insistent on tasting her, on putting my mouth "there" and secretly imagining an unspoken bargain being struck that would lead her, someday, to suck me as well. I stayed awake most of the night while she slept next to me, staring at the ceiling in utter disbelief and, in the grip of a kind of conversion, realized that some of my religious beliefs required, shall we say, modification.

Perhaps the real naiveté is not so much in the younger selves but in the hardheaded efforts to leave them all behind. The startled and intrigued five-year-old segues easily into the fifteen-year-old boy who can't sleep at the wonder of it all. Those two, and others as well, find their way into the embrace of our lovemaking, and I am so grateful that in this old dharma of giving up fear we have made this much room in our bed for this little community that inhabits the domain of our marriage.

BIOGRAPHIES

Carolyn Banks's collection *Tart Tales: Elegant Erotic Stories* was published recently. She is also the author of a new lighthearted mystery, *Death by Dressage*, the first book in an amateur sleuth series set in the horse world, which Banks, former editor of "Horse Play" magazine, knows well. Banks has also written many suspense novels including *The Girls on the Row* and *Mr. Right*.

Susan Block is a practicing sex therapist, nationally syndicated radio and television talk show host, columnist and bestselling author. She is the director of the Dr. Susan Block Institute for the Erotic Arts & Sciences, and co-publisher of "Dr. Susan Block's Journal of Voluptuous Reading," written by her listeners and viewers. She graduated magna cum laude from Yale University, and received her doctorate in philosophy from Pacific Western University. She is a princess by marriage.

Wickham Boyle is the founder and producing director of Under One Roof and the former director of La MaMa E.T.C. For sixteen years, this Yale graduate has headed a successful management consulting company specializing in the problems and issues that affect not-for-profit organizations. Boyle is an adjunct professor, teaching arts management, at NYU and Sarah Lawrence. Her writing has been seen in collections, magazines, and journals. She is a dedicated resident of Tribeca and the mother of two.

Edward Buskirk has written professionally since leaving the architectural engineering business in a rush of inspiration several years ago. Fearing another such rush, he has quit drinking. His short-story credits range from confession to crime-thriller, and his erotic fiction has appeared, under various pseudonyms, in numerous adult-oriented publications. He lives in Michigan, is writing a novel called *Midnight Confessions*, and has, at age forty-six, finally traded in his lifelong dream of playing shortstop for the Detroit Tigers for one of becoming their ace third-base coach.

Kim Chernin is a writer who lives in Berkeley, California. She has written "The Hunger Trilogy" (*The Obsession, The Hungry Self, Reinventing Eve*), *In My Mother's House* (an autobiography), *The Flame Bearers* (a novel), *The Hunger Song* (a collection of poetry), and *Sex and Other Sacred Games* (an erotic dialogue in story form) with Renate Stendhal. Her most recent book is *Crossing the Border: A Memoir of Passion* (Random House, 1994). She is presently at work on a book of tales set in Berkeley.

Clark Demorest, originally from the Rockies, is the pseudonym of a marketing and forecasting executive for a small telephone company in the South. This is his first venture into erotic writing. Demorest is active in local community and college theatre groups—both on the stage and behind. He is currently writing short stories for the fantasy/science fiction market and has taken time off from his novel-in-progress to try his hand at playwriting.

Katherine DeRosa is a pseudonym for a woman who lives with her husband in Austin, Texas, where she is currently writing a mystery novel. The author hopes her story will make both men and women smile at themselves and the attitudes they bring to sex.

Michael Ortiz Hill is a writer and registered nurse. He is the author of the forthcoming *Dreaming the End of the World: Apocalypse as* *a Rite of Passage* (Spring Publications, 1994) and is currently working on a book on white and black peoples' dreams about one another. He lives half-time in Santa Cruz, California, with his teen-age daughter, Nicole, and half-time in Topanga, California, with his wife, Deena Metzger.

Erik Jendresen is the author of three plays: "Malice Aforethought," "The Killing of Michael Malloy," and "Excuse My Dust, an Evening with Dorothy Parker." He has written four screenplays and chron-icled Dr. Alberto Villoldo's adventures in the Amazon in two books: *The Four Winds* and *Journey to the Island of the Sun*. He lives on a sailboat in Sausalito, California.

Hope Katz is a journalist, poet and writer of children's stories. Her goal is to start a publishing company for children's books. She has worked for "The Miami Herald" and "New Miami" magazine and currently is the West Coast correspondent for "US/Latin Trade" magazine based in Miami. Katz is also the president of a not-for-profit corporation, The Writing's On the Wall, a national project designed to help abused children heal through art, photography, and writing. She is currently working on her first children's book, the *Night Knight*.

Maximillian R. Lobkowicz has been the publisher of erotic magazines since 1972, including "The L.A. Star," "Love," "Finger," "The La-dies Room" (first erotica magazine written entirely by women), "The Brentwood Bla Bla," "Beverly Hills, The Magazine," and "Dr. Susan Block's Journal of Voluptuous Reading." He was involved in several first amendment cases regarding publishing erotica. He produces the Dr. Susan Block Show and is associate director of the Dr. Susan Block Institute for the Erotic Arts and Sciences. He is a prince on both the Czechoslovakian and the Italian sides of his family.

Carroll Mavis-Raine is the pseudonym for a full-time writer living in Manassas, Virginia, the site of two famous Civil War battles. Her erotic short stories have appeared in London's "For Women," "Forum" and "Erotic Stories." With "Phantom Grey," she makes her American publishing debut in erotic fiction. At present, she is at work on a mainstream novel about Northern Ireland.

Deena Metzger is a poet/healer and writer. Her books include *Writing for Your Life: A Guide and Companion to the Inner Worlds*; the novels *What Dinah Thought, The Woman Who Slept with Men to Take the War Out of Them*, and *Tree*, also two recent books of poetry—*A Sabbath Among the Ruins* and *Looking for the Faces of God*. She lives at the end of the road in Topanga Canyon with her wolves Isis and Owl and her husband, Michael Ortiz Hill.

Suzanne Miller holds a doctorate in psychoanalysis. She has published two books of poetry, produced and directed her own play, published short stories and written a novel. She is a founding member of the Lacanian School of Psychoanalysis based in Berkeley. Her private psychoanalytic practice is in Marin County. She is writing a new novel entitled *The Question of Naming* and is co-authoring a psychoanalytic book on female sexuality and gender identity.

Anna Nymus is a pseudonym for a journalist who has spent many years in different European countries where she has been actively engaged in the women's movement. She has published erotic short stories in several European women's magazines under this pen name. Currently, she is living in Berkeley, California, working on an erotic novel.

Marsha Powers divides her time between freelance writing and operating a retail sales manufactured home lot with her husband of eighteen years. She attributes her successful writing career and her successful marriage to her personal motto, "Don't sweat the small stuff." Her work has appeared in numerous major publications, including "Playgirl," "Cavalier," "Genesis," "Velvet," and "Pillow Talk," as well as many small press publications, including "Eldritch Tales," "After Hours," "Amazing Zoo," and "Women's Household." She is currently working on a screenplay.

Rob Scott is the pseudonym of an up-and-coming (he hopes) writer of science fiction, fantasy, and horror. He has a Ph.D. in French literature and has been a teacher, a translator, and a farmer. He lives in Vermont with his wife and two children. This is his first, but probably not his last, published piece of erotica.

B. J. Simmons, a retired instrument technician, works as a security guard at an old plantation in Pawley's Island, South Carolina. He is a published poet, and this is his second published short story. Simmons lives with his sister and two dogs, Barney and Little Debbie.

Shimon-Craig Van Collie has been a freelance journalist and writer since 1979, during which time he has published numerous articles and three books. Erotica has always been one of his muses. A native of Connecticut, where sex was a four-letter word, he now lives in California with his wife and son.

Dina Vered is the pseudonym for a woman who has worked as a journalist in the Middle East and Asia. Her articles appear regularly in major U.S. newspapers and magazines.

Bruce Zimmerman is a novelist, screenwriter, and retired fast-food cook. His published books are *Blood Under the Bridge, Thicker Than Water*, and *Full-Bodied Red*, the first of which was nominated for an Edgar Award as Best First Mystery in 1989. He is currently working on his fourth mystery and a novel-length adaptation of the short story included in this anthology. Zimmerman lives with his two sons and problematic dog in San Miguel de Allende, Mexico.

PILLOW TALK